Herbal, Food and Pharmaceutical Products

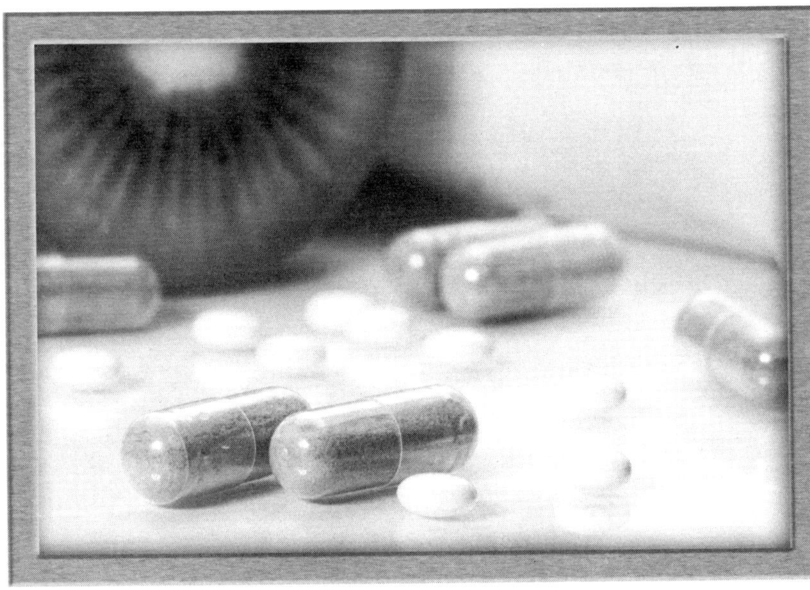

Herbal, Food and Pharmaceutical Products

Ranjan Magazine
Plant Head
Manufacturing and Marketing
Sunny Allied Industries
Jammu, J & K

CBSPD
CBS Publishers & Distributors Pvt Ltd

New Delhi • Bengaluru • Chennai • Kochi • Kolkata • Lucknow • Mumbai
Hyderabad • Jharkhand • Nagpur • Patna • Pune • Uttarakhand

Herbal, Food and Pharmaceutical Products

ISBN: 978-93-86217-714

First Edition: 2017
Reprint: 2020, 2025

Published by Satish Kumar Jain and produced by Varun Jain for

CBS Publishers & Distributors Pvt Ltd
4819/XI Prahlad Street, 24 Ansari Road, Daryaganj, New Delhi 110 002, India
Ph: 011-23289259, 23266838 Website: www.cbspd.com
e-mail: delhi@cbspd.com

Corporate Office: 204 FIE, Industrial Area, Patparganj, Delhi 110 092
Ph: 011-4934 4934 Fax: 011-4934 4935 e-mail: publishing@cbspd.com; publicity@cbspd.com

Branches

- **Bengaluru:** Seema House 2975, 17th Cross, K.R. Road, Banasankari 2nd Stage, Bengaluru 560 070, Karnataka, India
  Ph: +91-80-26771678/79 Fax: +91-80-26771680 e-mail: bangalore@cbspd.com
- **Chennai:** 18/8B, Subbarayan Street, Shenoy Nagar, Chennai 600 030, Tamil Nadu, India
  Ph: +91-44-42032115, 26681266 e-mail: chennai@cbspd.com
- **Kochi:** 42/1325, 1326, Power House Road, Opp KSEB, Power House, Ernakulam 682 018, Kerala, India
  Ph: +91-484-4059061-65 Fax: +91-484-4059065 e-mail: kochi@cbspd.com
- **Kolkata:** 147, Hind Ceramics Compound, 1st Floor, Nilgunj Road, Belghoria, Kolkata-700056, West Bengal, India
  Ph: 033-25633055, 033-25633056 e-mail: kolkata@cbspd.com
- **Lucknow:** Basement, Khushnuma Complex, 7-Meerabai Marg (Behind Jawahar Bhawan), Lucknow 226001, India
  Ph: 0522-4000032 e-mail: tiwari.lucknow@cbspd.com
- **Mumbai:** PWD Shed. Gala no. 25/26, Ramchandra Bhatt Marg, Next to JJ Hospital Gate no. 2, Opp. Union Bank of India Noorbaug Mumbai-400009, Maharashtra, India
  Ph: 022-66661880/89 e-mail: mumbai@cbspd.com

Representatives

- **Hyderabad** 0-9885175004 • **Jharkhand** 0-9811541605 • **Nagpur** 0-8692091830
- **Patna** 0-9334159340 • **Pune** 0-9664372571 • **Uttarakhand** 0-9716462459

Printed at Glorious Printers, Delhi, India

Preface

Herbal, food and pharmaceutical products are most important to maintain best health of body and mind. These food products have no adverse reactions in the body if taken in small quantities. Direct heat method is best food formulation, second best method of food formulation is boiling and third best method of food formulation is frying. Herbal and food products are formed in solids, semisolids and liquids. Chemicals are mixed to build smell, taste, stability, antioxidation, flavor, and strength and to preserve food formulations. If kept unformulated, food products will decompose and will cause various infections in body system. Chemicals and microbiological testing is needed for solids, semisolids and liquids formulations of food products. List of chemicals are written and explained. Chemicals and microbiological tests are written and explained. Contacts of pharmaceutical, cosmetics, herbal, food companies are explained. In order to control normal blood levels of various organs have been written and explained. Many recipes' with many method of food preparation is written and explained.

Suggestions from readers are most welcome.

Ranjan Magazine

ranjan.magazine@gmail.com

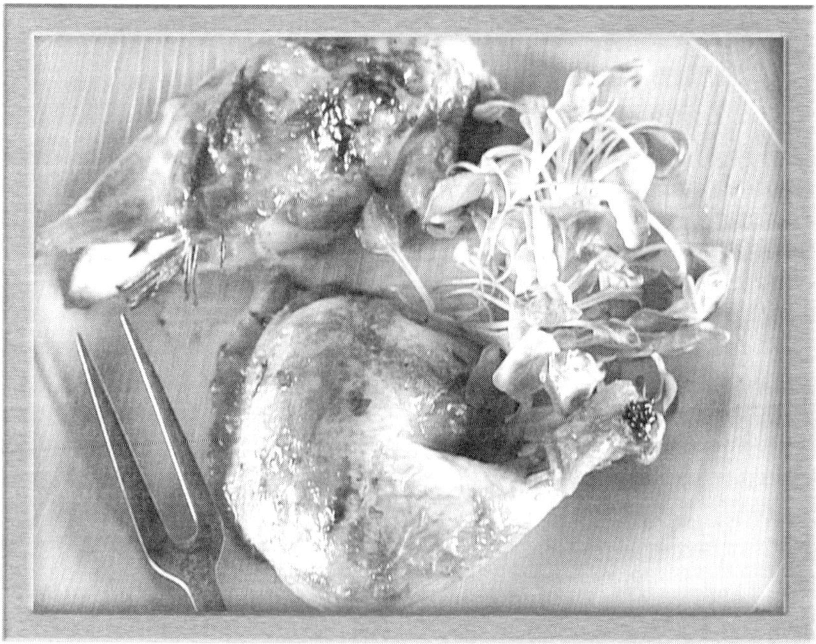

Contents

1 Ayurvedic Concepts

INTRODUCTION TO AYURVEDA

Ayurveda (Science of life) is the traditional medicine and natural healing system of India and its cultural sphere. Its foundation comes from the Vedic Era, the primitive age around 5000 years ago. It is appropriate to say that it is the Mother of all healing systems. Ayurveda is one of the most comprehensive healing systems in the world, dealing integrally with body, mind and spirit. Ayurveda has classified the body system according to the theory of Tridosha to overcome all ailments by eliminating the basic cause.

The basic objective of Ayurveda is to educate people on how to take care of their health by themselves and increase their span of healthy life. One can achieve this goal by monitoring and balancing one's nutritional diet and lifestyle. Keeping good habits to heal and prevent illness and inadequacy of body functioning. This system is related to the soul, body and mind simultaneously. Psychosomatic theory recognizes that the mind can create illness in the body.

To understand the ayurvedic system, the following fundamental section must be understood in detail:

1. Five elements (Base of constitution of the universe).
2. Three doshas—their normal and abnormal stage.
3. Three types of doshas and their significance.
4. Diseases caused by individual doshas.
5. Application of treatment as per symptoms of doshas.
6. Pathya-Apathya (Precaution and care of diet) (Foods to be taken - Foods to be avoided)
7. Three types of vitalities and their relation with the human being and the basis of their healing treatment. These are known as qualities of mind (Satva Rajas-Tamas) and should be considered.
8. Six tastes: Sweet, salty, bitter, sour, pungent and astringent. These become the cause of different diseases when aggravated.

Creation of Five Elements

The whole universe is made-up of five essential elements—Building blocks that all life forms contain: Ether, air, fire, water and earth. We can easily see how life was created from the subtlest to the grossest matter. From eternity, the subtlest form of matter is ether. Ether mixing with eternity creates air, more observable or experiential element. As air moves, it eventually creates friction, which creates heat or fire. Heat produces moisture, thus creating water, the densest element; if one tries to walk through water, one is slowed by its density. Finally, water produces the densest form of matter, earth. Ayurveda says that all of the creations, including humans, are made-up of the combination of all five elements. These elements are the subtlest aspects of human life, finer than the molecular, atomic, or subatomic levels. This is the level that Ayurveda healing works on. Focusing on the cause of the grosser levels of life, the denser aspects will be taken care of since they are made of these five elements. Just as a strong foundation supports a strong building, the five elements (the foundation of all matter) when strong and balanced in a person, they will automatically balance the more material levels. Thus, Ayurveda does not need to look at isolated parts of the human anatomy, or at the vitamin, chemical, or nutritional level of health. It simply balances the elements, and this balances the more physical levels.

A person diagnosed with a duodenal ulcer is an example of this balancing. Rather than creating a name for a symptom, Ayurveda identifies the illness as an excess of the fire elements. Acid is a by-product of heat. Ayurveda will look to see in what part of the patient's life overheating occurs. It may be due to eating excessive fiery foods and spices like tomatoes and peppers. One's career may be causing undue anger (i.e. hot temper). Perhaps the person drinks alcohol (fire water).

Once the cause is learned, suggestions for reducing a person's excessive intake of fire are discussed. Simultaneously, the patient is advised to use more of the air and water elements to balance the heat with coolness (air cools heat, water puts out the fire).

Thus, the holistic approach of Ayurveda seeks the cause of an illness and restores balance, using the insight of the elemental creation of the universe.

Description of the Five Elements

1. **Space-Sky-Akash (Ether):** It is an omni present and all prevailing element, which serves as an abode (dominating or controlling) to all the other four elements and objects in the universe. It is due to space that one can separate or differentiate various objects and different parts of the objects. The same space exists in the body, which creates differentiation and division in the tissues of the body.
2. **Air-Vayu:** Air contains oxygen, which is a vital element for the existence of all living creatures. Wind is responsible for all the movement in nature. It is in the presence of oxygen in the air that fire can exhibit its action. Wind, in the form of a storm, can cause the destruction of trees, crops, houses, etc. The same term as "Vata" applies to the body, which acts in the body as commanding all activities and functions for its betterment and its abnormalities. The knowledge of these facts, helps in the treatment of disease.
3. **Energy-Agni (Heat) (Pitta):** The sun and fire are the main sources of energy in nature. The sun maintains equitable environmental temperature and light. These properties of the sun are essential and vital for survival of life. The sun's heat is the source for ripening of plants, vegetables, fruits as well human body cells. It also causes evaporation of water, forming clouds which supply the water to the earth, mountains, hills and streams, etc. These elements of nature constitute the life of human beings. The same heat is known as Agni or "Pitta" in Ayurveda. It has the role of chemical changes in the body helping digestion, forming various secretions and enzymes.
4. **Water-Apa (Kapha):** Water is found in the atmosphere, the sea, lakes, rivers, etc. Water is the basic element for sustaining life. It has the cooling effect in the environment. It

also feeds the plants, crops, etc. The same element in Ayurveda is Kapha. It constitutes the various cells of the body and provides strength as well as life to human beings.

5. **Solid or Earth:** This element itself is predominantly solid. It gives shelter and protection to human beings to work and move on the surface of earth. It is also a source of life and existence. The solid (Earth) maintains life and stability in the nature. The same element represents the development and stability of the body. All the solid elements in the body, such as the bones, teeth, etc. are of the Earth constitution. The Earth property is the base of the constitution of the body.

Tri-Doshas

Parallel to the three qualities of mind in creation are the three doshas or constitutions in human body.

Vata, Pitta and Kapha are the three biological elements, which constitute the structural and fundamental units of all the living cells, tissues, organs and the body as a whole. The three doshas originate from five elements, i.e. the doshas are the basis of five elements.

Relation of the five elements with the three doshas:

1. Vata has relation with air.
2. Pitta has relation with Heat-Energy-Fire (Agni).
3. Kapha has the relation with liquid substances of nature, i.e. Water (Earth).
4. Akash (Space) forms the space in the body and division in the various cells.
5. Earth forms the solid parts of the body.

Therefore, the doshas act in the body in accordance with the five elements that are the base of nature as well as Ayurvedic theory of treatment.

The functioning and existence of the body entirely depends on Vata, Pitta, Kapha. To the three elements of constitution, i.e. air, water and heat, the Sanskrit names have been given according to their significance (properties) i.e. Vata, Pitta and Kapha.

The name themselves show their properties and foundation:

Details of doshas

Vata: Vata or air means movement in the universe. Vata is responsible for all the movements. Vata molecules are light, minute, clear, rough and dry. They are always mobile and move in all directions. They quickly spread throughout the body. Vata is cold in nature and causes the diseases related to cold. Because of its minute nature, it cannot be visualized in any form in the body but its presence can be proved by its actions. It is the electricity, setting the organism into motion, marinating the equilibrium between Pitta and Kapha (inerts). It is the sole power to control all the movements of nerves, tissues, cells and systems.

Vata may be understood as nerve force, electromotor, physical activity or that which is responsible for motion. It controls the actions of the prefrontal lobe, motor cortex and spinal cord. It carries all the sensory impulses to their centers and also maintains the efficiency of the sense organs. Vata has five divisions or responsibilities in the body, which exist in the different parts of the body.

Pran is located in the head and governs the chest, throat, mind, heart, sense organs, intelligence, expectorating, sneezing, belching, inspiration, and swallowing of food-outward movement.

Udan resides in the chest and controls the nose, navel, throat, and is responsible for initiating speech, effort, enthusiasm, the capacity to work, complexion, and memory-upward movement.

Vyan is found in the heart and rapidly moves throughout the body. It regulates all body movements, including walking, raising and lowering of the body parts, and opening and closing the eyes.

Saman is located near the digestive fire. It works in the alimentary tract, and other abdominal organs. It holds food in the alimentary tract (absorbing nutrients and excreting wastes), helps digest foods, separates nutrients from waste, and eliminates the waste-equalized movement.

Apan is seated in the colon, and controls the waist, bladder, genitals, and thighs. Its main function is downward movement of wastes (feces, urine), reproductive fluid, menstrual fluid, and it also controls the downward movement of the fetus.

Pitta (Heat)

Pitta represents energy or heat (Calorie) in the body. Further, Pitta is the combination of energy (heat) and liquid. Heat is the active principle whereas liquid acts as a vehicle. Life on earth depends on energy derived from the Sun. Digestion entirely depends on Pitta (Agni). The process of digestion continues in the gastrointestinal tract and in the tissues by means of various digestive and tissue enzymes (known as Pitta).

Character of Pitta

Pitta is hot, light, clear and viscous and has a penetrating power, mobile, pungent, sour and has strong foul smell. It tends to move upward and downward (on the principle of gravity). It increases heat and body temperature as well as appetite and thirst. It maintains the complexion, color and luster of skin. It renders the skin soft and thin. It also maintains the vision. Its main sites are digestive tract, body fluids, blood, sweat, skin, eyes and brain.

There are five types of Pitta in the body which exist in the different parts of the body.

Pachak Pitta (digestive fire): The gastrointestinal tract is the seat of Pachak Pitta. The fire digests and transforms food, emulsifying food fats and separating absorbable nutrients from wastes, so they may be passed to lacteals by absorption (Food becoming partially digested in the stomach is called chyme. This chyme passes into the small intestine where it becomes digested by the pancreatic juice and bile. The usable byproduct is lymph and fatty matter, or chyle. The chyle moves through lacteals, or lymphatic vessels which carry chyle from small intestine to the thoracic duct. From the thoracic duct, the chyle is sent into the blood). Pachak (digestive enzymes), through digestion, automatically nourishes the other four Pittas.

1. **Ranjak Pitta:** The main sites of this Pitta are the liver, spleen, stomach and small intestines. It is represented by the bile, enzymes and bone marrow. Its function is synthesis of hemoglobin and imparting red color to the blood.
2. **Sodhaka Pitta:** The brain is the main site of Shodak Pitta. It is represented by the cellular enzymes of nerve cells. It helps in performing mental function, such as knowledge, intelligence and consciousness by maintaining rhythmic and cardiac contractions.
3. **Alochak Pitta:** It exists in the eyes. It is represented by the enzymes in the rode and cones in the retina. It functions in perception of light.

4. **Bhrajak Pitta:** The skin is the main site of this Pitta. It keeps the skin warm and is responsible for its normal complexion and luster by keeping secretions from the sweat and sebaceous glands of the skin active.
5. **Kapha:** The Biological element of Kapha is derived from the two basic physical elements namely earth and water. Kapha molecules are heavy, stable, smooth, soft, viscous, shiny and moist, white in color and predominantly have a sweet and slightly salty taste. Kapha constitutes the main body mass and is responsible for the shape and form of the body. Kapha fills the intercellular spaces of the body as connective tissues including mucus, synovial fluids and tendons. All the cells, tissues and organs of the body are predominantly composed of Kapha elements.

The biological combination of solid and liquids in varying proportions is responsible for the varying structure and composition of various tissues like body fluids (Rasa), semen, blood, muscle, fat, bone marrow and brain.

The fluid component of Kapha is responsible for the maintenance and formation of body fluids. Because of its heavy and stable qualities, it is responsible for strength stability and firmness of body and mind. Because of its oily nature, it prevents friction between the two parts of the body. In muscles, it gives strength to the body. In fact, it gives shape (form) to it. In the semen, it is responsible for fertility. The brain and nerves tissues predominantly contain Kapha molecules. Kapha of inferior quality in the brain produces a stab of ignorance, delusion, laziness and jealousy.

Five sites of Kapha in body

1. **Kledak:** It is present in the stomach and intestines up to the colon. It is the mucus secretion in the gastrointestinal tract. It dilutes the food taken, and also helps the digestion and supports the Kapha elements to work properly throughout the body.
2. **Avalambak:** It is present in the chest. It constitutes the myocardial and alveoli (lungs tissue), pleural and pericardial fluids. It supports and gives strength to the heart, lungs and bone cage of the body.
3. **Bodhak:** Present in the oral cavity and throat, represented by saliva. It helps to appreciate taste by the tongue. It also helps to moisten the food for easy ingestion and digestion.
4. **Tarpak Kapha:** Situated in the cranial cavity and is represented by Kapha molecule of brain, cerebrospinal fluids. It supports the nutrition of brain and nourishes the sense organs.
5. **Shleshak Kapha:** Known as sinovial fluid in the joints. It provides nutrition to the ends of the bones and its presence prevents friction during joint movements and, particularly supports to constitute and strength to the body.

Vayu/Pitta, Vayu/Kapha, Pitta/Kapha, and a combination of all three (tridosha). Although finding the cause of an illness is still a mystery to modern science, it was and continues to be the main goal of Ayurveda. Six stages of the development of disease were known, including aggravation, accumulation, overflow, relocation, a build-up in a new site, and manifestation into the recognizable disease. Modern equipment and diagnosis can only detect a disease during the fifth and sixth stages of illness. Ayurvedic physicians can recognize an illness in the making before it creates more serious imbalances in the body. Health is seen as a balance of the biological humors, whereas disease is an imbalance of the humors. Ayurveda creates balance by supplying deficient humors and reducing the excess ones. Surgery is seen as a last resort. Modern medicine is just beginning to realize the need to supply rather than to remove, but still does not know how or what to supply?

Additionally, there are over 2,000 medicinal plants classified in India's materia medica. A unique therapy, known as Pancha Karma (five actions), completely removes toxins from the body. This method reverses the disease path from its manifestation stage, back into the bloodstream, and eventually into the gastrointestinal tract (the original site of the disease). It is achieved through special diets, oil massage, and steam therapy. At the completion of these therapies, special forms of emesis (vomiting), purgation, and enemas remove excesses from their sites of origin. Finally, Ayurveda rejuvenates—rebuilding the body's cells and tissues after toxins are removed.

Significance of Doshas

Disease is caused by imbalancing of the doshas. For example, if a Pitta dosha eats much ginger, it will create excess fire in the digestive system (body). This results in Pitta disorders like acid indigestion. Disease may be caused by deficient, improper or excess contact with seasons (e.g. excess cold in winter), sensory objects (e.g. excessive light/sound), and activities (e.g. over exercise).

Vata Symptoms and Significance

The following symptoms show the causes of Vata and significance (existence) in the body:

1. **Joints and muscles:** Pain all over the body or in individual parts, i.e. joints, muscles, nerves, etc. (Arthritis).
2. **Muscles:** Myalgia, muscular pain, tenderness in the muscles.
3. **Nerves:** Neuralgia, other stages of Vata disease—hemiplagia, facial paralysis, trigerminal, neuralgia, neurotic pain in any part of the body—other diseases of the nervous system.
4. **Convulsions hysteria:** Epilepsy–spasm, tremors—stiffness.
5. **Abdominal pain:** Accumulation of wind in the digestive tract.
6. **Renal colic:** colic pain.
7. **Liain in the joints:** Pain in the chest, pain in the back.

General Symptoms

Loss of weight, pain in the eye-ear-head, fingers, etc. prostate enlargement (hardness), stiffness of thighs, stiffness of body, (emacian), reduction of body tissues, (tremring).

Treatment of Vata Dosha

General Treatment

For most of the complaints caused by Vata dosha—the following procedures should be applied:

- Massage, fomentation and purgative procedures should be adopted regularly.
- Mild taste, salty, astringent, hot foods.
- Covering of the affected parts by woolen clothes or bandages.
- Dry herbal formulations and tonics.

- Mild and small doses of alcohol.
- Digestive, palatable and light food.

Use of herbal supplements

1. **In the stage of neurotic disease like neuralgia, hemiplegics, seitier, pain all over body, etc.**
    1. Yograj guggal: 2 pills twice daily
    2. Rasnadi Qwath: One cup twice or Maha Rasnadi Qwath 1 or 2 pills twice daily
    3. Meat of pegeon: Meet soup.
2. **In the stage of abdominal pain (Flati lens)**
    1. Garlic: 1 pills three times daily
    2. Gastro care: One pill after every meal
    3. Hingvastika churna: One tea spoon twice.
3. **Joint pain**
    1. Guggual Formulation (item #600-618): 2 Pills twice daily
    2. Ashwagandha powder/tablets: Tea spoon twice/1 tablets twice daily.
4. **Pain in back**
    1. Chandar prabha Vati: 2 pills daily with milk.
5. **Convulsions, hysteria etc.**
    1. Vacha churn: Jata mansi powder/tablets
    2. Shankh Pushpi powder/tablets with cows milk
    3. Brahmi powder/tablets
    4. Tinet: Jaipal (Croten seeds or Nishottara), javil, long.

Pitta Symptoms and Significance

The following symptoms show the cause and significance (existence) of Pitta in the body:

1. Burning sensation: Hot feeling in the body.
2. Inflammation: In different organs, i.e. throat, tongue, eyes, skin erulitions, itching
3. Thirst
4. Excess heat in the digestive system, gastritis, blood mixed in the stool, bleeding piles.
5. Functional disease: Hepatitis, jaundice, neliotistic, colitis, acidity, etc.
6. Fever caused by hot climate, hot food, drinks.
7. Yellowish discoloration of urine, eyes, stool and skin.
8. Foul smell of the body, sweating.
9. Bitter or acidic taste in the mouth: Supportive

General Treatment

1. Use of Ghee.
2. Massage by Ghee.
3. Sweet, bitter food and herbs.
4. Cold water and drinks.
5. Icy cold swalis on the forehead.

6. Bath with cold water.
7. Mild, cold, heart tending (pleasing) atmosphere.
8. Ice cream, jelly, milk shake, icy cold milk, etc.

Use of Herbal Medicine

1. Sandal or Khas drink, Kutki (picorrhiza Kurroa), Guduchi, Gokhru, Shatavari, lieral calcium, Blood cleaner, Mahamanjistha Kwat
2. For local application-Silfina Oil, Glories oil.

Kapha Symptoms and Significance

The following symptoms show the cause and significance (existence) of Kapha dosha in the body:

1. Numbness in the body, coldness in the extremities, palm and sole.
2. Desire for hot food and hot environment.
3. Drowsiness and sleepy habit (excessive sleep).
4. lioor intelligence, or dullness, laziness.
5. Increase phlegm in the chest, mouth and throat.
6. Spitting of saliva and sputum
7. Coldness of body and head.
8. Obesity and heaviness of the body.
9. Nasal frontal and maxillary sinuses obstruction.
10. Sinking of heart, respiratory obstruction.
11. Inactivity and sluggishness.
12. Weak digestive liower.
13. Cause of diabetes.
14. Sweet taste in the mouth.
15. Increased quantity of urine and stool.
16. Cause of Asthma.
17. Obstruction in the nasal—Bronchial passage.

General Treatment

1. Dry and hot foods.
2. Hot environment.
3. Hot clothes.
4. Fast emetic (vomiting) and purgatives emetic.
5. Old wine.
6. Avoid sleepiness.
7. Exercises.
8. Dry massage by dry powders (Bhos Bhesan-chik lieas powder).
9. Fat reduction agents (medicine and diet).
10. Periodical fast.
11. Honey with water and lemon drops.

Use of herbal medicine

Reslim, Gluco health (Glubeta), Chanderprabha, Respiton, Sitopladi churna, Talisadi churna, Trikatu, Antma syrup

Kapha Oil for local application or steaming

Tastes:

Tastes have crucial significance in Ayurveda. According to Ayurvedic theory, there are six tastes existing in every food, plants, herbs, etc. and these play a vital role in human body:

1. Sweet (Madhus)
2. Sour (Amal)
3. Salty (Lawan)
4. Pungent (Kattu)
5. Bitter (Tikt)
6. Astringent (Kashaya)

These tastes have the direct relation with doshas. These tastes may either aggravate or pacify the doshas: Vata (air), Pitta (fire), Kapha (water).

For example:

1. Sweet (Madhu): Increases the Kapha and subsides the Vayu (Vata) and pitta.
2. Sour (Amal): Increases the pitta and subsides the Vayu (Vata) and Kapha.
3. Salty (Lawan): Increases the pitta and Kapha and subsides the Vayu (Vata).
4. liungent (Kattu): Increases the pitta and subsides Kapha and Vayu (Vata).
5. Bitter (Tikta): Increases the Vayu (Vata) and subsides the pitta and Kapha.
6. Astringent (Kashaya): Increases the Vayu (Vata) and subsides the pitta and Kapha.
7. Sweet, sour, salty: Subsides the Vayu and increases the Kapha and pitta.
8. liungent, bitter, astringent: Subsides the Kapha and increases the pitta and Vayu.
9. Astringent, bitter, sweet: Subsides the pitta and increases the Kapha and Vayu.
10. Sweet, Sour, Salty: Increase Kapha and pitta, subsides the Vayu.
11. Pungent, bitter, sweet: Increase the Kapha and subsides the pitta.
12. Astringent, bitter, sweet: Increase the Kapha and subsides the pitta.

The six tastes have the relation with five elements also:

1. Sweet, pungent, astringent: (Relation with): Water
2. Salty: (Relation with): Earth
3. Sour, salty: (Relation with): Fire (Heat)
4. Astringent, bitter: (Relation with): Vayu (Air)

Omni Present: *Akash (ether)*

Sweet taste is the most nourishing and as each taste becomes less nourishing, it becomes more bitter, until it is astringent – the least nourishing. That is why meals should be tasteful. In aggravated doshas, to maintain health, a little of each taste is prescribed in Ayurveda.

Qualities of the Brain: *Satva-Rajas-Tamas*

1. Satva means good quality of mind.
2. Rajas means undesirable/medium quality of mind.
3. Tamas means bad quality of mind.

Parallel to the three qualities of mind in creation are the three doshas or constitutions in human body. These are the three qualities of mind, which are formed at the time of imbedding of the fetus in the human being and just compared with the formation of genes, which sustain throughout life. They have a deep relation with the Ayurvedic system and treatment. Treatment of Satva persons is maintained and applied according to nature of the Satva person; similarly Rajas and Tamas persons are treated according to their nature.

Description

1. Satva persons are holy, steady, clear minded, religious and follow the path of truth. They are persons of good manners and characters. They posses a great degree of self-control and never become upset or angry. They remain calm, quiet, mentally strong, less sleepy and respectful. They are always dedicated to improving their knowledge, efficiency and skill. They are persons of strong and correct decisions and many times they are found like saints.
2. Rajas persons have involvement in worldly affairs. These persons are egoistic, proud, ambitious and have a tendency to rule on others as they are persons of uncertain decisions. Though inattentive they are hard working. They lack proper planning and direction. Their mental make-up is not strong. A wavering mind, emotions like anger, joy, attachment, jealousy and selfishness rules them and are good friends with others for their own interest.
3. Tamas persons are less intelligent, depressed and lazy. The slightest mental exertion tires them. They a have tendency to feel sleepy even during the day. They indulge in eating, drinking, sleeping and sex affairs. They are extremely greedy, irritable and have no interest in the affairs of others. They go to the extent of harming others to safeguard their own interests.

These qualities are transferred by parents to their children during fertilization. Environment and diet plays a decisive role in the formation of all the above noted three qualities (Satva, Rajas, Tamas).

Some considerable factors

Ayurvedic system of healing takes a long time to fix any problem as the problem is fixed from the roots and the basic cause of the problem is eliminated. So that's why Ayurvedic herbal products are supposed to be taken with confidence, regularity, and should be used for a long time. Ayurvedic treatment has no side effects.

Instead of filling the body with vitamins, minerals and other components Which are synthetic or extracted, and cannot have all of them at a time. Why not take vitamins, minerals and other nutritious components required by body from herbs? Which are in colloidal form, eassily and naturally get absorbed in the body whole having nutritional, assimilating and absorption values, without any side effects. For example, one Emblica Officinalis (Amla fruit) provides 20 times more vitamin C than a whole orange. Besides, it has herbal curative properties also.

How can a problem be fixed so quickly when it took a long time to develop? It is advisable to use natural products for a long time for better results, as herbal products take time to show any significant results and these results last forever.

There is more stress put on the carrier, i.e. the type of liquid that is used to take herbal formulas, and precautions (food habits). The properties of many herbs change simply whether they are taken with cold water or hot water. This shows how the carrier plays a key role in the effectiveness of herbal formulations.

The herbal formulation acts faster in a physically weak person, as compared to a healthy person.

"These statements have not been evaluated by the Food and Drug Administration. This product is not intended to diagnose, treat, cure or prevent any Disease."

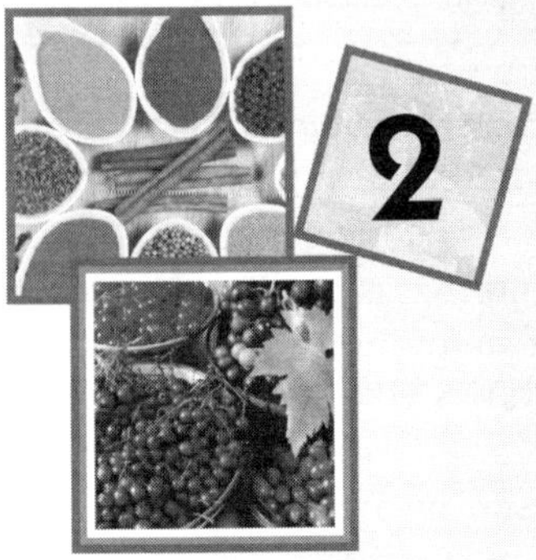

2 Principles of Ayurveda

Ayurvedic formulations are amalgamation of various herbs used to cure various lifestyle diseases. The secret of the natural health is based on the laws of Ayurveda and on standardization of ayurvedic formulation that are well documented in the great treatises, such as Charakasamhita, Sushrut Samhita and Ashtanga a Granthavali. These ayurvedic herbal formulations are processed under the most hygienic condition and are available in vacuum-sealed packaging in different quantities.

Trikatu

Trikatu is an ancient formula made of three herbal stimulants Pippali, Maricha, and Sunthi in equal amounts. It is a powerful stimulant for both digestive and respiratory systems. The special blend of Trikatu is useful in cases of obesity, weak digestion, high cholesterol, high triglycerides, hypothyroid, slow metabolism, congestion, cough and edema.

Trifla

Trifala is an effective Ayurvedic formulation made by mixing equal proportion of powder of Emblica Officinalis, Terminalia Belerica and Terminalia Chebula. It is widely used to promote appetite and digestion. Trifala is good for gentle, slow detoxification of the digestive tract and then the deep tissue. It is perfect for all body type.

Chyawanprash

Based on centuries old Ayurvedic formulation, our special blend of Chyawanprash strengthens body's internal defense mechanism and immune system. It has an antioxidant property and provide protection against infections, cough, cold and stress and more. Our Chyawanprash has a tangy sweet-sour taste with the consistency of jam.

Yograj

Yograj is a combination of variety of Ayurvedic herbs and gugguls. It has been traditionally used for painful joints and muscles, rheumatoid arthritis and osteoarthritis. It also rejuvenates and strengthens the skeletal and neuromuscular system. The yograj supports overall body function by removing toxins and maintaining healthy metabolism.

Guggul

Guggul is organic Ayurvedic herbal remedy formulated with selected Indian Ayurvedic herbs. The versatile Ayurvedic formulation is used for supporting rheumatoid arthritis and 'Ama' based disorders. Its rejuvenating action assists in the general well-being of all the tissues but are highly beneficial for nervous system, genitourinary system, digestive system and the skin.

Mahayograj Guggul

Mahayograj Guggul is an anti-arthritic herbal supplement composed of variety of gugguls. Guggul herbs are a collective name of various guggul gum resins extracted from trees. The Maha Yograj Guggul has been traditionally used to treat inflammatory conditions, such as osteoporosis, bone density, arthritis, especially rheumatism and gout. It is a powerful anti-oxidant, and stimulates the immune system's white blood cells.

Aasavs

Asavas are fermented medicines that are mildly alcoholic in nature. They are prepared by soaking organic herbal drugs in unboiled water along with the specific ingredients. Asavas are useful for various conditions including rickets, bronchitis, gonorrhea, spermatorrhea and loss of appetite, cough and general debility.

Bhasms

Bhasms are generally fine powder of metal prepared in herbal juices at a very high temperature. The metallic powder is combined with appropriate herbs for treatment of critical ailments as stated in Ayurveda. The Bhasms are very potent and should only be taken according to the recommended dosage.

Ayurvedic Churna

Ayurvedic churna are coarse powder made by certain herbs or combination of different herbs. The main reason behind using churans is the fact that effectiveness of herbs multiplies in the powdered form. We are leading ayurvedic churna manufacturer which is used for treatment of various disorders and diseases.

Avleh

Avleh is one of the most popular Ayurvedic tonics made from valuable bhasams, herbs and dry fruits. The special formulation of Avleh improves the immunity, vigor, blood, weight and general health. The high content natural antioxidant rejuvenates both body and mind and bring balance in the life.

Vati

Vati was traditionally used as an ayurvedic remedies for various disorders and diseases in the form of pills. It is a herbo-mineral compound made with strong herbs in the soluble base. Some of the commonly used Vati are Arogyavardhini vati, Arshoghani bati, Kankayana bati, Kutajghana bati, Chandraprabha bati, Chitrakadi bati, Pranada bati and more.

Isabagol

Isabgol is an excellent bulking agent used widely used as laxative for constipation. It consists of natural fibres and helps those persons who do not take a good quantity of roughage, salad or leafy vegetables in their diet. Isabgol is useful for cardiac patients, during pregnancy and in all conditions where straining at stools must be avoided.

Husk

Husk is a primarily insoluble fiber that is not absorbed or digested by the body. They are mostly used as laxative to restore proper bowel movement. Husk is also useful in inflammatory conditions of mucous membrane of gastrointestinal and genitourinary tracts.

Customized Formulations are for various disorders. These formulations are made from a mixture of pure natural herbs processed under the most hygienic conditions. The customized formulations are available in special packages in different quantities as per the requirement of the clients. Various actual example are mentioned below.

Contents for HIV/Aids treatment

Each Capsule Contains	*Wt/unit*
Cressa Cretica	20 mg
Leptadenia reticulate	20 mg
Tinospora cordifolia	20 mg
Picrorhiza Kurroa	20 mg
Asparagus adscendens	20 mg
Zingiber officinale	20 mg
Tribulus terrestris	20 mg
Caesalpinia crista	20 mg
Asparagus racemosus	20 mg
Piper Longum	20 mg
Swertia chirata	20 mg
Phaseolus radiatus	20 mg
Piper Nigrum	20 mg
Withania Somnifera	20 mg
Ocimum Sanctum	20 mg
Mineral Pitch	20 mg
Mucuna Prurita	20 mg
Commifera mukul	20 mg
Glycyrrhiza glabra	20 mg
Holarrhena Antidysenterica	20 mg
Feroso Revie Oxide	20 mg
Pueraria Tubeursa	20 mg
Curcuma longa	20 mg
Azadirachta Indica	20 mg
Terminalia Chebula	20 mg

Contents for the treatment of black spots or pigmentation

Composition	*Wt (%)*
Pterocarpus santalivus	10%
Symplucos recemosa	10%
Santalum Album	10%
Inula racemosa	10%
Nelumbo nucifera	10%
Berberis aristata	10%
Myristica fragrans	10%
Termanalia Arjuna	10%
Multani	10%
Khapariya	10%

Contents for the treatment of sperm production

Each capsule contains	*Wt/unit*
(Cressa Cretica)	200 mg
Mineral Pitch	200 mg
Mucuna Prurita	200 mg
Withania Somnifera	100 mg
Asparagus Racemonus	100 mg
Zinc	100 mg
Boitite	50 mg
Iron	50 mg

Contents for the treatment of hypertension

Each capsule contains	*Wt (%)*
Rauwolfia serpentina	150 mg
Convolvulus pluricaulis	100 mg
Santalum album	50 mg
Symplocos racemosus	50 mg
Tinospora cordifolia	50 mg
Terminalia Chembulla	25 mg
Piper Longum	100 mg
Termanalia Arjuna	25 mg
Hyoscymus niger	25 mg

Contents for the treatment of type 2 diabetes

Composition	*Wt (%)*
Cressa Cretica	10 %
Vitex negundo	10 %
Terminatia Chebula	10 %
Elugenia Jamboloma	10 %
Picrorhiza Kurroa	20 %
Enicostama Littorale	20 %
Azadirachta IndicaS	20 %

Contents for increasing strength

Each capsule contains	*Wt/unit*
Mineral Pitch	50 mg
Feroso Revie oxide	50 mg
Piper longum	50 mg
Pueraria Tubeursa	50 mg
Swertia chirata	50 mg
Asparagus adscendens	100 mg
Cressa Cretica	150 mg

Contents for the treatment of allergy

Each capsule contains	*Wt/unit*
Solanum Indicum	150 mg
Cressa Cretica	150 mg
Ocimum Sanctum	100 mg
Piper longum	100 mg

Contents for the treatment of strong hair

Composition	*V/V (%)*
Cressa Cretica	5 %
Berberis aristata	5 %
Eclipta alba	5 %
Vitex negundo	5 %
Bacopa monniera	5 %
Azadirachta Indica	QS

Contents for the treatment of strong hair

Composition	*V/V (%)*
Cressa Cretica	5 %
Berberis aristata	5 %
Eclipta alba	5 %
Vitex negundo	5 %
Bacopa monniera	5 %
Azadirachta Indica	QS

Contents for the treatment to reduce cholesterol (LDL)

Each capsule contains	*Wt/unit*
Termanalia Arjuna	300 mg
Annona Cherimolia	150 mg
Piper longum	50 mg

Contents for the treatment of baldness

Composition	*V/V (%)*
Cressa Cretica	10 %
Berberis aristata	10 %
Eclipta alba	5 %
Vitex negundo	5 %
Bacopa monniera	5 %
Azadirachta Indica	QS

3 Quality Control

Herbs Forever Inc is proud to carry on the tradition of our founders since 1932. We are a team of herbalists, biochemists, pharmacists and microbiologists to bring you safe and high quality traditional products.

FACTORS TO CONSIDER

Our naturally grown wild crafted herbs come from their natural habitat. Natural habitat plays a key role in the potency of herbs, which is why we use wild crafted herbs, as opposed to less effective cultivated ones. Every herb is collected at its proper harvest time for higher potency.

High quality extracts/Standardized extract of wild crafted herbs from their natural habitat.

In all our proprietary formulas and single formulas, we use high quality extracts (amount used is dependent on the potency and quality of the plants). Our extraction process uses the methodology most appropriate for each specific herb.

GMP and ISO Certified manufacturing facility in India : Laboratory tested for quality purity and heavy metal standards.

ISO 9001 (International quality standard) Certified

No preservatives or artificial colors.

All binding ingredients used are taken from a natural source.

All herbs and ingredients used in our products have a safe history of use in Ayurveda (Indian Vedic herbal system) for many centuries.

Every herb is collected during the full-ripened time; tested for its genuiness and strength of its active constituents. Naturally-grown herbs are preferable to cultivated herbs. Aromatic herbs or herbs having volatile oil are used in the natural form. The rest of the herbs are used in standardized extract form because active principals vary from region to region and habitat to habitat. Total extract of herbs is used instead of isolated salts. Ancient Ayurveda has suggested many methods for analyzing the various herbs, but at that time herbs were used in their original form to powder, pills or juice of fresh herbs or distillate of herbs. All the suggestions and methods for identifying a particular herb were physical and taste based. Now, since a lot of work has been done, chemical tests are available for identification of true herbs and quantity of active constituents. We are equipped with a modern plant, machinery and quality assurance system and the herbs are tested for their complete strength, efficacy and safety. Good manufacturing practices are applied with a neat, clean and sanitary environment. Herbs are procured in season and stored in extract form. All the requirements regarding purity, quality and efficacy are totally complied with and given top priority from the time of procurement till ready for consumption.

Manufacturing activities are carried out in newly-built premises and laboratory in India. Quality control measurements are taken under the guidelines of a highly experienced and qualified person, having a vast knowledge of analytical chemistry and an Associate of Institute of Chemists to maintain strict standards and comply with all requirements from the time of procurement to finished product.

EXTRACTION SYSTEM

Extraction is the process in which the plant tissues are treated with specific solvents whereby the medicinally active constituents are dissolved out, cell tissues and most of inactive or inert components remain undissolved. The plant material used for extraction should be properly identified. The choice of the plant material for extraction depends on its nature and the components required to be isolated. The solvents used for extraction purposes is known as "Menstruum" and residue left after extracting the desired constituents is known as "Marc".

The medicinal value of natural herb of the plant is due to the active constituents. It is generally advantages to extract the active constituents to formulate a control doses form of that active constituents rather than using the bulk quantity.

Solvents Used for the Extraction of Herbs

From the stand point of pharmacy, the purpose of a solvent is to remove from a solid, either in part or in its entirety such substances that may be rendered to a liquid.

When the material has extracted, the "Menstruum" is known as "Vehicle" or "Carrier" of the extracted materials. Solvents differ widely from each other, not only in differing boiling points, but how they act or react with substances in which they come in contact.

An ideal solvent for the extraction of the herbs should meet the following criteria:-

1. It should be non-toxic and selective, i.e. it should dissolve only the required constituent with minimum amount of the inert materials.
2. It should not cause the extract to complex or dissociate.
3. It should be preservative in action.
4. It should promote rapid physiologic absorption of the extract.
5. It should be easily evaporated at low heat.

Alcohol (Ethanol) will meet all above criteria

There are large number of solvents (Menstruum) used for extraction of herbs, but the selection of the suitable solvents capable of extracting the active constituents depends upon the chemical properties of active constituents as well as the qualities of the solvent. The solvents commonly used for the extraction of the herbs include water, alcohol and there different dilutions.

a. **Water:** It is a good solvent for the extraction of many types of active constituents, such as alkaloidal salts, colouring agents, glycosides, gums, sugars, anthraquinone derivatives and tannins. It can also act as menstruum for many organic acids and small proportions of volatile oils.

Water is not a suitable menstruum (Solvent) for constituents like waxes, fats, fixed oil and alkaloidal bases due to there insolubility in water. Water is not selective as it can dissolve a wide range of substances and leads to hydrolysis of many substances.

Water soluble herbs are aloe, glycyrrhiza, linseed, senna leaves, senna pods, ginger, etc.

b. **Alcohol:** Alcohol or ethanol can dissolve a large number of chemical constituents, such as alkaloids, alkaloidal salts, glycosides, tannins, anthraquinone derivatives, volatile oils and resins, but constituents like albumin, gums, waxes, fats, fixed oils and sucrose are insoluble in alcohol.

Generally dilute alcohols (hydroalcoholic solutions) are used for many extractions, but in some cases stronger alcohol may be used to prevent the extraction of unwanted substances, such as gums.

It is nontoxic in the quantities present in medicinal substances. It is reasonably selective. In a herb containing a number of chemical substances, such as alkaloidal salts, glycosides, albumin and gum, water will dissolve all the substances. Whereas dilute alcohol will dissolve only the alkaloidal salts and glycosides.

Alcohol soluble herbs are benzoin, asafoetida, ginger, valerian, myrrh, etc.

Other solvents Used for Extraction of Herbs Include Ether (Anesthetic Ether), chloroform, glycerin, light petroleum, benzene, propylene glycol, acids, such as acetic acid and tannic acid.

c. **Ether:** Soluble constituents are oils, fats, waxes, resins and alkaloidal bases. Highly inflammable produces physiologically effects. Ether soluble herbs are capsicum, male fern, linseed, nutmeg, etc.
d. **Chloroform:** Soluble constituents are oils, fats, waxes, resins and alkaloidal bases. Non-inflammable.
e. **Glycerin:** Soluble constituents are tannins. Noninflammable and viscous liquid.
f. **Light Petroleum:** Soluble constituents are oils, fats, waxes, resins and alkaloidal bases. Highly inflammable and very volatile.
g. **Fixed Oils:** Soluble constituents (Arachis Oil) can act as menstruum for camphor. Non-inflammable and viscous.
h. **Propylene Glycol:** Soluble constituents are progesterone, phenobarbitone sodium. Clear, colorless, odorless, viscous liquid, miscible with water, alcohol and chloroform.

Extraction of organic bases like alkaloids usually necessitates basification of plant material, if a water immiscible solvent is to be used, whereas for aromatic acids and phenols, acidification may be required. The glycosides are soluble in water and alcohol but are insoluble in nonpolar solvents. Tannins are phenolic matter soluble in water, alcohol and ethyl acetate.

Location of Active Constituents in Plants

Cell inclusions (ergastic substances of plants): The nonliving substances of plant metabolism are known as ergastic substances. They may be reserve foods, secretory and excretory or end products of metabolism.

a. **Reserve foods:** The materials which occur as reserve foods in cell are the carbohydrates, proteins and lipids. They are present in insoluble forms. Their conversion to soluble form is covered by enzymatic processes.

b. **Secretory products:** Enzymes, coloring substances, nectar are the examples of secretory products. Enzymes are nitrogenous water soluble compounds carrying out hydrolysis of carbohydrates and proteins. Coloring substances or pigments like chlorophyll are essential for photosynthesis and several others, flavonoid glycosides giving attractive color to various flowers and leaves. Nectar is the sugary solution secreated by many flowers in special cells or glands to attract the insects for effective pollination.

c. **Excretory products (compounds):** Animals are able to get rid of their excretory products in liquid or solid form. Plants being unable to do so, their wastes are excreted in the form of insoluble products and are stored inside the cells only. Excretory products (compounds) of the plants are named as tannins, resins, latex, volatile oils, chemicals like alkaloids, glycosides and mineral crystals, such as calcium oxalate, calcium carbonate, silica, etc.

In extraction, a solvent is employed which is capable of penetrating the tissues of the herb and dissolve the active principles contained in it cell. Any method will be a good technique, if it will accelerate:

1. Wetting of the surface of the herb particles.
2. Permeability of cell walls.
3. Rate of dissolution of cell contents in the solvent.
4. Outward diffusion of the solution.

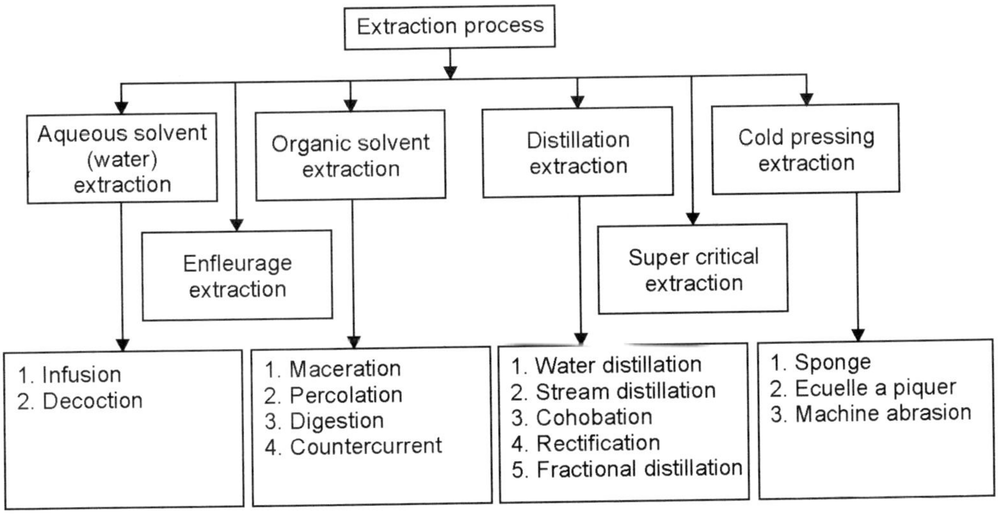

Quality Control and Quality Assurance

At herbal, we recognize that our reputation for high quality work is our most important asset. Our Quality Assurance (QA) department continuously conducts general inspections of our operations to ensure that production operations comply with the strict GMP standards and that products of consistently high quality leave our premises. The QA department is the final and highest hurdle that a product must clear before receiving our stamp of approval for being despatched to you, the clients. Quality control checks are applied in the following areas: Control of raw materials, packing materials, intermediate and finished products. Stability testing related to normal and simulated climatic conditions. Microbiological tests cleaning validation impurity profiling.

Research and Development

With our in-house R & D facility working round the clock, and with the assistance of various technical personnel we are able to develop products that are superior in nature and functionality. Our R & D department concentrates on the following:

- Morphological and microscopic studies of medicinal plants.
- Maintains control samples herbarium of phytopharmaceutical material.
- Seeks to study the mechanism of action to active ingredients of plant material.
- Works on developing immunoprotective material for immunodeficiency.

Various tests like HPLC, TLC, microbial, lead precipitate, toxicity, etc. required to adhere to the strict norms of GMP are also carried out prior to the clinical tests. Our result oriented original formulations are clinically tried out on at least 500 individuals with laboratory reports of each one before being put into the open market.

WHO Guidelines for Quality Standardized Herbal Formulations

a. Quality control of crude drugs material, plant preparations and finished products.
b. Stability assessment and shelf life.
c. Safety assessment; documentation of safety based on experience or toxicological studies.
d. Assessment of efficacy by ethnomedical informations and biological activity evaluations.

The bioactive extract should be standardized on the basis of active principles or major compounds along with the chromatographic fingerprints (TLC, HPTLC, HPLC and GC). The standardization of crude drug materials include the following steps:

1. Authentication (Stage of collection, parts of the plant collected, regional status, botanical identity like phytomorphology, microscopical and histological analysis, taxonomical identity, etc.)
2. Foreign matter (herbs collected should be free from soil, insect parts or animal excreta, etc.)
3. Organoleptic evaluation (sensory characters – taste, appearance, odor, feel of the drug, etc.)
4. Tissues of diagnostic importance present in the drug powder.
5. Ash values and extractive values.
6. Volatile matter.
7. Moisture content determination.
8. Chromatographic and spectroscopic evaluation. TLC, HPTLC, HPLC methods will provide qualitative and semi quantitative information about the main active constituents present in the crude drug as chemical markers in the TLC fingerprint evaluation of herbals (FEH). The quality of the drug can also be assessed on the basis of the chromatographic fingerprint.
9. Determination of heavy metals, e.g. cadmium, lead, arsenic, etc.
10. Pesticide residue: WHO and FAO (Food and agricultural organization) set limits of pesticides, which are usually present in the herbs. These pesticides are mixed with the herbs during the time of cultivation. Mainly pesticides like DDT, BHC, toxaphene,

aldrin cause serious side effects in human beings if the crude drugs are mixed with these agents.

11. Microbial contamination—usually medicinal plants containing bacteria and molds are coming from soil and atmosphere. Analysis of the limits of *E. coli* and molds clearly throws light towards the harvesting and production practices. The substance known as afflatoxins will produce serious side-effects if consumed along with the crude drugs.

4 Microbiological Tests

LIMITS FOR MICROBIAL CONTAMINATION

Microorganism	*Finished product*	*Raw materials*
E. coli	10^1	10^4
Salmonella	–	–
Total aerobic bacteria	10^5	–
Enterobacteria	10^3	–

Aflatoxins should be completely removed or should not be present.

Radioactive contamination: Microbial growth in herbals are usually avoided by irradiation. This process may sterilize the plant material but the radioactivity hazard should be taken into account. The radioactivity of the plant samples should be checked accordingly to the guidelines of International Atomic Energy (IAE) in Vienna and that of WHO.

In order to obtain quality oriented herbal products care should be taken right from the proper identification of plants; season and area of collection, extraction, isolation and verification process.

Chemical and instrumental analyses are routinely used for analyzing synthetic drugs to confirm its authenticity. In the case of herbal drugs, however the scene is different especially for polyherbal formulation, as there is no chemical or analytical methods available. Therefore biological-screening methods can be adopted for routine check-up of herbal drugs and formulations. In the case of herbal drugs, the quality of raw materials and products can be furnished by regular pharmacognostic identifications and phytochemical analysis. The herbal formulations in general can be standardized schematically as to formulate the medicament using raw materials collected from different localities and a comparative chemical efficacy of different batches of formulation are to be observed. The preparation with better clinical efficacy are to be selected. After all the routine physical, chemical and pharmacological parameters are to be checked for all the batches to select the final finished product and to validate the whole manufacturing process.

The stability parameters for the herbal formulations which includes physical parameters, chemical parameters, and microbiological parameters.

Physical parameters include color, appearance, odor, clarity, viscosity, moisture content, pH, disintegration time, friability, hardness, flowability, flocculation, sedimentation, settling rate and ash values. Chemical parameters includes limit tests, extractive values, chemical assays, etc.

Chromatographic analysis of herbals can be done using TLC, HPLC, HPTLC and GC, UV, Fluorimetry, GC-MS, etc.

Microbiological parameters include total viable content, total mold count, total enterobacterial and their count. Limiters can be utilized as a quantitative or semiquantitative tool to ascertain and control the amount of impurities like the reagents used during abstraction of various herbs, impurities coming directly from the manufacturing vessels, impurities from the solvents, etc.

Chemical decomposition of substances present in the formulation also produces several toxic or impure compounds during storage in undesirable conditions. Contaminants may come directly from the atmosphere also. This include mainly dust, sulfur dioxide, H_2S, CO_2, Arsenic, moisture, etc.

The guidelines set by WHO can be summarized as follows:

a. Reference to the identity of the drug. Botanical evaluation – sensory characters, foreign organic matter, microscopical, histological, histochemical evaluation, quantitative measurements, etc.

b. Reference to the physiochemical character of the drug. Chromatographic profiles, ash values, extractive values, refractive index, polarimetric readings, moisture content, volatile oil content, etc.

c. Reference to the pharmacological parameters. Biological activity profiles, bitterness values, haemolytic index, astringency, swelling factor, foaming index, etc.

d. Toxicity details – heavy metals like cadmium, lead, arsenic, mercury, etc. Pesticide residues.

   Maximum residue limits =

$$\frac{\text{Acceptable daily index} \times \text{body weight} \times \text{extraction factor}}{\text{Mean daily intake of drug} \times \text{safety factor} \times 100} \times \text{Therapeutic doses}$$

e. Microbial contamination—Total viable aerobic count, pathogenic bacteria like enterobacteria, *E. coli*, salmonella, *Pseudomonous aeruginosa*, *Staphylococcus aureus*, etc. and presence of aflatoxins, etc.

f. Radioactive contamination.

Modern Herbal Ayurvedic Monographs

In the modern herbal Ayurvedic monographs the standardization parameters are discussed in a comprehensive way. According to the modern Ayurvedic monograph the quality control protocols include the following: Title, synonyms, publications related to that plant, constituents present, analytical methods.

Descriptive evaluation: Description of the drug, phytomorphological, microscopical, organoleptic evaluations, foreign matter, foreign minerals, etc.

Physicochemical Parameters

Identity: Physical and chemical identity, chromatographic fingerprints, ash values, extractive values, moisture content.

Strength: Ethanol and water extractive values, volatile oil and alkaloidal assays, quantitative estimation protocols, etc.

Biological Activity Evaluation

Bitterness values, astringency, swelling factor, form index, hemolytic index, etc.

Toxicological Evaluation

Pesticide residues, heavy metals, microbial contamination like total viable aerobic count, pathogens like *E. coli*, Salmonella, *P. aeruginosa*, *S. aureus*, Enterobacteria, etc.

Aflatoxins

The presence of aflatoxins can be determined by chromatographic methods using standard aflatoxins B_1, B_2, G_1, G_2 mixtures. Aflatoxin is a product of the microbial strain *Aspergillus flavus*.

Radioactive Contaminants

Therapeutic Evaluation

Classical evaluation as per Ayurvedic literatures

Classical therapeutical attributes like Rasna, Guna, Virya, Vipaka and Karma classical formulations, doses, storage conditions.

The quality of the raw materials can be tested according to the following format:

Name of the drug (English, Regional names, Exact botanical nomenclature)

Part of the plant used

Area of collection

Distribution details

Season of Crop

Time and year of collection

Pesticide and insecticides

Condition of the drug (fresh or dry)

Form of the drug (powdered or intact or cuttings like, etc.)

CONCLUSION

The subject of herbal drug standardization is massively wide and deep. There is so much to know and so much seemingly contradictory theories on the subject of herbal medicines and its relationship with human physiology and mental function.

For the purpose of research work on standardization of herbal formulations and nutraceuticals a profound knowledge of the important herbs found in India and widely used in Ayurvedic formulation is of utmost importance.

India can emerge as the major country and play the lead role in production of standardized, therapeutically effective Ayurvedic formulation. India needs to explore the medicinally important plants. This can be achieved only if the herbal products are evaluated and analyzed using sophisticated modern techniques of standardization, such as UV-visible, TLC, HPLC, HPTLC, GC-MS, spectrofluorimetric and other methods.

5 Herbal Formulations

Herbal Formulations developed by our company is by keeping in mind our motto "natural solutions for better living". Recently, we have developed two unique formulations, which are launched after an extensive research on lifestyle disorders.

The product offered is among the best in comparison to the other alternatives available in the market, in its effect to rectify the disorder and also has as price competitiveness. And the best thing about the product is that they are free from any side effects. Formulations offered are as below:

1. Slimming herbal formulation in capsule
2. Men Health Herbal Formulation in capsule

Phytochemicals

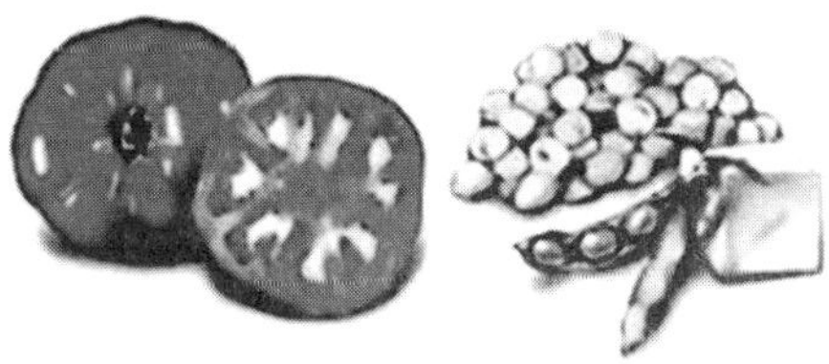

Phytochemicals offered are known for their at most purity and standardized strength. The Products provide distinctive health benefits by finding wide application in pharma and food industry. The range of phytochemicals we offer are listed below.

- Andrographolides 95%
- Capsaicin 95%
- Curcumin 95%
- Forskohlin 95%
- Guggulsterones 95%
- Levodopa 90%
- Methoxsalen 99%
- Piperine 95%
- Polycosanol 60–80%
- Raubasine 95%

Herbal Extracts

At "herbal." We offer a wide range of herbal extracts, which has been carefully obtained from pure herbs after in-depth research.

Renowned for accurate compositions and standardized strength, they come with an assurance of having no side effects.

Our comprehensive range of herbal extracts are:

Sr No.	*Extracts*	*Standardised for*	*Grades Available*
1.	Cassia angustifia (sena)	Sennosides (UV)	10–60%
2.	Gymnema sylvestre (Gurmar)	Gymnemic acids	25 and 75%
3.	Garcinia cambogia (Vilayati imli)	Hydroxycitric acid (HPLC)	50–60%
	Garcinia extract (water soluble)	Hydroxycitric acid (HPLC)	40–70%
4.	Garcinia mangostana	Mangosteen (HPLC)	10–20%
	Garcinia mangostana (water soluble)	Mangosteen	3–10%
5.	Mucuna pruriens (Kaunch)	Natural Levodopa	10–40%
6.	White Kidney Bean	Amylase Inhibition activity	4000–10000 Units

Rejuvenative for muscles, bone marrow and semen.

Helps to cure stress, weakness, tissue deficiency, the elderly.

HERBAL SYRUPS

We are engaged in offering a huge gamut of Herbal syrups. These syrups are very effective for treating various illnesses. Being economically priced, these syrups are very popular due to their accurate composition and swift action. Thus, these are prescribed by reputed hospitals, clinics and medical practitioners. We offer the following range of products:

Nostone Syrup

Our esteemed clients can avail from us the best quality range of nostone syrup. This Nostone syrup is very popular in the market, as these are pure, hygenically prepared, securely packed and has a long shelf life. These syrups are highly effective in getting rid of renal stones and burning micturition found in urine infection patients. The recommended dosage of this syrup is for adult is 2 TSF twice a day.

Composition: Each 10 ml contains

Sr No.	Drug name	Latin name	Qty.
1.	Gokshur	Tribulus Terrestris	250 mg
2.	Varun	Crataevia Nurvala	300 mg
3.	Yavakshar		100 mg
4.	Palash Pushp	Butea Monosperm	100 mg
5.	Suryakshar		100 mg
6.	Daruhaldi	Berberis Aristata	300 mg
7.	Shudh Guggulu	Commiphora Mukul	150 mg
8.	Apamarg Kshar		150 mg
9.	Swet Parpati		200 mg
10.	Lajwanti	Mimosa Pudica	200 mg
11.	Mulakshar		
12.	Narikel Lavan		100 mg
13.	Kulatha	Dolichos Biflorus	300 mg

Macliv Syrup

We are engaged in offering a huge gamut of Macliv syrup. This syrup is formulated by making use of the best quality ingredients, coupled with latest technology. The Macliv syrup is highly recommended to treat various Liver disorders and is very useful in treating hepatitis effectively. The recommended dosage for adult is 1–1.5 tsf twice a day and for children it is prescribed 1/2 tsf twice a day.

Composition: Each 5 ml contains

Sr. No.	Drug name	Latin name	Qty.
1.	Kasni	Cichorium Intybus	30 mg
2.	Kakamachi	Solanum Nigrum	10 mg
3.	Arjuna chal	Terminalia Arjuna	10 mg
4.	Kasmarda	Cassia Occidentalis	10 mg
5.	Jhavuka	Tamariz Croupii	10 mg
6.	Kutki	Picrrohiza Kurroa	20 mg
7.	Bhringraj	Eclipta Alba	34 mg
8.	Bhoomiamla	Phyllanthus Nirrui	34 mg
9.	Punernava	Boerrhavia Diffusa	34 mg
10.	Gudchi	Tinospora Cordifolia	16 mg
11.	Daruharidra	Berberis Aristata	34 mg

(Contd.)

Composition: Each 5 ml contains *(Contd.)*

Sr. No.	*Drug name*	*Latin name*	*Qty.*
12.	Munaka	Vitis Vinifera	8 mg
13.	Chitrak	Plumbago Zeylinca	8 mg
14.	Vidang	Emblia Ribes	16 mg
15.	Pitpapra	Fumaria Parviflora	8 mg
16.	Haritiki	Terminalia Chebula	8 mg
17.	Preservatives		

R. Koff Syrup

Banking on our enriched domain experience, we are engaged in offering a huge assortment of R. Koff syrup. This cough syrup is very effective in treating bronchitis and rhinitis. The usually prescribed dosage for adults is 10 ml twice or thrice a day and for children, it is 5 ml twice or thrice a day. We source this syrup from highly well-known manufacturers of the industry.

Composition: Each 10 ml contains

Sr. No.	*Drug Name*	*Latin Name*	*Qty.*
1.	Vasa	Adhatoda Vasica	280 mg
2.	Somlata	Ephedra Vulgaris	120 mg
3.	Gajavaan		110 mg
4.	Jufa	Chyssopua Officinalis	120 mg
5.	Kakrasinhghi	Pistacia Intigirrima	50 mg
6.	Bharangi	Cleodendron Serratum	120 mg
7.	Kantkari	Solanum Xanthocarpum	55 mg
8.	Pushkarmool	Inula Racemosa	120 mg
9.	Arkmool	Calotropis Procera	50 mg
10.	Dalchini	Cinnamomum Zeylanicum	110 mg
11.	Mulathi	Glycrrhiza Glabra	120 mg
12.	Talispatra	Abies Webbiana	50 mg
13.	Karpura	Camphor	4 mg

Acidend Syrup

Leveraging on our wide vendor contact base, we are able to deliver the best quality range of Acidend syrup. This syrup is highly appreciated for its unique properties, such as high effectiveness, homogeneity, accurate composition and long shelf life. These are very effective in treating various ailments like hyperacidity and heartburn. The dosage for adults is 1 tsf thrice a day and for children it is 1/2 tsf thrice a day.

Composition: Each 10 ml contains

Sr. No.	*Drug name*	*Latin name*	*Qty.*
1.	Amla	Emblica Officinalis	200 mg
2.	Vacha	Acorus Calamus	60 mg
3.	Trikatu		120 mg
4.	Mulathi	Glycrrhiza Glabra	125 mg
5.	Nishoth	Operculina Turpethum	120 mg
6.	Shankh Bhasm		35 mg
7.	Kapardika Bhasm		25 mg
8.	Tamra Bhasm		6 mg
9.	Pravala Pisthi		10
10.	Mishri		150 mg
11.	Swarna Gairik		20 mg

Gyanicol Syrup

With the active support of our team of experts, we are engaged in offering a wide range of Gyanicol syrup. This syrup is highly appreciated for its distinctive attributes, such as high quality, accurate composition and is available in industry approved packaging. The Gyanicol Syrup is highly recommended for the treatment of Leucchorea. The prescribed dosage for adults is 1–2 tsf twice a day, or as per doctor's advice.

Composition: Each 10 ml contains

Sr. No.	*Drug name*	*Latin name*	*Qty.*
1.	Ashok	Saraca Asoca	950 mg
2.	Dhatki	Woodfordia Fructicosa	150 mg
3.	Lodhra	Symplocos Racemosa	210 mg
4.	Udumber	Ficus Glomerata	65 mg
5.	Preservatives		

Heamapure Syrup

We are engaged in offering a huge assortment of Heamapure syrup. This syrup is sourced from highly placed vendors of the industry. Our Heamapure Syrup is widely recommended for the treatment of various skin diseases. The commonly recommended dosage of this medicine to adults is 2 tsf twice a day and for children, it is 1 tsf twice a day or as per the advice of the doctor.

Composition: Each 10 ml contains

Sr. No.	*Drug name*	*Latin name*	*Qty.*
1.	Sariva	Ichnocarpus Fruiticens	25 mg
2.	Manjistha	Rubia Cordifolia	25 mg
3.	Karella	Momordhica Clarentia	25 mg
4.	Neem Chaal	Azadirachta Indica	50 mg
5.	Chopchini	Smilax China	15 mg
6.	Gorakhmundi	Sphaenthus Indicus	5 mg
7.	Shisham Chaal	Dalbergia Sisso	10 mg
8.	Suranjan	Colchichum Luetum	15 mg
9.	Gandhak Rasyan		50 mg
10.	Bakuchi	Psorelliya Corylifolia	50 mg
11.	Bakuchi	Curcuma Longa	25 mg
12.	Siah Jeera	Carum Bulbocastum	10 mg
13.	Pravala Pisthi		
14.	Mishri		150 mg
15.	Swarna Gairik		20 mg

Safurti Syrup

Our esteemed clients can avail from us a wide assortment of safurti syrup. This syrup is highly effective for treating general debility. The prescribed dosage for adults is 2 tsf thrice a day and for children-1 tsf thrice a day. These syrups are highly appreciated for their unique features, such as high quality, quick action, accurate composition and long shelf life.

Composition: Each 10 ml contains

Sr. No.	*Drug name*	*Latin name*	*Qty.*
1.	Gokshur	Tribulus Terrestris	12 mg
2.	Vidhara	Argyreia Speciosa	12 mg
3.	Kaunch Beej	Mucuna Pruruita	12 mg
4.	Rasna	Pluchea Lanceolata	20 mg
5.	Ashwangdha	Withania Somnifera	60 mg

(Contd.)

Composition: Each 10 ml contains *(Contd.)*

Sr. No.	*Drug name*	*Latin name*	*Qty.*
6.	Manjistha	Rubia Cordifolia	20 mg
7.	Chaturjaat		20 mg
8.	Trifla		20 mg
9.	Katu		15 mg
10.	Shatawari	Asparagus Racemosus	50 mg
11.	Akarkara	Anacyclus Pyrethrum	30 mg
12.	Jaiphal	Myristica Fragrans	22 mg
13.	Vidarikand	Pueraria Tuberosa	35 mg
14.	Shilajeet	Asphaltum	15 mg
15.	Musli Safed	Asparagus Ascendens	25 mg
16.	Preservatives		

Risizyme Syrup

Leveraging on our enriched domain experience, we are engaged in offering a huge gamut of Risizyme syrup. This syrup is highly recommended by famous doctors, medical personnel and health care workers. These products are highly effective in giving immediate relief from digestive problems like indigestion, gastritis and flatulence. The recommended dosage in adult is 10 ml twice a day and in children it is 5 ml twice a day.

Composition: Each 10 ml contains

Sr. No.	*Drug name*	*Latin name*	*Qty.*
1.	Yastimadhu	Glycrhizza Glabra	425 mg
2.	Saunf	Foeniculum Vulgare	200 mg
3.	Harataki	Terminalia Chebula	175 mg
4.	Pitpapra	Fumaria Parviflora	110 mg
5.	Jeera	Cyumin Cummi	100 mg
6.	Pipali	Piper Longum	50 mg
7.	Badi Elaichi	Amomum Subulatum	100 mg
8.	Tulsi	Ocimum Sanctum	50 mg
9.	Ajwain	Trachyspermum Ammi	95 mg
10.	Saunth	Zingiber Officinale	105 mg
11.	Kali Marich	Piper Nigrum	55 mg
12.	Dalchini	Cinnamomum Zeylanica	50 mg
13.	Punarnava	Boerrhavia Diffusa	100 mg
14.	Pudina	Mentha Spicata	60 mg
15.	Saindha Namak		10 mg
16.	Kala Namak		20 mg

Jas Koff Syrup

We are engaged in offering a wide range of Jas Koff syrup. This syrup is highly appreciated for it unique properties, such as homogeneity, purity, long shelf life and high effectiveness. These are very effective in curing cough, sinusitis and bronchial asthma. The recommended dosage for adults is 10 ml twice or thrice a day and for children it is 5 ml twice or thrice a day.

Composition: Each 10 ml contains

Sr. No.	*Drug name*	*Latin name*	*Qty.*
1.	Kutki	Picrorhhiza Kurroa	250 mg
2.	Kakrasinghi	Pistacia Intigirrima	150 mg
3.	Yastimadhu	Glycrrhiza Glabra	100 mg
4.	Tulsi	Ocimum Sanctum	120 mg
5.	Anantmool	Ichnocarpus Frutescens	50 mg
6.	Banefsa	Viola Odorata	50 mg
7.	Talispatra	Abies Webbiana	50 mg
8.	Preservatives		

Macliv-DS Syrup

Our company is renowned as a specialist in offering a huge assortment of Macliv-Ds syrup. This syrup is been formulated by making use of high quality ingredients, coupled with latest technology. Thus, this syrup is highly effective in curing Liver disorders and is very helpful in the treatment of hepatitis. Adults are prescribed a dosage of 1/2 tsf twice a day and Children-1/4 tsf twice a day.

Composition: Each 5 ml contains the following extracts

Sr. No.	*Drug name*	*Latin name*	*Qty.*
1.	Kasni	Cichorium Intybus	60 mg
2.	Kakamachi	Solanum Nigrum	20 mg
3.	Arjuna Chal	Terminalia Arjuna	20 mg
4.	Kasmarda	Cassia Occidentalis	20 mg
5.	Jhavuka	Tamariz Croupii	20 mg
6.	Kutki	Picrrohiza Kurroa	40 mg
7.	Bhringraj	Eclipta Alba	68 mg
8.	Bhoomiamla	Phyllanthus Nirrui	68 mg
9.	Punernava	Boerrhavia Diffusa	68 mg
10.	Gudchi	Tinospora Cordifolia	32 mg

(Contd.)

Composition: Each 5 ml contains the following extracts *(Contd.)*

Sr. No.	*Drug name*	*Latin name*	*Qty.*
11.	Daruharidra	Berberis Aristata	68 mg
12.	Munaka	Vitis Vinifera	16 mg
13.	Chitrak	Plumbago Zeylinca	16 mg
14.	Vidang	Emblia Ribes	32 mg

HERBAL CAPSULES

Banking on our vast domain experience, we are able to offer a wide range of Herbal capsules. We offer these products under reputed brands formulated by reputed manufacturers. These capsules are recommended for treating rheumatic and joint pains, and offers instant relief from headache. Our capsules are highly recommended by renowned doctors, as these are free from any side effects. We offer the following range of capsules:

Hamrid Capsule

The superior quality Hamrid capsule offered by us is highly recommended by reputed doctors and medical experts. Our capsules are formulated in line with the industry set quality standards and norms. Thus, these capsules are very effective in preventing and curing bleeding and dry piles. The recommended dosage for adults is 1 capsule thrice a day or as per the prescription of the doctor.

Composition: Each capsule contains

Sr. No.	*Drug name*	*Latin name*	*Qty.*
1.	Guggulu	Commiphora Mukul	150 mg
2.	Neem	Azadirachta Indica	150 mg
3.	Shilajeet	Asphaltum Punjabimum	20 mg
4.	Harar	Terminalia Chebula	15 mg
5.	Amla	Emblica Officinalis	30 mg
6.	Daru Haldi	Berberis Aristata	100 mg
7.	Excipients		

EG Slim Capsule

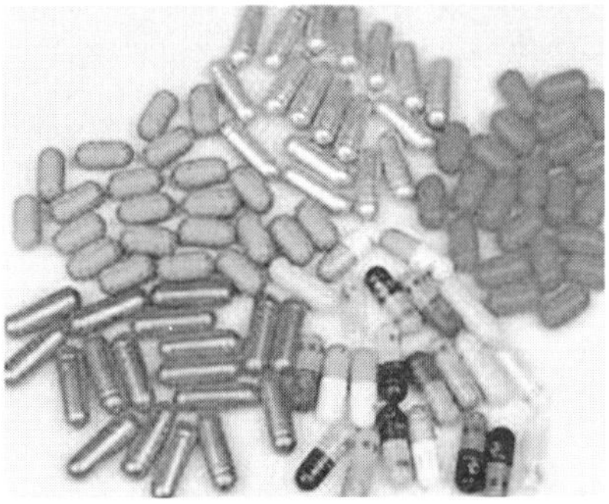

We are considered as one of the pioneers engaged in offering a wide range of EG Slim capsule. These tablets are widely appreciated for their distinctive qualities, such as accurate composition, long shelf life, high quality, swift action and high effectiveness. Our EG Slim Capsule is very helpful in fighting and preventing the problem of obesity. The recommended dosage for adults is 2 capsules thrice a day with water and for children is 1 capsule thrice a day.

Composition: Each capsule contains

Sr. No.	*Drug name*	*Latin name*	*Qty.*
1.	Trifla		60 mg
2.	Loh Bhasm		50 mg
3.	Vidang	Emblia Ribes	25 mg
4.	Pipali	Piper Longum	25 mg
5.	Kali Marich	Piper Nigrum	25 mg
6.	Chitrak Mool	Plumbago Zeylanica	25 mg
7.	Nagarmotha	Cyperus Rotundus	50 mg
8.	Saunth	Zingiber Officinale	25 mg
9.	Vasa	Adhatoda Vasica	25 mg
10.	Khadir Chaal	Acacia Catechu	25 mg
11.	Giloy	Tinospora Cordifolia	25 mg
12.	Excipients		

Mentone Capsule

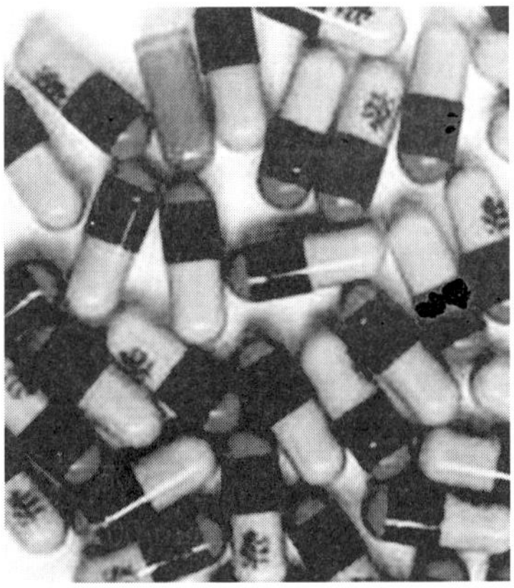

Our renowned clients can avail form us the best quality range of Mentone capsule. These capsules are widely recommended by reputed doctors for treating stress and hypertension in patients. The prescribed dosage in adults is 2 capsules thrice a day with water and for children it is 1 capsule thrice a day or as per the advice of the doctor. We offer these capsules at industry leading prices.

Composition: Each capsule contains

Sr. No.	*Drug name*	*Latin name*	*Qty.*
1.	Sudh Kupilu	Strychnos Nux Vomica	30 mg
2.	Jatamansi	Nordostychus Jatamansi	30 mg
3.	Vacha	Acorus Calamus	60 mg
4.	Jyotismati	Celastrus Paniculatus	30 mg
5.	Mandukparni	Centella Asiatica	30 mg
6.	Brahmi	Bacopa Monneri	30 mg
7.	Bhringraj	Eclipta Alba	20 mg
8.	Mulathi	Glycrrhiza Glabra	20 mg
9.	Godanti Bhasm		60 mg
10.	Kusmand	Benincasa Hispida	20 mg
11.	Ustukhudus	Lavandula Stoechas	20 mg

Macliv Capsule

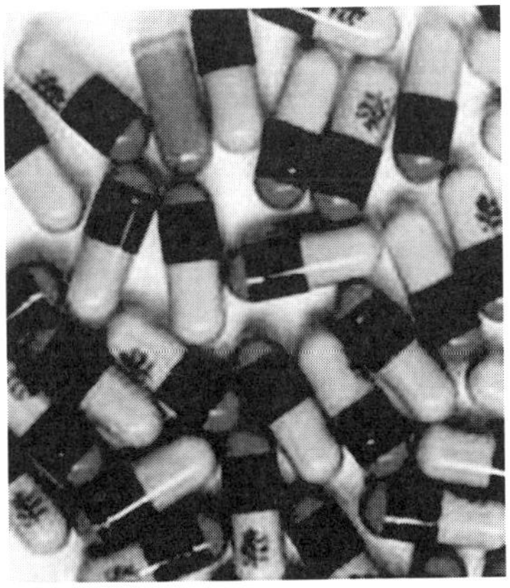

We are highly instrumental in offering a huge gamut of Macliv capsule. These capsules are usually prescribed to treat various liver disorders, anorexia and indigestion in patients. The recommended dosage for adults is 2 capsules thrice a day and for children is 1 capsule thrice a day under strict medical supervision. These capsules are procured form reliable vendors of the market.

Composition: Each capsule contains

Sr. No.	*Drug name*	*Latin name*	*Qty.*
1.	Vidang	Emblia Ribes	30 mg
2.	Chirayata	Swertia Chirayata	25 mg
3.	Chitrakmool	Plumbago Zeylanica	20 mg
4.	Shilajeet	Asphaltum Punjabimum	6 mg
5.	Bhringraj	Eclipta Alba	45 mg
6.	Kutki	Picrorhhiza Kurroa	25 mg
7.	Bhoomiamla	Phyllanthus Nirrui	20 mg
8.	Sarpankha	Tephrosia Purpurae	20 mg
9.	Punarnava	Boerrhavia Diffusa	20 mg
10.	Giloy	Tinospora Cordifolia	60 mg

(Contd.)

Composition: Each capsule contains *(Contd.)*

Sr. No.	*Drug name*	*Latin name*	*Qty.*
11.	Neem Beej	Azadirachta Indica	60 mg
12.	Kasmard	Cassia Occidentalis	45 mg
13.	Rohitaki	Tecoma Undulata	55 mg
14.	Mandur Bhasm		
15.	Ghritkumari	Aloe Barbedensis	15 mg
16.	Excipients		

Ignite Capsule

Our esteemed clients can avail from us the best quality range of Ignite capsule. These capsules are highly recommended for treating oligospermia and general debility successfully in patients. The generally prescribed dosage in adults is 1–2 capsules twice a day or as per the recommendations of the doctor. These capsules are highly appreciated for their long shelf life, immediate effectiveness and accurate composition.

Composition: Each capsule contains

Sr. No.	*Drug name*	*Latin name*	*Qty.*
1.	Shilajeet	Asphaltum Punjabimum	50 mg
2.	Rajat Bhasm		5 mg
3.	Shatawari Pili	Asparagus Racemosus	30 mg
4.	Pipali	Piper Longum	35 mg
5.	Kali Musli	Curculigo Orchide	30 mg
6.	Vang Bhasm		70 mg
7.	Loh Bhasm		10 mg
8.	Kesar	Crocus Sativus	3 mg
9.	Ashwgandha	Withania Somnifera	100 mg
10.	Kaunch Beej	Mucuna Pruritis	50 mg
11.	Jaiphal or Javitri	Myristica Fragrans	45 mg
12.	Laung	Caryophyllus Aromaticus	45 mg
13.	Excipients		

Herbilox Capsule

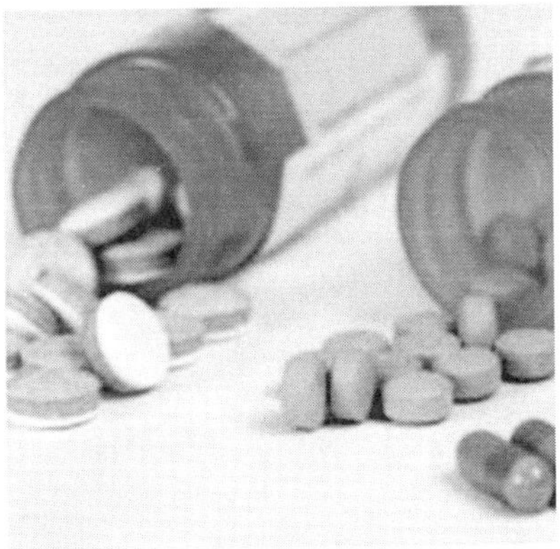

We are engaged in offering a huge gamut of Herbilox capsule. These capsules are being formulated by making use of pure and original ingredients. Thus, these are widely recommended by reputed doctors for preventing and treating constipation in patients. The recommended dosage for adults is 1 capsule daily with water. We offer these capsules at market leading prices to attain optimum client satisfaction.

Composition: Each capsule contains

Sr. No.	*Drug name*	*Latin name*	*Qty.*
1.	Harar	Terminalia Chebula	80 mg
2.	Jaiphal	Croton Tiglium	20 mg
3.	Excipients	q.s.	

Arthrva Capsule

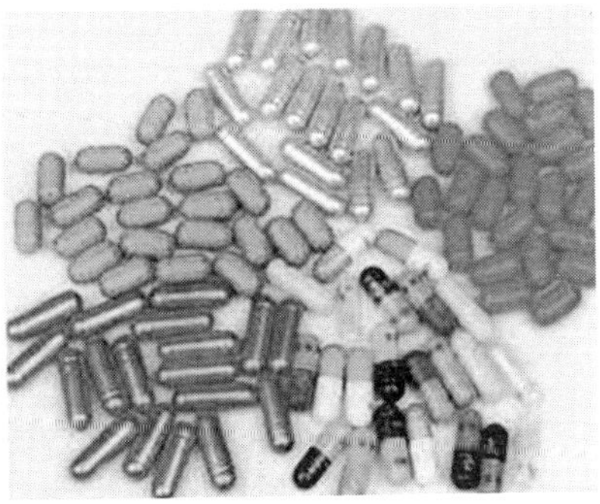

Our company is regarded as a specialist in offering a wide range of Arthrva capsule. these capsules are sourced form reliable manufacturers of the industry. They employ the best technology to formulate these capsules. Our arthrva capsules are highly recommended for treating infections like gout, ra, and synovitis. The prescribed dosage for adults is 1–2 capsules twice a day.

Flushme Capsule

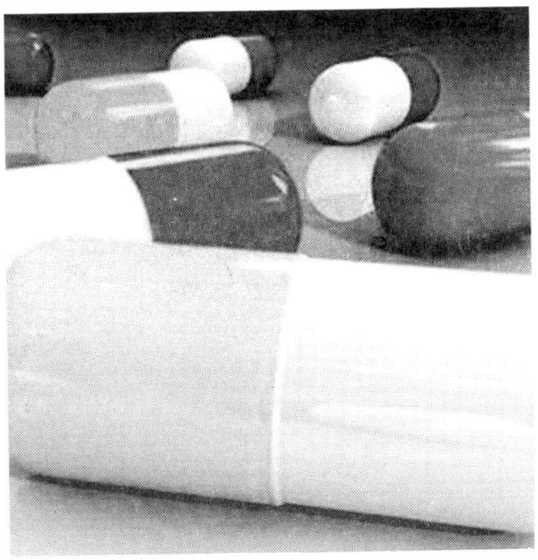

We are engaged in offering the most preferred range of Flushme capsule. These capsules are highly recommended by renowned doctors for their superior quality, long shelf life and effectiveness. Thus, these capsules are generally recommended for getting immediate relief from painful menstruation and secondary amenorrhea in women. The prescribed dosage for adults is 1 capsule thrice a day.

Composition: Each capsule contains

Sr. No.	*Drug name*	*Latin name*	*Qty.*
1.	Ulatkambal	Abroma Augusta	50 mg
2.	Vansh	Bambusa Arundinatia	25 mg
3.	Shan	Crotolaria Juncea	25 mg
4.	Karpas	Gossipium Herbaccum	240 mg
5.	Guggulu Sudh	Commiphora Mukul	25 mg
6.	Hingu Powder	Ferula Narthrex	50 mg
7.	Ajmodadi Powder		

Gyanicol Capsule

The superior quality Gyanicol capsule offered by us is highly appreciated for instant effects and long-term relief from various illnesses. These capsules are very effective in successfully treating anemia, leukorrhea and low backache. The adults are prescribed a dosage of 1 capsule thrice a day for getting relief from these above mentioned health problems.

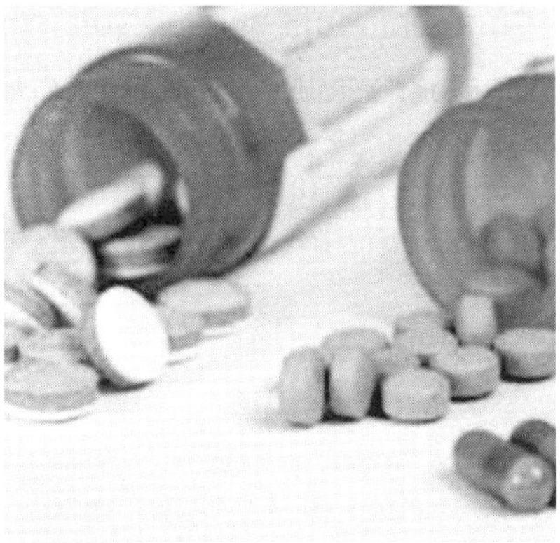

Composition: Each capsule contains

Sr. No.	*Drug name*	*Latin name*	*Qty.*
1.	Trivang Bhasma	–	45 mg
2.	Lodhra	Symplocos Racemosa	115 mg
3.	Ashoka	Saraca Asoca	95 mg
4.	Loh Bhasm	–	50 mg
5.	Chandan Safed	Santalum Album	50 mg
6.	Guggulu Sudh	Commiphora Mukul	145 mg
7.	Excipients	–	

6 Herbal Products

Our company is regarded as one of the pioneers engaged in offering a huge assortment of **Herbal Products**. These herbal products are highly effective and made from pure ingredients. Thus, these products are highly recommended for different health benefits.

We offer the following range of products:

Macliv Drops

We offer our clients with **Macliv drops**. These drops are very popular in the medical segments for their accurate composition and purity. Our Macliv drops are generally recommended for treating various liver disorders and are very effective in curing diseases, such as hepatitis. The recommended dosage for adults is 1–2 tea spoons, three a day. For children, it is 10–20 drops three times a day.

DROPS

Composition: Each 1 ml contains extracts of

Sr. No.	*Drug name*	*Latin name*	*Qty.*
1.	Kasni	Cichorium Intybus	20 mg
2.	Kakamachi	Solanum Nigrum	5 mg
3.	Arjuna Chal	Terminalia Arjuna	5 mg
4.	Kasmarda	Cassia Occidentalis	5 mg
5.	Jhavuka	Tamariz Croupii	4 mg
6.	Kutki	Picrrohiza Kurroa	20 mg
7.	Bhringraj	Eclipta Alba	20 mg
8.	Bhoomiamla	Phyllanthus Nirrui	20 mg
9.	Punernava	Boerrhavia Diffusa	10 mg
10.	Guduchi	Tinospora Cordifolia	8 mg
11.	Daruharidra	Berberis Aristata	10 mg

(Contd.)

Composition: Each 1 ml contains extracts *(Contd.)*

Sr. No.	*Drug name*	*Latin name*	*Qty.*
12.	Munaka	Vitis Vinifera	4 mg
13.	Chitrak	Plumbago Zeylinca	4 mg
14.	Vidang	Emblia Ribes	16 mg
15.	Pitpapra	Fumaria Parviflora	4 mg
16.	Haritiki	Terminalia Chebula	4 mg
17.	Preservatives		

Sun Lotion

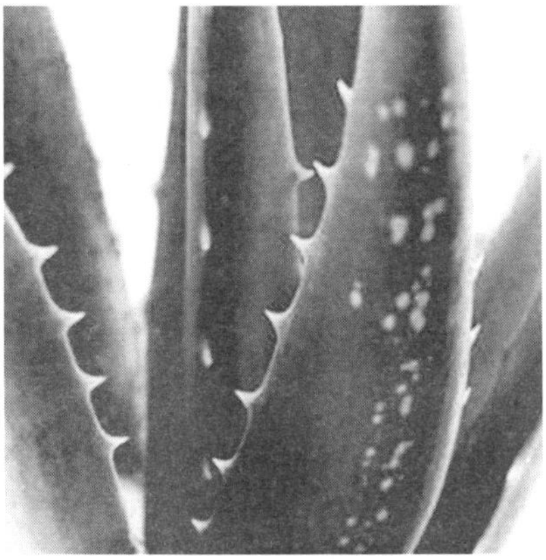

Our renowned clients can avail from us a wide assortment of **Sun Lotion**. These lotions are available in easy to use tubes and are offered in attractive packaging. Our Sun Lotion is very helpful in preventing the harmful and skin damaging effects of UV rays of the sun. Thus, these sun lotions are widely recommended by beauticians and dermatologists to protect the skin from harsh sun rays in summer and hot seasons.

Following are the compositions of this lotion:

- **adov** avobenzene 1. 5% + oxybenzone 1. 5% w/v + octyl methoxycinnamate 3. 75% w/v + titanium dioxide micronized 1% w/v **lotion**

Nutritional supplement:

- **Adrovit** lycopene + vitamins + minerals **capsules**
- **Adrovit** l-lysine + multivitamins + zinc **syrup**
- **Adrovit** zinc sulphate + vitamin B complex **drops**
- **Adrovit-g** proteins + multivitamins + multiminerals **powder**
- **Adrovit plus** ferric ammonium citrate 160 mg + folic acid 0. 5 mg + vitamin B_{12} 7. 5 mcg **syrup**
- **Fulace** multivitamins + multiminerals + beta carotene **capsule**
- **Vigrow** ginseng + multivitamins + antioxidants **capsule**.

Samran Syrup

We are engaged in offering a huge gamut of **Samran syrup**. This syrup is very helpful in enhancing the memory power of students and people who are prone to memory loss. The recommended dosage of this syrup for adults is 10 ml twice or thrice a day. For children it is recommended consuming 5 ml twice or thrice a day. We source this syrup from reliable manufacturers of the industry.

Composition: Each 10 ml contains

Sr. No.	*Drug name*	*Latin name*	*Qty.*
1.	Shatapushpa	Foeniculum Vulgare	200 mg
2.	Ashwagandha	Withania Somnifera	95 mg
3.	Guduchi	Tinospora Cordifolia	100 mg
4.	Jatamansi	Nordostychus Jatamansi	100 mg
5.	Vacha	Acorus Calamus	100 mg
6.	Brahmi	Bacopa Moneri	145 mg
7.	Jyotismati	Celastrus Paniculatus	45 mg
8.	Elaichi	Amomum Subulatum	25 mg
9.	Tagar	Valeriana Wallichhi	95 mg
10.	Saunth	Zingiber Officinale	15 mg
11.	Lavang	Caryophyllus Aromaticus	20 mg
12.	Sarpgandha	Rauwolfia Serpentina	50 mg
13.	Shankhpushpi	Convolvulus Pluricaulis	90 mg
14.	Behra	Terminalia Bellerica	20 mg
15.	Arjun	Terminalia Arjuna	45 mg
16.	Preservatives		

Mixed Infections

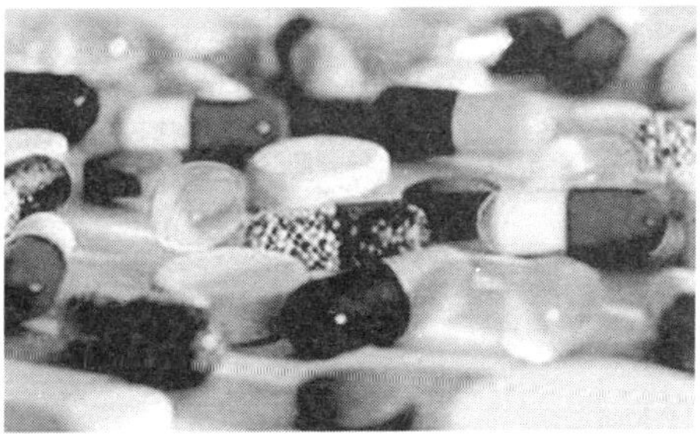

Our renowned clients can avail form us the best quality range of **mixed infections** formulations. These formulations are made from superior quality ingredients. Thus, these formulations, are widely prescribed to treat various infections, such as viral and bacterial infections. The chemical formulations of these products enable to effectively destroy these pathogens with the recommended dosage for a particular span of time.

Following are the composition of this product:

- **CORGE-C** Beclomethasone Dipropionate 0.025% w/v + Gentamycin Sulphate 0.1% w/v + Clotrimaxole 1% w/v **Cream**
- **CORGE-BC** Beclomethasone Dipropionate 0.025% w/v+ Clotrimazole 1%w/v + Benzyl Alcohol 1% w/v + Methyl Paraben 0.15% w/w + Sodium Propyl Paraben 0.05% w/w **Cream**
- **CORGE-CM** Centamycin Sulphate eq to Gentamycin 0.10% w/w + Clobetasol 0.05% w/w + Miconazole Nitrate 2% w/w **Cream**

7 Energy Kilojoules/ Kilocalories

Energy has traditionally been expressed as calories or kilocalories. More recently, the units of energy have been changed to kilojoules. There are 4.2 kilojoules in 1 kilocalorie. For convenience, both units are shown on the chart. Someone having 2000 kilocalories each day would be having 8400 kilojoules, also known as 8.4 megajoules. The energy value of a food indicates its value to the body as a fuel. This may be less than the heat value obtained experimentally by 'burning' the food outside the body in what is called a 'bomb calorimeter'. After a food is ingested, some of its energy may be 'lost' during digestion and metabolism. Although the energy value of some foods has been found by combustion in a bomb calorimeter, more usually the amounts of the macronutrients—fat, protein, **carbohydrate** and alcohol (ethanol) - in a food are taken into account when assessing the total energy value of the food. The energy value for each macronutrient must be known, and an allowance made for body losses. The first system for giving energy values to the macronutrients was described by Dr WO Atwater in 1899. Modified, the '**Atwater factors**' are:

Food charts list: beverages cereals, biscuits, cakes, deserts egg and cheese dishes fats and oils fish and seafoods fruit meat and meat products milk and milk products nuts sauces and condiments soups (as served) sugars, jams and spreads sweets vegetables.

	Kilojoules per gram	Kilocalories per gram
Fat	37	9
Alcohol	29	7
Protein	17	4
Carbohydrate	16	4

The energy value of a particular food is calculated from a knowledge of macronutrient composition and the modified Atwater factors for these macronutrients. The energy values shown in the chart have been obtained with this approach.

Fat is the most energy-dense macronutrient, followed by alcohol, protein and carbohydrate. For example, one double Scotch has about twice as many kilocalories as a glass of soft drink; a glass of full-cream milk has about twice the kilocalories as a glass of soft drink or of skimmed milk. Dietary fibre or roughage is not usually ascribed an energy value for humans, but it is now recognized that some dietary fibre components are used as fuels by the microflora (bacteria) of the gut, especially in the large intestine. Some of the products of dietary fibre digestion may provide energy for the gut lining and some may actually be absorbed for general bodily metabolism. Vitamins and elements have no energy value.

Energy requirement can be thought of as the amount needed to maintain the basic processes of life at rest, that is, basal metabolism, plus the amount needed for physical activity under a variety of circumstances. Body weight is an important factor in determining how much energy we need, since more energy will be needed to sustain and move a greater body mass.

You should refer to the charts of energy requirement according to age, sex and level of physical activity, together with the energy values of foods. However, remember that there is a great deal of individual variation in the efficiency with which ingested food energy is utilized for work by the body. If your body is relatively inefficient in its use of food energy, loss will occur in feces and by relatively more heat production.

The word 'energy' has been used here in the nutritional sense of 'provider of fuel' and not in the sense of providing zest and vitality. High-energy foods do not necessarily affect how we feel. Food products are sometimes promoted as mood-changers on the basis of their energy value, but this is simply a reflection of the double-meaning of 'energy'.

ENERGY FOOD CHARTS

BEVERAGES

kJ/kcal	*Beverages*
165/40	Beer (240 g)
150/35	Cider, dry, alcoholic (180 g)
175/40	Sweet, alcoholic (180 g)
188/45	Sweet, nonalcoholic (220 g)
1300/310	Cocoa powder (5 g)
8/2	Coffee, percolated (230 g)
170/40	Cola-type drinks (240 g)
140/35	Cordil, diluted 1:4 (240 g)
1555/365	Drinking chocolate (10 g)
160/40	Lemonade, carbonated drinks (240 g)
1785/425	Milo (10 g)
1700/400	Ovaltine (10 g)
655/155	Port (60 g)
480/115	Sherry, dry (60 g)
490/120	Medium (60 g)
570/130	Sweet (60 g)
920/220	Spirits, e.g. whisky (30 g)
2/1	Tea, infusion (230 g)
285/70	Wine, red (100 g)
275/65	White, dry (100 g)
310/70	Medium (100 g)
315/75	Sparkling (100 g)
395/95	Sweet (100 g)

Cereals, Biscuits, Cakes, Deserts

kJ/kcal	*Cereals, Biscuits, Cakes, Deserts*
510/120	Barley, pearl, boiled (–)
2200/525	Biscuit, chocolate (20 g)
2095/500	Cream-filled (20 g)
1365/320	Crispbread, rye (20 g)
1640/390	Wheat, starch-red (11 g)
1925/455	Gingernut (15 g)
1925/455	Semi-sweet (15 g)
1965/470	Short-sweet (15 g)
870/205	Bran, wheat (8 g)
1015/240	Bread, brown, slice (25 g)
1205/285	Lebanese (pita) (¼ = 25 g)
1015/240	White, slice (25 g)
985/235	Wholemeal, slice (25 g)
1230/290	Roll, brown (35 g)
1630/385	Starch-reduced (35 g)
1230/290	White (35 g)
1490/355	Cake, fruit (60 g)
1650/390	Plain (60 g)
1940/465	Cake, sponge (60 g)
1415/335	Chapati (60 g)
1745/420	Cheesecake (120 g)
1590/380	Cornflakes (30 g)
1045/250	Crumpet (50 g)
495/120	Custard (70 g)
1200/285	Custard tart (120 g)
1465/350	Doughnut (40 g)
1570/375	Eclair (50 g)
1460/350	Flour, corn (–)
1505/360	Plain (–)
1525/365	Self-raising (–)
1870/445	Soya, full-fat (–)
1490/350	Low-fat (–)
1440/345	Wholemeal (–)
1555/370	Fruit pie (150 g)
1615/385	Jam tart (35 g)
250/60	Jelly, made with water (100 g)
1485/355	Lamington (60 g)
1360/325	Lemon meringue pie (120 g)
1620/380	Meringue (15 g)
550/130	Milk pudding (e.g. sago) (160 g)
1790/425	Muesli (30 g)
625/150	Noodles (chow mein) (250 g)
1285/305	Pancake (75 g)
500/115	Pasta, macaroni, boiled (150 g)

500/115	Spaghetti, boiled (120 g)
250/60	Canned in tomato sauce (120 g)
2355/565	Pastry, flaky (–)
2200/525	Short crust (–)
980/235	Pizza, cheese and tomato (150 g)
190/45	Porridge (30 g)
520/125	Rice, boiled (160 g)
930/220	Fried (120 g)
1590/380	Puffed (25 g)
1560/370	Scone (30 g)
1445345	Sponge pudding, steamed (100 g)
675/160	Triffle (100 g)
1570/375	Wheat, breakfast biscuit (35 g)
715/170	Yeast, dried, baker's (–)

Egg and Cheese Dishes

kJ/kcal	*Egg and Cheese dishes*
470/115	Cauliflower, cheese (100 g)
1030/250	Cheese souffle (100 g)
610/145	Egg, boiled (55 g)
960/230	Egg, fried (60 g)
785/190	Omelette (100 g)
645/155	Poached (55 g)
610/145	Raw (55 g)
1020/245	Scrambled (70 g)
725/175	Macaroni cheese (180 g)
1625/390	Ouiche lorraine (150 g)

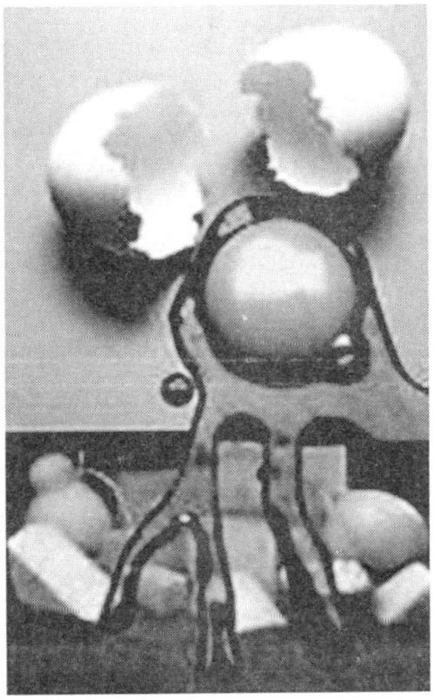

Fats and Oils

kJ/kcal	*Fats and Oils*
3045/730	Butter, salted (10 g)
3665/890	Dripping, beef (–)
3665/890	Lard (–)
3045/730	Margarine (10 g)
3695/900	Vegetable oils (–)

Fish and Other Seafoods

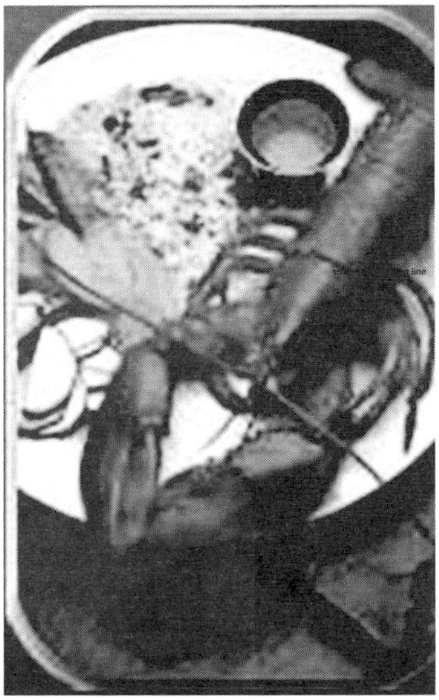

kJ/kcal	*Fish and Other Seafoods*
425/100	Bream, steamed (100 g)
410/95	Cod, baked (100 g)
835/200	Tried in batter (100 g)
395/95	Poached (100 g)
350/85	Steamed (100 g)
535/125	Crab, boiled (150 g)
340/80	Canned (90 g)
785/190	Fish cakes, fried (4 = 100 g)
975/235	Fingers, fried (5 = 100 g)
1060/250	in batter, fried (120 g)
845/200	Flounder, baked (100 g)
730/175	Haddock, fried (100 g)
415/100	Steamed (100 g)
500/120	Lobster, boiled (120 g)
365/85	Mussels, boiled (12 = 120 g)
215/50	Oysters, raw (12 = 120 g)
450/105	Prawns, boiled (6 = 120 g)
845/200	Roe, cod, fried (100 g)
650/155	Salmon, canned (100 g)
1380/330	Sardines, canned (60 g)
445/105	Scallops, steamed (10 = 100 g)
1200/290	Tuna, canned in oil (120 g)
800/190	Whiting, crumbed, fried (100 g)
390/90	Steamed (100 g)

Fruit

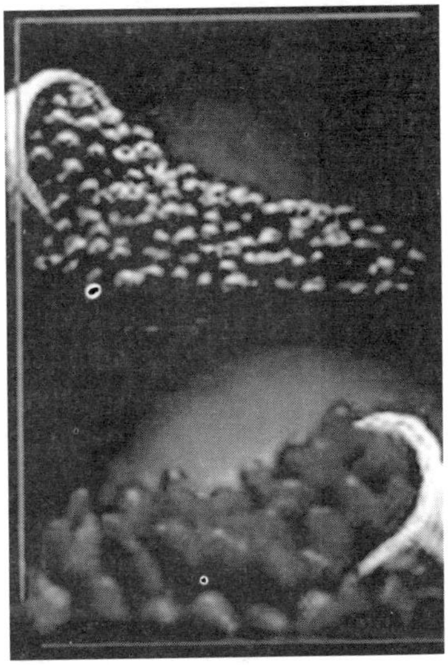

kJ/kcal	*Fruit*
150/35	Apple (inc, skin, core 100 g)
135/30	Baked, no sugar (inc. skin 110 g)
135/30	Stewed, no sugar (110 g)
110/25	Apricots (inc. stones 3 = 100 g)
450/105	Apricots, canned (100 g)
775/180	Dried (25 g)
90/20	Stewed, no sugar (inc. stones 110 g)
920/225	Avocado pear (½ = 150 g)
340/80	Banana (100 g)
125/30	Blackberries (100 g)
105/25	Stewed, no sugar (100 g)
65/15	Cantaloup (inc. skin 120 g)
175/40	Cherries (inc. stones 20 = 100 g)
140/35	Stewed, no sugar (inc. stones 100 g)
120/30	Currants, black (90 g)
1040/245	Dried (15 g)
90/20	red (90 g)
1055/250	Dates, dried (6 = 35 g)
175/40	Figs (2 = 75 g)
910/215	Dried (2 = 40 g)
405/95	Fruit salad, canned (120 g)
215/50	Grapes, black (20 = 100 g)
255/60	White (20 = 100 g)
45/10	Grapefruit, whole (200 g)
255/60	Canned (100 g)
130/30	Juice, canned (120 g)
260/60	Guavas, canned (100 g)
65/15	Lemon, slices (2 = 15 g)
30/7	Juice (15 g)
75/15	Loganberries (100 g)
430/100	Canned (100 g)
65/15	Stewed, no sugar (100 g)
290/70	Lychees, canned (100 g)
195/46	Mandarins (2 = 100 g)
235/55	Canned (50 g)
255/60	Mango (100 g)
330/75	Canned (100 g)
200/45	Nectarines (inc. stones 3 = 100 g)
340/80	Olives, in brine (5 = 20 g)
115/25	Orange, whole (130 g)
160/40	Juice, fresh (120 g)
145/35	Canned (120 g)
60/15	Passion fruit, whole (30 g)
170/40	Pawpaw (100 g)

275/65	Canned (100 g)
135/30	Peach (inc. stones 120 g)
375/85	Canned (120 g)
905/210	Dried (25 g)
335/80	Peach, stewed, no sugar (120 g)
125/30	Pear (inc. skin. core 120 g)
325/75	Canned (120 g)
130/30	Stewed, no sugar (120 g)
195/45	Pineapple (80 g)
330/75	Canned (80 g)
225/55	Juice, canned (120 g)
145/35	Plums (inc. stones 3 = 100 g)
125/30	Stewed, no sugar (inc. stones 100 g)
570/135	Prunes (inc. stones 8 = 80 g)
315/75	Stewed, no sugar (inc. stones 120 g)
105/25	Quince, raw (100 g)
1050/245	Raisins, dried (20 g)
105/25	Raspberries (100 g)
370/85	Canned (100 g)
110/25	Stewed, no sugar (100 g)
25/6	Rhubarb, stewed, no sugar (120 g)
110/25	Strawberries (10 = 100 g)
345/80	Canned (100 g)
1065/250	Sultanas, dried (15 g)
45/10	Watermelon (260 g)

Meat and Meat Products

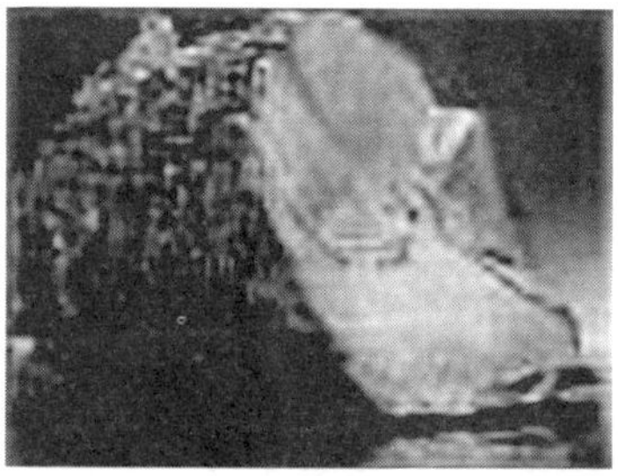

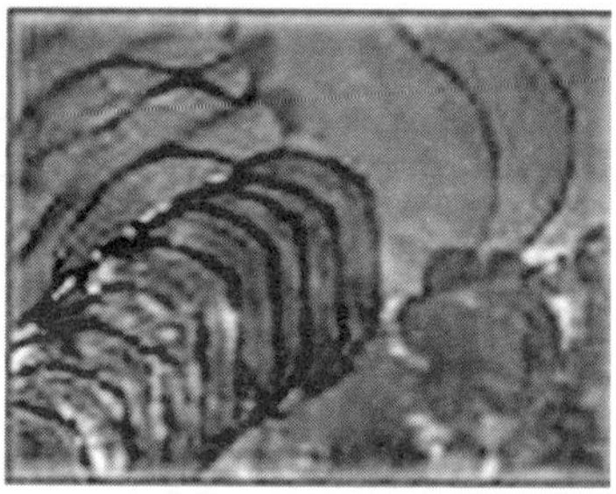

kJ/kcal	*Meat and Meat Products*
1975/475	Bacon rashers, middle, fried (2 = 40 g)
1720/415	Grilled (40 g)
905/215	Beef, corned, canned (90 g)
835/200	Fillet steak, grilled (130 g)
955/230	Mince, stewed (100 g)
1025/245	Rump steak, fried (150 g)
910/220	Grilled (150 g)
1010/240	Silverside, salted, boiled (120 g)
1180/285	Sirloin, roast (120 g)
930/225	Stewing steak, stewed (120 g)
895/215	Topside, roast (120 g)
1100/265	Beefburger, frozen, fried (60 g)
500/120	Beef stew (250 g)
580/140	Bolognes sauce (100 g)
765/185	Chicken, boiled (100 g)
1380/330	Crumbed, no bone (140 g)
900/215	roast (130 g)

390/90	Leg quarter (inc. bone 130 g)
310/75	Wing quarter (inc. bone 130 g)
810/195	Chicken livers, fried (130 g)
1405/340	Duck, roast (100 g)
1435/340	Gelatin (–)
500/120	Ham, canned (90 g)
950/225	Hamburger (170 g)
1100/260	With cheese (190 g)
475/115	Lrish stew (250 g)
525/125	Lamb, brain, boiled (150 g)
1145/275	Chops, loin, grilled (inc. bone 120 g)
1015/245	Cutlets, grilled (inc, bone 100 g)
990/235	Heart, roast (140 g)
650/155	Kidney, fried (100 g)
1105/265	Leg, roast (120 g)
970/230	Liver, fried (130 g)
1310/315	Shoulder, roast (120 g)
1195/290	Tongue, stewed (100 g)
1300/315	Luncheon meat, canned (90 g)
960/230	Meat pie (180 g)
810/195	Moussaka (200 g)
1390/330	Pastie (160 g)
1075/260	Pork, chop, ooin, grilled (100 g)
1190/285	Leg, roast (120 g)
770/185	Sweet and sour (250 g)
1565/375	Pork pie (180 g)
380/90	Rabbit, stewed (inc. bone 170 g)
2030/490	Salami, slices (3 = 90 g)
1285/310	Sausage, liver (60 g)
1210/290	Sausage roll (100 g)
1125/270	Sausages, beef, fried (2 = 120 g)
1105/265	Grilled (2 = 120 g)
1135/275	Frankfurter (2 = 100 g)
1315/275	Pork, fried (2 = 120 g)
1320/320	Grilled (2 = 120 g)
1090/260	Saveloy, large (2 = 150 g)
1400/335	Spring roll, fried (200 g)
1350/325	Steak and kidney pie (180 g)
730/175	Stewed steak in gravy, canned (100 g)
885/215	Tongue, canned (100 g)
420/100	Tripe, stewed (100 g)
720/170	Turkey, roast (120 g)
905/215	Veal, cutlet, fried (110 g)
965/230	Fillet, roast (100 g)
1335/320	Schnitzel (140 g)

Milk and Milk Products

kJ/kcal	*Milk and Milk Products*
1245/300	Cheese, camembert (25 g)
1680/405	Cheddar (25 g)
1175/285	Cheese spread (10 g)
400/95	Cottage (25 g)
1805/440	Cream cheese (15 g)
1470/355	Danish blue (25 g)
1260/305	Edam (25 g)
1695/410	Parmesan (10 g)
1290/310	Processed (25 g)
1915/460	Stilton (25 g)
1585/375	Swiss (25 g)
1525/365	Cream, 35% fat (30 g)
950/230	Sterilized, canned (15 g)
705/170	Ice cream (60 g)
690/165	non-dairy (60 g)
1140/265	Milk, cow's, cond, skim, sweet (30 g)
1360/320	Cond, whole, sweet (30 g)
1510/355	Dried, skimmed (12 g)
2050/490	Dried, whole (10 g)
660/160	Evap, whole, unsweet (30 g)
360/85	Flavored (230 g)
140/35	Fresh, skimmed (230 g)
275/65	Fresh, whole (230 g)
275/65	Longlife, UHT (230 g)
290/70	Goat's (230 g)
290/70	Human (100 g)
510/120	Milkshake, flavored (340 g)
420/100	Yoghurt, flavored (200 g)
405/95	Fruit, low-fat (200 g)
215/50	Natural, low-fat (200 g)
325/75	Plain (200 g)

Nuts

kJ/kcal	*Nuts*
2325/565	Almonds (10 = 15 g)
2545/620	Brazil nuts (5 = 20 g)
2405/575	Cashews, roast (10 = 20 g)
720/170	Chestnuts (4 = 20 g)
2490/605	Coconut, desiccated (15 g)
1570/380	Hazel nuts (10 = 15 g)
2960/705	Macadamia nuts (8 = 20 g)
2365/385	Peanuts, raw, in shells (5 = 25 g)
1630/570	Roasted, salted (30 = 25 g)
2485/590	Pistachio nuts, shelled (25 = 15 g)
2165/525	Walnuts (5 = 20 g)

Sauces and Condiments

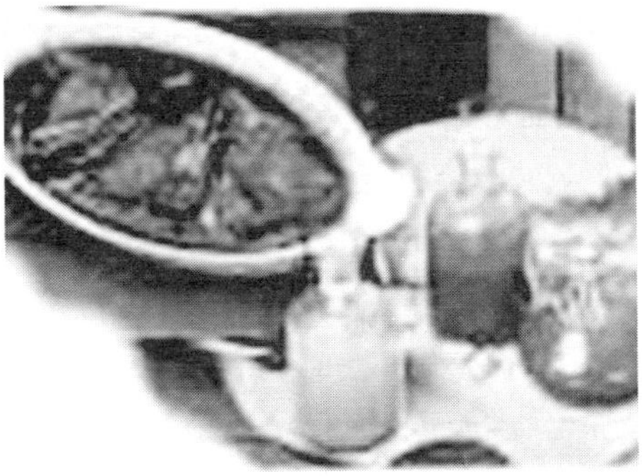

kJ/kcal	*Sauces and Condiments*
380/90	Barbecue sauce (10 g)
90/20	Chilli sauce (–)
660/155	Chutney, tomato (20 g)
920/220	Curry powder (–)
2705/660	French dressing (15 g)
1085/260	Ginger (ground) (–)
2950/720	Mayonnaise (20 g)
1940/460	Mustard powder (–)
970/230	Oxo cubes (–)
1310/310	Pepper (–)
140/35	Pickles, mustard (20 g)
570/135	Sweet (20 g)
1290/310	Salad cream (25 g)
0/0	Salt, table (–)
2355/560	Sesame seeds (–)
285/70	Soy sauce (–)
2095/500	Tartare sauce (20 g)
360/85	Tomato sauce (25 g)
15/4	Vinegar (–)
335/80	Worcestershire sauce (–)

Soups (as served)

kJ/kcal	*Soups (as served)*
205/50	Chicken, condensed (230 g)
85/20	Chicken coodle, dried (230 g)
100/25	Minestrone, dried (230 g)
220/55	Mushroom, canned (230 g)
260/60	Tomato, condensed (230 g)
130/30	Tomato, dried (230 g)
160/35	Vegetable, canned (230 g)

Sugars, Jams and Spreads

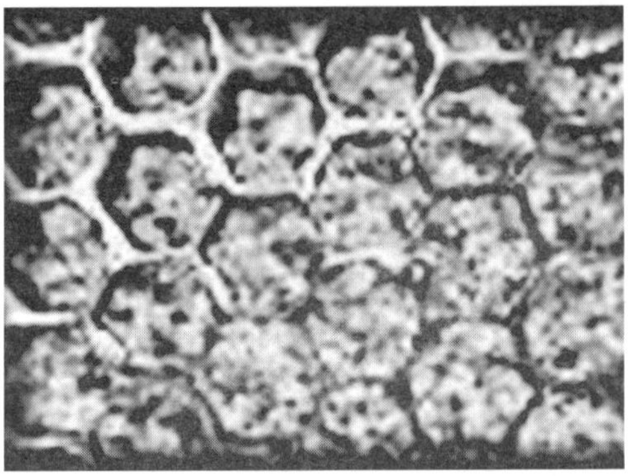

kJ/kcal	*Sugars, Jams and Spreads*
705/170	Fish paste (5 g)
1230/295	Honey (30 g)
1115/260	Jam, fruit edible seeds (30 g)
1115/260	Jam, stone fruit (30 g)
1115/260	Marmalade (30 g)
720/175	Meat paste (5 g)
2580/625	Peanut butter (20 g)
1680/395	Sugar, white (–)
1270/300	Syrup, golden (30 g)
565/135	Topping, flavored (40 g)
1095/255	Treacle, black (30 g)
725/174	Vegemite (3 g)

Sweets

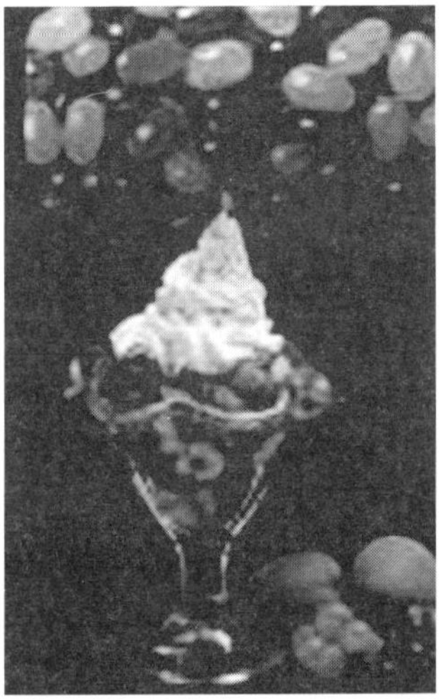

kJ/kcal	*Sweets*
1395/325	Boiled sweed (5 g)
1760/420	Butterscotch (5 g)
1710/405	Caramel (5 g)
1775/425	Carob bar (75 g)
2215/530	Chocolate square, milk (5 g)
1745/415	Fruit and honey bar (50 g)
1465/350	Jelly bean (5 g)
1335/315	Liquorice allsort (7 g)
1080/255	Pastille (5 g)
1670/390	Peppermint (4 g)
1605/380	Popcorn, plain unsalted (15 g)
1720/410	Sesame bar (50 g)
1810/430	Toffee, mixed (5 g)

Vegetables

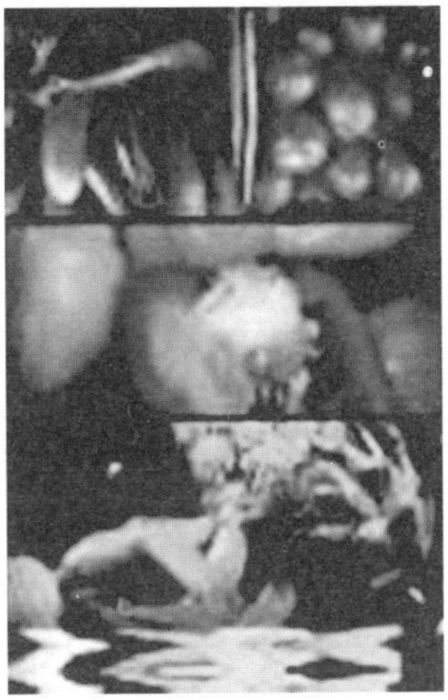

kJ/kcal	*Vegetables*
30/7	Artichoke, globe, boiled (100 g)
40/9	Asparagus, boiled (5 = 100 g)
105/25	Bamboo shoots (50 g)
30/7	Beans, french, boiled (100 g)
270/65	Baked, in tomato sauce (125 g)
215/50	Broad, boiled (100 g)
395/95	Kidney (and haricot), boiled (100 g)
445/105	Mung, cooked dal (100 g)
545/130	Soya, boiled (100 g)
190/45	Beetroot, slices, boiled (2 = 30 g)
145/35	Canned (2 = 30 g)
80/20	Broccoli, boiled (100 g)
75/20	Brussels sprouts, boiled (7 = 70 g)
110/25	Cabbage, raw (50 g)
40/9	Boiled (100 g)
100/25	Carrots, raw (50 g)
80/20	Boiled (50 g)
80/20	Young, canned (50 g)
55/15	Cauliflower, raw (50 g)
40/9	Boiled (100 g)
60/15	Celery, boiled (3 = 60 g)
35/8	Celery, raw (50 g)
20/5	Boiled (50 g)
610/145	Chickpeas, cooked dal (60 g)
45/10	Cucumber, slices (5 = 30 g)
250/60	Egg plant, baked (½ = 100 g)
50/10	Endive, raw leaves (3 = 15 g)
105/25	Leeks, boiled (4 = 100 g)
420/100	Lentils, split, boiled (100 g)
50/10	Lettuce, raw leaves (2 = 20 g)
30/7	Marrow, boiled (100 g)
55/15	Mushrooms, raw (3 = 30 g)
865/210	Fried (6 = 60 g)
100/25	Onions, raw (¼ = 20 g)
55/15	Boiled (100 g)
1425/345	Fried (70 g)
150/35	Spring (4 = 20 g)
90/20	Parsley, sprigs (2 = 5 g)
240/55	Parsnip, boiled (½ = 60 g)
200/45	Peas, conned (60 g)
340/80	Canned, processed (60 g)
225/50	Fresh, boiled (60 g)
175/40	Frozen, boiled (60 g)
505/120	Split, boiled (60 g)

65/15	Peppers, green, raw (¼ = 15 g)
60/15	Boiled (50 g)
365/85	Potato, baked (inc. skin 120 g)
345/80	Boiled (120 g)
1065/250	Chips, fresh, fried (12 = 120 g)
1215/290	Chips, frozen, fried (8–14 = 120 g)
2225/535	Crisps (10 = 25 g)
500/120	Mashed (100 g)
300/70	Instant, cooked (100 g)
325/75	New, boiled (2 = 100 g)
225/55	New, canned (2 = 100 g)
660/155	Roast (120 g)
65/15	Pumpkin (100 g)
60/15	Radishes (2 = 20 g)
130/30	Spinach, keaves, boiled (3 = 60 g)
75/20	Swede, boiled (80 g)
520/125	Sweetcorn, on cob, boiled (150 g)
325/75	Canned kernels (80 g)
365/85	Sweet patato, boiled (100 g)
60/15	Tomato, raw (120 g)
50/10	Canned (120 g)
290/70	Fried (120 g)
65/15	Juice, canned (120 g)
60/10	Turnip, boiled (80 g)
510/120	Yam, boiled (100 g)

8 Water

Water is perhaps the most essential of nutrients since we can do without it for only a short time-days at the outside. This is because, without an adequate flow of urine, waste products would build-up in the body, and with the absence of moisture loss it would not be possible to regulate body temperature. However, we can obtain water from a number of sources. Water may be taken as a beverage and as part of food; water is produced in our body cells following the metabolism (chemical breakdown) of fat, alcohol, protein and carbohydrate. Food usually provides more than half our daily water requirement.

The more water a food contains, the less energy dense it is, that is, water-rich foods have few kilocalories (or kilojoules) per 100 grams.

The need for water is influenced by environmental conditions. For example, in a hot climate a great deal of water can be lost not only as sweat, but also in expired air.

Making water supplies hygienic has contributed greatly to human health. More recently, the addition of fluoride to water supplies deficient in it has reduced dental decay. In Australia, nutritionists are encouraging people to drink water in preference to other beverages and to drink it in adequate amounts in dry conditions and with increased physical activity. It is sensible to have four or five glasses of 200 milliliters each day; by so doing, less energy and alcohol will be consumed. With that much water you will be less thirsty for alcohol, coffee and other beverages and probably eat less food. Fluoride intake will be improved for many. Urine flow will increase and the risk of kidney stones decrease.

WATER INTAKE

Safe and adequate daily intake of water

	All sources (Millilitres)	*Drinks*
Adult in a temperate climate	2500	1000 (800–1600)
Adult during exercise and thermal stress	up to 9000–10000	up to 6000–7000

Toxic Level of Intake

It is a most unusual event to be able to overload the body with water by drinking too much. The body compensates by increasing urine output. However, there can be an accumulation of body water in certain disease states. Occasionally, for psychological reasons, over-consumption of water does occur.

WATER

Beverages

grams per 100 grams	*Beverages*
96	Beer (240 g)
93	Cider, dry alcoholic (180 g)
91	Sweet, alcoholic (180 g)
88	Sweet, nonalcololic (220 g)
3	Cocoa powder (5 g)
100	Coffee, percolated (230 g)
90	Cola-type drinks (240 g)
91	Cordial, diluted 1:4 (240 g)
2	Drinking chocolate (10 g)
90	Lemonade, carbonated drinks (240 g)
3	Milo (10 g)
2	Ovaltine (10 g)
72	Port (60 g)
82	Sherry, dry (60 g)
81	Medium (60 g)
75	Sweet (60 g)
68	Spirits, e.g. whisky (30 g)
100	Tea, infusion (230 g)
88	Wine, red (100 g)
89	White, dry (100 g)
86	Medium (100 g)
86	Sparkling (100 g)
81	Sweet (100 g)

Cereals, Biscuits, Cakes, Deserts

grams per 100 grams	*Cereals, Biscuits, Cakes, Deserts*
70	Barley, pearl, boiled (–)
2	Biscuit, chocolate (20 g)
3	Cream-filled (20 g)
6	Crispbread, rye (20 g)
5	Wheat, starch-red (11 g)
3	Gingernut (15 g)
3	Semi-sweet (15 g)
3	Short-sweet (15 g)
8	Bran, wheat (8 g)
39	Bread, brown, slice (25 g)
27	Lebanese (pita) (¼ = 25 g)
39	White, slice (25 g)
40	Wholemeal, slice (25 g)
29	Roll, brown (35 g)
9	Starch-reduced (35 g)
29	White (35 g)
20	Cake, fruit (60 g)
20	Plain (60 g)
15	Cake, sponge (60 g)
29	Chapati (60 g)
35	Cheesecake (120 g)
3	Cornflakes (30 g)
35	Crumpet (50 g)
75	Custard (70 g)
48	Custard tart (120 g)
26	Doughnut (40 g)
35	Eclair (50 g)
12	Flour, corn (–)
13	Plain (–)
13	Self-raising (–)
7	Soya, full-fat (–)
7	Low-fat (–)
14	Wholemeal (–)
23	Fruit pie (150 g)
19	Jam tart (35 g)
84	Jelly, made with water (100 g)
24	Lamington (60 g)
35	Lemon meringue pie (120 g)
2	Meringue (15 g)
72	Milk pudding (e.g. sago) (160 g)
6	Muesli (30 g)
70	Noodles (chow mein) (250 g)
43	Pancake (75 g)

72	Pasta, macaroni, boiled (150 g)
72	Spaghetti, boiled (120 g)
83	Canned in tomato sauce (120 g)
7	Pastry, flaky (–)
7	Short crust (–)
51	Pizza, cheese and tomato (150 g)
89	Porridge (30 g)
70	Rice, boiled (160 g)
50	Fried (120 g)
8	Puffed (25 g)
22	Scone (30 g)
29	Sponge pudding, steamed (100 g)
65	Triffle (100 g)
8	Wheat, breakfast biscuit (35 g)
5	Yeast, dried, baker's (–)

Egg and Cheese Dishes

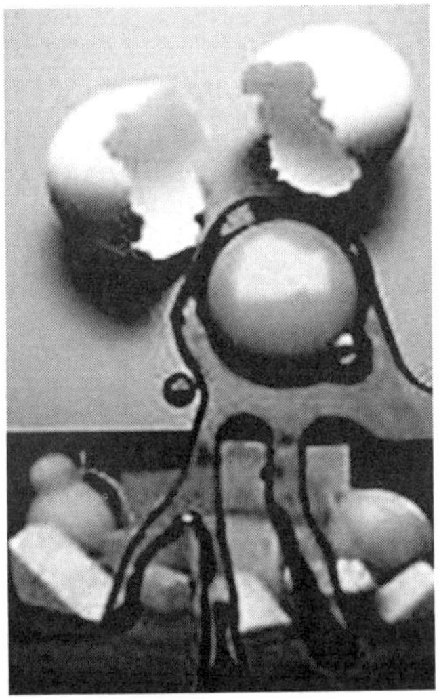

grams per 100 grams	*Egg and Cheese dishes*
78	Cauliflower, cheese (100 g)
57	Cheese souffle (100 g)
75	Egg, boiled (55 g)
63	Egg, fried (60 g)
69	Omelette (100 g)
75	Poached (55 g)
75	Raw (55 g)
62	Scrambled (70 g)
67	Macaroni cheese (180 g)
35	Ouiche lorraine (150 g)

Fats and Oils

grams per 100 grams	*Fats and Oils*
16	Butter, salted (10 g)
1	Dripping, beef (–)
1	Lard (–)
16	Margarine (10 g)
Tr	Vegetable oils (–)

Fish and Other Seafoods

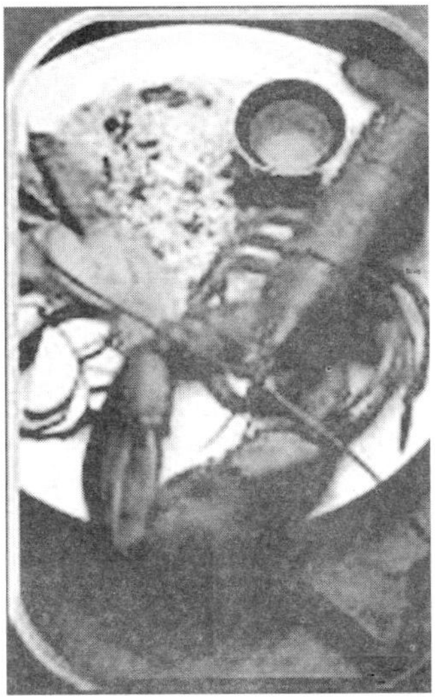

grams per 100 grams	*Fish and Other Seafoods*
77	Bream, steamed (100 g)
77	Cod, baked (100 g)
61	Tried in batter (100 g)
78	Poached (100 g)
79	Steamed (100 g)
73	Crab, boiled (150 g)
79	Canned (90 g)
63	Fish cakes, fried (4 = 100 g)
56	Fingers, fried (5 = 100 g)
55	in batter, fried (120 g)
60	Flounder, baked (100 g)
65	Haddock, fried (100 g)
75	Steamed (100 g)
72	Lobster, boiled (120 g)
79	Mussels, boiled (12 = 120 g)
86	Oysters, raw (12 = 120 g)
70	Prawns, boiled (6 = 120 g)
62	Roe, cod, fried (100 g)
70	Salmon, canned (100 g)
49	Sardines, canned (60 g)
73	Scallops, steamed (10 = 100 g)
55	Tuna, canned in oil (120 g)
63	Whiting, crumbed, fried (100 g)
77	Steamed (100 g)

Fruit

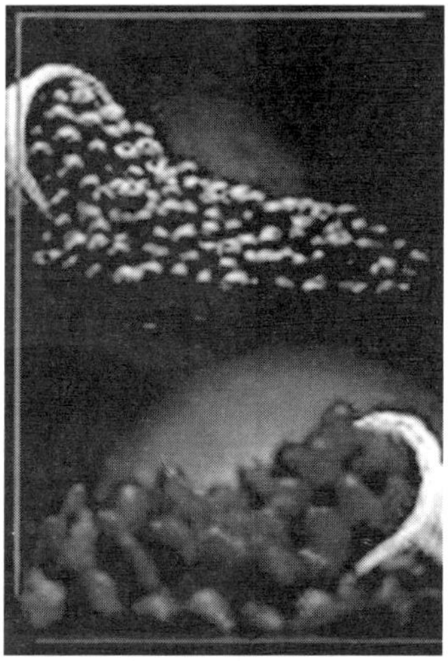

grams per 100 grams	*Fruit*
65	Apple (inc, skin, core 100 g)
68	Baked, no sugar (inc. skin 110 g)
88	Stewed, no sugar (110 g)
80	Apricots (inc. stones 3 = 100 g)
68	Apricots, canned (100 g)
15	Dried (25 g)
83	Stewed, no sugar (inc. stones 110 g)
69	Avocado pear (½ = 150 g)
71	Banana (100 g)
82	Blackberries (100 g)
85	Stewed, no sugar (100 g)
57	Cantaloup (inc. skin 120 g)
71	Cherries (inc. stones 20 = 100 g)
73	Stewed, no sugar (inc. stones 100 g)
77	Currants, black (90 g)
22	Dried (15 g)
83	Red (90 g)
15	Dates, dried (6 = 35 g)
85	Figs (2 = 75 g)
17	Dried (2 = 40 g)
71	Fruit salad, canned (120 g)
65	Grapes, black (20 = 100 g)
76	White (20 = 100 g)
44	Grapefruit, whole (200 g)
82	Canned (100 g)
90	Juice, canned (120 g)
78	Guavas, canned (100 g)
85	Lemon, slices (2 = 15 g)
91	Juice (15 g)
85	Loganberries (100 g)
66	Canned (100 g)
86	Stewed, no sugar (100 g)
79	Lychees, canned (100 g)
87	Mandarins (2 = 100 g)
84	Canned (50 g)
83	Mango (100 g)
75	Canned (100 g)
74	Nectarines (inc. stones 3 = 100 g)
61	Olives, in brine (5 = 20 g)
65	Orange, whole (130 g)
88	Juice, fresh (120 g)
89	Canned (120 g)
31	Passionfruit, whole (30 g)

88	Papaw (100 g)
80	Canned (100 g)
75	Peach (inc. stones 120 g)
74	Canned (120 g)
16	Dried (25 g)
69	Peach, stewed, no sugar (120 g)
60	Pear (inc. skin. core 120 g)
76	Canned (120 g)
86	Stewed, no sugar (120 g)
84	Pineapple (80 g)
77	Canned (80 g)
86	Juice, canned (120 g)
70	Plums (inc. stones 3 = 100 g)
74	Stewed, no sugar (inc. stones 100 g)
19	Prunes (inc. stones 8 = 80 g)
55	Stewed, no sugar (inc. stones 120 g)
84	Quince, raw (100 g)
22	Raisins, dried (20 g)
83	Raspberries (100 g)
74	Canned (100 g)
82	Stewed, no sugar (100 g)
95	Rhubarb, stewed, no sugar (120 g)
89	Strawberries (10 = 100 g)
79	Canned (100 g)
18	Sultanas, dried (15 g)
47	Watermelon (260 g)

Meat and Meat Products

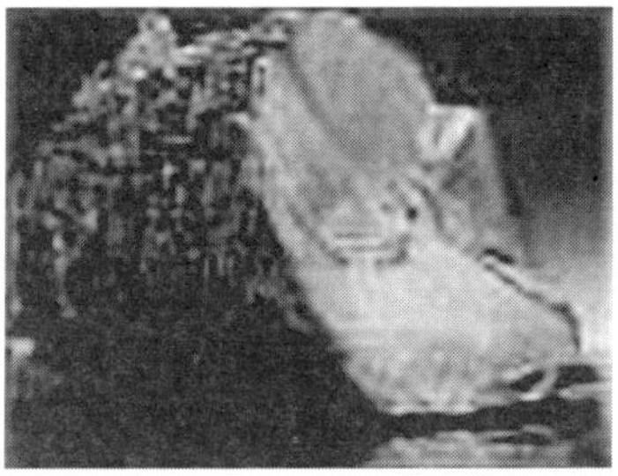

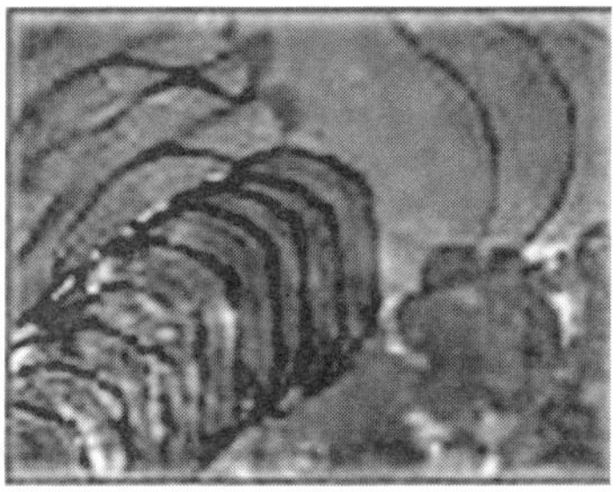

grams per 100 grams	*Meat and Meat Products*
29	Bacon rashers, middle, fried (2 = 40 g)
35	Grilled (40 g)
59	Beef, corned, canned (90 g)
62	Fillet steak, grilled (130 g)
59	Mince, stewed (100 g)
56	Rump steak, fried (150 g)
59	Grilled (150 g)
55	Silverside, salted, boiled (120 g)
54	Sirloin, roast (120 g)
57	Stewing steak, stewed (120 g)
60	Topside, roast (120 g)
53	Beefburger, frozen, fried (60 g)
78	Beef stew (250 g)
75	Bolognes sauce (100 g)
63	Chicken, boiled (100 g)
45	Crumbed, no bone (140 g)
62	Roast (130 g)
42	Leg quarter (inc. bone 130 g)
34	Wing quarter (inc. bone 130 g)
64	Chicken livers, fried (130 g)
50	Duck, roast (100 g)
13	Gelatin (–)
73	Ham, canned (90 g)
51	Hamburger (170 g)
48	With cheese (190 g)
69	Lrish stew (250 g)
77	Lamb, brain, boiled (150 g)
36	Chops, loin, grilled (inc. bone 120 g)
30	Cutlets, grilled (inc, bone 100 g)
57	Heart, roast (140 g)
67	Kidney, fried (100 g)
55	Leg, roast (120 g)
58	Liver, fried (130 g)
54	Shoulder, roast (120 g)
57	Tongue, stewed (100 g)
52	Luncheon meat, canned (90 g)
51	Meat pie (180 g)
66	Moussaka (200 g)
39	Pastie (160 g)
36	Pork, chop, ooin, grilled (100 g)
52	Leg, roast (120 g)
60	Sweet and sour (250 g)
37	Pork pie (180 g)

33	Rabbit, stewed (inc. bone 170 g)
28	Salami, slices (3 = 90 g)
52	Sausage, liver (60 g)
42	Sausage roll (100 g)
48	Sausages, beef, fried (2 = 120 g)
48	Grilled (2 = 120 g)
60	Frankfurter (2 = 100 g)
45	Pork, fried (2 = 120 g)
45	Grilled (2 = 120 g)
57	Saveloy, large (2 = 150 g)
40	Spring roll, fried (200 g)
43	Steak and kidney pie (180 g)
70	Stewed steak in gravy, canned (100 g)
64	Tongue, canned (100 g)
79	Tripe, stewed (100 g)
65	Turkey, roast (120 g)
55	Veal, cutlet, fried (110 g)
55	Fillet, roast (100 g)
49	Schnitzel (140 g)

Milk and Milk Products

grams per 100 grams	*Milk and Milk Products*
48	Cheese, camembert (25 g)
37	Cheddar (25 g)
51	Cheese spread (10 g)
79	Cottage (25 g)
46	Cream cheese (15 g)
41	Danish blue (25 g)
44	Edam (25 g)
28	Parmesan (10 g)
44	Processed (25 g)
28	Stilton (25 g)
38	Swiss (25 g)
56	Cream, 35% fat (30 g)
70	Sterilized, canned (15 g)
64	Ice cream (60 g)
66	non-dairy (60 g)
27	Milk, cow's, cond, skim, sweet (30 g)
26	Cond, whole, sweet (30 g)
4	Dried, skimmed (12 g)
3	Dried, whole (10 g)
69	Evap, whole, unsweet (30 g)
82	Flavored (230 g)
90	Fresh, skimmed (230 g)
88	Fresh, whole (230 g)

88	Longlife, UHT (230 g)
87	Goat's (230 g)
87	Human (100 g)
75	Milkshake, flavored (340 g)
79	Yoghurt, flavored (200 g)
75	Fruit, low-fat (200 g)
86	Natural, low-fat (200 g)
84	Plain (200 g)

Nuts

grams per 100 grams	*Nuts*
5	Almonds (10 = 15 g)
9	Brazil nuts (5 = 20 g)
4	Cashews, roast (10 = 20 g)
52	Chestnuts (4 = 20 g)
2	Coconut, desiccated (15 g)
41	Hazel nuts (10 = 15 g)
2	Macadamia nuts (8 = 20 g)
3	Peanuts, raw, in shells (5 = 25 g)
5	Roasted, salted (30 = 25 g)
5	Pistachio nuts, shelled (25 = 15 g)
24	Walnuts (5 = 20 g)

Sauces and Condiments

grams per 100 grams	*Sauces and Condiments*
81	Barbecue sauce (10 g)
94	Chilli sauce (–)
58	Chutney, tomato (20 g)
–	Curry powder (–)
24	French dressing (15 g)
–	Ginger (ground) (–)
28	Mayonnaise (20 g)
–	Mustard powder (–)
9	Oxo cubes (–)
Tr	Pepper (–)
86	Pickles, mustard (20 g)
59	Sweet (20 g)
53	Salad cream (25 g)
Tr	Salt, table (–)
5	Sesame seeds (–)
63	Soy sauce (–)
34	Tartare sauce (20 g)
82	Tomato sauce (25 g)
95	Vinegar (–)
80	Worcestershire sauce (–)

Soups (as served)

grams per 100 grams	*Soups (as served)*
91	Chicken, condensed (230 g)
94	Chicken coodle, dried (230 g)
93	Minestrone, dried (230 g)
89	Mushroom, canned (230 g)
85	Tomato, condensed (230 g)
91	Tomato, dried (230 g)
86	Vegetable, canned (230 g)

Sugars, Jams and Spreads

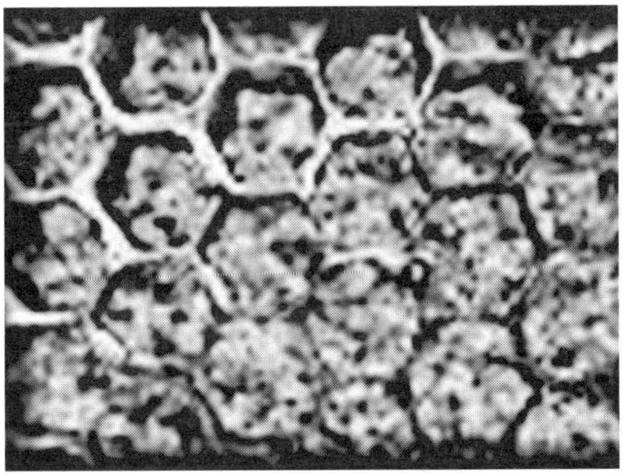

grams per 100 grams	*Sugars, Jams and Spreads*
67	Fish paste (5 g)
23	Honey (30 g)
30	Jam, fruit edible seeds (30 g)
30	Jam, stone fruit (30 g)
28	Marmalade (30 g)
67	Meat paste (5 g)
1	Peanut butter (20 g)
Tr	Sugar, white (–)
20	Syrup, golden (30 g)
66	Topping, flavored (40 g)
29	Treacle, black (30 g)
37	Vegemite (3 g)

Sweets

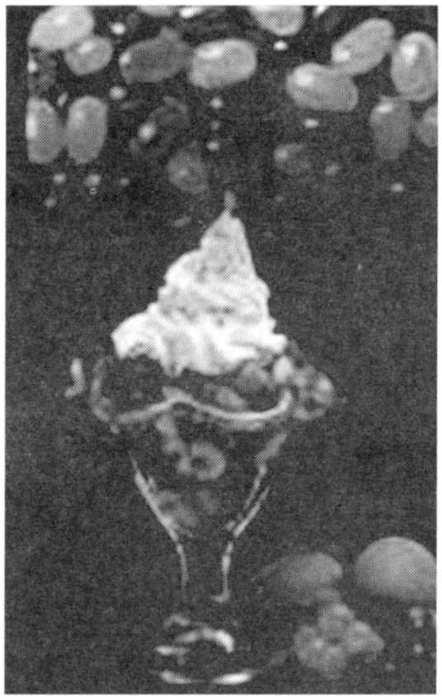

grams per 100 grams	*Sweets*
Tr	Boiled sweed (5 g)
2	Butterscotch (5 g)
7	Caramel (5 g)
4	Carob bar (75 g)
2	Chocolate square, milk (5 g)
11	Fruit and honey bar (50 g)
9	Jelly bean (5 g)
7	Liquorice allsort (7 g)
10	Pastille (5 g)
Tr	Peppermint (4 g)
4	Popcorn, plain unsalted (15 g)
11	Sesame bar (50 g)
5	Toffee, mixed (5 g)

Vegetables

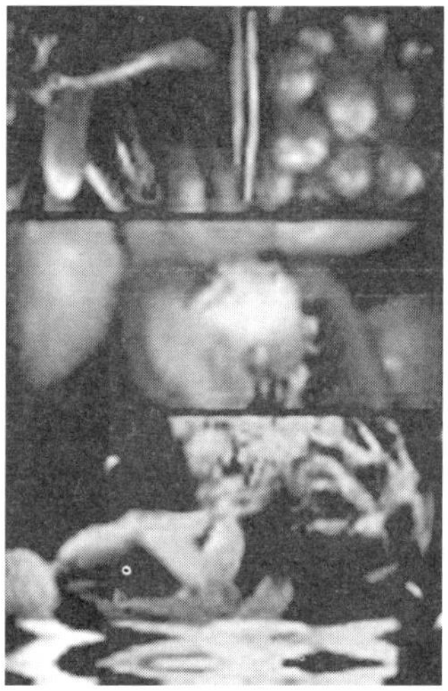

grams per 100 grams	*Vegetables*
36	Artichoke, globe, boiled (100 g)
46	Asparagus, boiled (5 = 100 g)
91	Bamboo shoots (50 g)
96	Beans, french, boiled (100 g)
74	Baked, in tomato sauce (125 g)
84	Broad, boiled (100 g)
70	Kidney (and haricot), boiled (100 g)
73	Mung, cooked dal (100 g)
70	Soya, boiled (100 g)
83	Beetroot, slices, boiled (2 = 30 g)
90	Canned (2 = 30 g)
90	Broccoli, boiled (100 g)
92	Brussels sprouts, boiled (7 = 70 g)
90	Cabbage, raw (50 g)
96	Boiled (100 g)
90	Carrots, raw (50 g)
92	Boiled (50 g)
91	Young, canned (50 g)
93	Cauliflower, raw (50 g)
95	Boiled (100 g)
90	Celery, boiled (3 = 60 g)
94	Celery, raw (50 g)
96	Boiled (50 g)
66	Chickpeas, cooked dal (60 g)
96	Cucumber, slices (5 = 30 g)
89	Egg plant, baked (½ = 100 g)

94	Endive, raw leaves (3 = 15 g)
91	Leeks, boiled (4 = 100 g)
72	Lentils, split, boiled (100 g)
96	Lettuce, raw leaves (2 = 20 g)
98	Marrow, boiled (100 g)
92	Mushrooms, raw (3 = 30 g)
64	Fried (6 = 60 g)
93	Onions, raw (¼ = 20 g)
97	Boiled (100 g)
42	Fried (70 g)
87	Spring (4 = 20 g)
79	Parsley, sprigs (2 = 5 g)
83	Parsnip, boiled (½ = 60 g)
82	Peas, conned (60 g)
72	Canned, processed (60 g)
80	Fresh, boiled (60 g)
81	Frozen, boiled (60 g)
67	Split, boiled (60 g)
94	Peppers, green, raw (¼ = 15 g)
94	Boiled (50 g)
58	Potato, baked (inc. skin 120 g)
81	Boiled (120 g)
47	Chips, fresh, fried (12 = 120 g)
48	Chips, frozen, fried (8–14 = 120 g)
3	Crisps (10 = 25 g)
77	Mashed (100 g)
79	Instant, cooked (100 g)
79	New, boiled (2 = 100 g)
84	New, canned (2 = 100 g)
64	Roast (120 g)
95	Pumpkin (100 g)
93	Radishes (2 = 20 g)
85	Spinach, keaves, boiled (3 = 60 g)
92	Swede, boiled (80 g)
65	Sweetcorn, on cob, boiled (150 g)
73	Canned kernels (80 g)
72	Sweet patato, boiled (100 g)
94	Tomato, raw (120 g)
94	Canned (120 g)
87	Fried (120 g)
93	Juice, canned (120 g)
95	Turnip, boiled (80 g)
66	Yam, boiled (100 g)

9 Dietary Fiber

Dietary fiber is a term that refers to a group of food components that pass through the stomach and small intestine undigested and reach the large intestine virtually unchanged. Most other nutrients are digested and are being used in other parts of the body by this stage. During its passage through the large intestine some components of dietary fiber are broken down to varying degrees and absorbed by the body; the remaining components are excreted in the feces.

To the extent that products of dietary fiber breakdown in the large intestine are absorbed, a small amount of energy is contributed, probably of the order of 13 kilojoules (3 kilocalories) per gram of dietary fiber ingested. Diets that are high in dietary fiber produce a slower rate of stomach emptying, and bulky feces which pass more quickly through the large intestine.

The current attention being given to the role of dietary fiber in prevention of certain diseases is largely due to the observation that patterns of disease observed in Africa and Asia were different from those in Western countries. It was suggested that the dietary fiber content was associated with this difference. Although it is not yet proven, there is evidence to suggest that a diet high in dietary fiber can be of value for treating or preventing such disorders as constipation, irritable bowel syndrome, diverticular disease, hiatus hernia and hemorrhoids. Some components of dietary fiber may also be of value in reducing the level of cholesterol in blood and thereby decreasing a risk factor for coronary heart disease and the development of gallstones. Dietary fiber is beneficial in the treatment of some diabetics.

The actual role of dietary fiber in many of these disorders is not known. It may be that dietary fiber as such is not the major factor. When high dietary fiber foods are eaten, other foods, which may be responsible for the disease, are either reduced in quantity or completely excluded. For example, diets that are high in fiber tend to be low in energy and these diets can be useful in weight control. People who are grossly overweight (more than 130 percent of desirable weight or with a body mass index of about 30 kilograms per square meter) are more prone to heart disease and diabetes.

The analysis of dietary fiber in food is very complex and only a limited number of foods have been examined in detail. Dietary fiber from different foods, and even different samples of the same food, contain varying quantities of the components that collectively make-up dietary fiber. Each of these components has different biological properties and it is frequently not clear which of these is most beneficial. The different components of dietary fiber and their sources. Foods of animal origin do not contain dietary fiber.

Component	Source
Cellulose	All food plants
Hemicellulose	All food plants, especially cerealbran
Pectin	Mainly fruit
Lignin	Mainly cereals and 'woody'vegetables
Gums and some foodthickeners	Food additives in processed foods

Intake of Dietary Fiber

There is no recommended dietary intake (RDI) for fiber, as such in Australia. However, the Australian Department of Health has among its dietary goals for Australians an increased intake of fruit, vegetables, bread and cereals, all of which are sources of dietary fiber. The greatest amount of dietary fiber in wheat is in the outer layer or bran, of the wheat grain. When white flour is produced, the bran layer is removed and the dietary fiber content of the flour is greatly reduced. Flour made from whole grains contains about three times as much dietary fiber as white flour. It is probably reasonable to aim for a dietary fiber intake of between 35 and 45 grams per day, compared with current intakes in Western countries of about 20 grams per day.

DIETARY FIBER FOOD CHARTS

Beverages

grams per 100 grams	*Beverages*
–	Beer (240 g)
–	Cider, dry alcoholic (180 g)
–	Sweet, alcoholic (180 g)
–	Sweet, nonalcololic (220 g)
–	Cocoa powder (5 g)
–	Coffee, percolated (230 g)
0	Cola-type drinks (240 g)
–	Cordial, diluted 1:4 (240 g)
–	Drinking chocolate (10 g)
0	Lemonade, carbonated drinks (240 g)
–	Milo (10 g)
–	Ovaltine (10 g)
–	Port (60 g)
–	Sherry, dry (60 g)
–	Medium (60 g)
–	Sweet (60 g)
–	Spirits, e.g. whisky (30 g)
–	Tea, infusion (230 g)
–	Wine, red (100 g)
–	White, dry (100 g)
–	Medium (100 g)
–	Sparkling (100 g)
–	Sweet (100 g)

Cereals, Biscuits, Cakes, Deserts

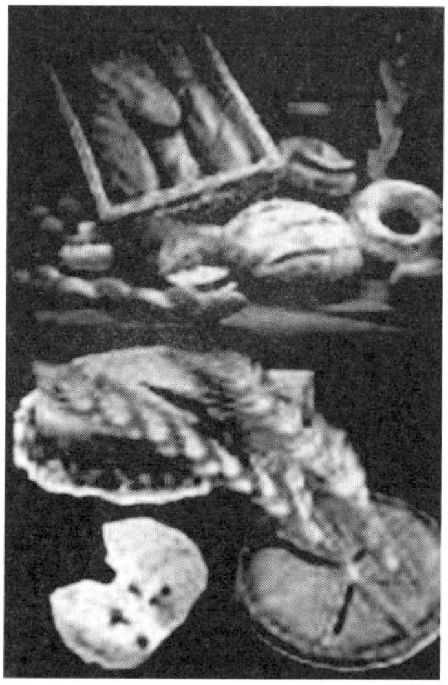

grams per 100 grams	*Cereals, Biscuits, Cakes, Deserts*
2	Barley, pearl, boiled (–)
3	Biscuit, chocolate (20 g)
–	Cream-filled (20 g)
12	Crispbread, rye (20 g)
5	Wheat, starch-red (11 g)
2	Gingernut (15 g)
2.5	Semi-sweet (15 g)
1.5	Short-sweet (15 g)
44	Bran, wheat (8 g)
5	Bread, brown, slice (25 g)
–	Lebanese (pita) (¼ = 25 g)
3	White, slice (25 g)
7	Wholemeal, slice (25 g)
7	Roll, brown (35 g)
2	Starch-reduced (35 g)
3	White (35 g)
3	Cake, fruit (60 g)
1.5	Plain (60 g)
1	Cake, sponge (60 g)
3.5	Chapati (60 g)
1	Cheesecake (120 g)
–	Cornflakes (30 g)
–	Crumpet (50 g)
–	Custard (70 g)
1	Custard tart (120 g)
–	Doughnut (40 g)
–	Eclair (50 g)
–	Flour, corn (–)
3.5	Plain (–)
3.5	Self-raising (–)
12	Soya, full-fat (–)
14.5	Low-fat (–)
9.5	Wholemeal (–)
2.5	Fruit pie (150 g)
1.5	Jam tart (35 g)
–	Jelly, made with water (100 g)
–	Lamington (60 g)
.5	Lemon meringue pie (120 g)
–	Meringue (15 g)
–	Milk pudding (e.g. sago) (160 g)
–	Muesli (30 g)
–	Noodles (chow mein) (250 g)
–	Pancake (75 g)

.5	Pasta, macaroni, boiled (150 g)
–	Spaghetti, boiled (120 g)
–	Canned in tomato sauce (120 g)
2	Pastry, flaky (–)
2	Short crust (–)
1.8	Pizza, cheese and tomato (150 g)
1	Porridge (30 g)
1	Rice, boiled (160 g)
–	Fried (120 g)
–	Puffed (25 g)
2	Scone (30 g)
1	Sponge pudding, steamed (100 g)
–	Triffle (100 g)
–	Wheat, breakfast biscuit (35 g)
22	Yeast, dried, baker's (–)

Egg and Cheese Dishes

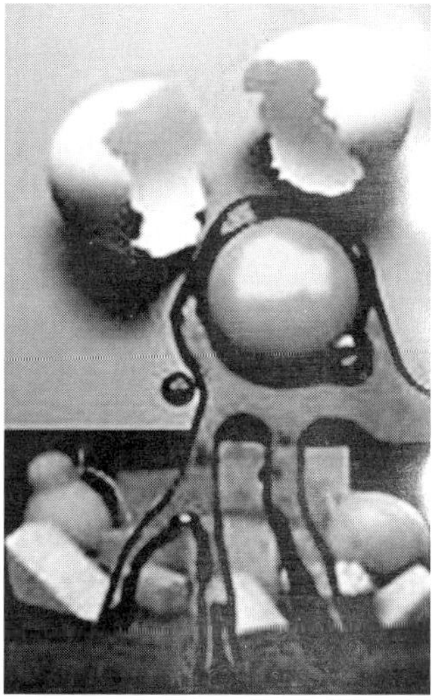

grams per 100 grams	*Egg and Cheese dishes*
1.2	Cauliflower, cheese (100 g)
.3	Cheese souftle (100 g)
–	Egg, boiled (55 g)
–	Egg, fried (60 g)
–	Omelette (100 g)
–	Poached (55 g)
–	Raw (55 g)
–	Scrambled (70 g)
.6	Macaroni cheese (180 g)
.8	Ouiche lorraine (150 g)

Fats and Oils

grams per 100 grams	*Fats and Oils*
–	Butter, salted (10 g)
–	Dripping, beef (–)
–	Lard (–)
–	Margarine (10 g)
–	Vegetable oils (–)

Fish and Other Seafoods

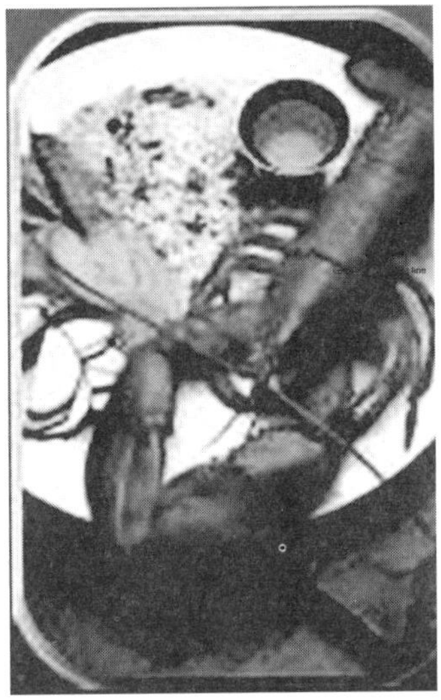

grams per 100 grams	*Fish and Other Seafoods*
–	Bream, steamed (100 g)
–	Cod, baked (100 g)
.3	Tried in batter (100 g)
–	Poached (100 g)
–	Steamed (100 g)
–	Crab, boiled (150 g)
–	Canned (90 g)
.7	Fish cakes, fried (4 = 100 g)
.7	Fingers, fried (5 = 100 g)
–	In batter, fried (120 g)
–	Flounder, baked (100 g)
–	Haddock, fried (100 g)
–	Steamed (100 g)
–	Lobster, boiled (120 g)
–	Mussels, boiled (12 = 120 g)
–	Oysters, raw (12 = 120 g)
–	Prawns, boiled (6 = 120 g)
–	Roe, cod, fried (100 g)
–	Salmon, canned (100 g)
–	Sardines, canned (60 g)
–	Scallops, steamed (10 = 100 g)
–	Tuna, canned in oil (120 g)
–	Whiting, crumbed, fried (100 g)
–	Steamed (100 g)

Fruit

grams per 100 grams	*Fruit*
1.5	Apple (inc, skin, core 100 g)
2	Baked, no sugar (inc. skin 110 g)
2	Stewed, no sugar (110 g)
2	Apricots (inc. stones 3 = 100 g)
1.5	Apricots, canned (100 g)
24	Dried (25 g)
1.5	Stewed, no sugar (inc. stones 110 g)
2	Avocado pear (½ = 150 g)
1.3	Banana (100 g)
7.5	Blackberries (100 g)
6.5	Stewed, no sugar (100 g)
.5	Cantaloup (inc. skin 120 g)
1.5	Cherries (inc. stones 20 = 100 g)
1	Stewed, no sugar (inc. stones 100 g)
8.5	Currants, black (90 g)

6.5	Dried (15 g)
8	Red (90 g)
8.5	Dates, dried (6 = 35 g)
2.5	Figs (2 = 75 g)
18.5	Dried (2 = 40 g)
1	Fruit salad, canned (120 g)
.5	Grapes, black (20 = 100 g)
1	White (20 = 100 g)
.5	Grapefruit, whole (200 g)
.5	Canned (100 g)
–	Juice, canned (120 g)
3.5	Guavas, canned (100 g)
5	Lemon, slices (2 = 15 g)
–	Juice (15 g)
6	Loganberries (100 g)
3.5	Canned (100 g)
3.5	Stewed, no sugar (100 g)
5.5	Lychees, canned (100 g)
–	Mandarins (2 = 100 g)
.5	Canned (50 g)
1.5	Mango (100 g)
1	Canned (100 g)
2	Nectarines (inc. stones 3 = 100 g)
3.5	Olives, in brine (5 = 20 g)
1.5	Orange, whole (130 g)
–	Juice, fresh (120 g)
–	Canned (120 g)
6.5	Passionfruit, whole (30 g)
–	Papaw (100 g)
.5	Canned (100 g)
1	Peach (inc. stones 120 g)
1	Canned (120 g)
14.5	Dried (25 g)
5.5	Peach, stewed, no sugar (120 g)
1.5	Pear (inc. skin. core 120 g)
1.5	Canned (120 g)
2.5	Stewed, no sugar (120 g)
1	Pineapple (80 g)
1	Canned (80 g)
0	Juice, canned (120 g)
4	Plums (inc. stones 3 = 100 g)
3	Stewed, no sugar (inc. stones 100 g)
13.5	Prunes (inc. stones 8 = 80 g)
7.5	Stewed, no sugar (inc. stones 120 g)
6.5	Quince, raw (100 g)
7	Raisins, dried (20 g)

7.5	Raspberries (100 g)
5	Canned (100 g)
7.8	Stewed, no sugar (100 g)
2.5	Rhubarb, stewed, no sugar (120 g)
2	Strawberries (10 = 100 g)
1	Canned (100 g)
7	Sultanas, dried (15 g)
–	Watermelon (260 g)

Meat and Meat Products

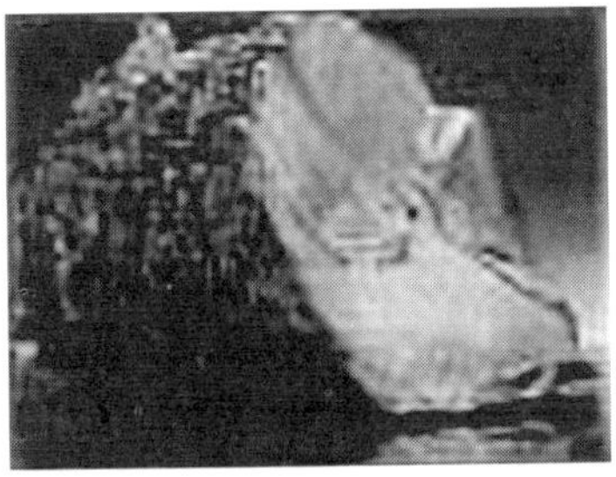

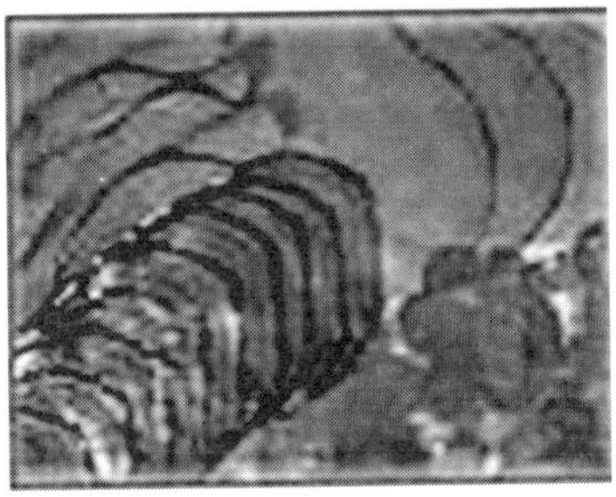

grams per 100 grams	*Meat and Meat Products*
–	Bacon rashers, middle, fried (2 = 40 g)
–	Grilled (40 g)
–	Beef, corned, canned (90 g)
–	Fillet steak, grilled (130 g)
–	Mince, stewed (100 g)
–	Rump steak, fried (150 g)
–	Grilled (150 g)
–	Silverside, salted, boiled (120 g)
–	Sirloin, roast (120 g)
–	Stewing steak, stewed (120 g)
–	Topside, roast (120 g)
.3	Beefburger, frozen, fried (60 g)
.7	Beef stew (250 g)
.2	Bolognes sauce (100 g)
–	Chicken, boiled (100 g)
–	Crumbed, no bone (140 g)
–	Roast (130 g)
–	Leg quarter (inc. bone 130 g)
–	Wing quarter (inc. bone 130 g)
–	Chicken livers, fried (130 g)
–	Duck, roast (100 g)
–	Gelatin (–)
–	Ham, canned (90 g)
–	Hamburger (170 g)
–	With cheese (190 g)
1.2	Lrish stew (250 g)
–	Lamb, brain, boiled (150 g)
–	Chops, loin, grilled (inc. bone 120 g)
–	Cutlets, grilled (inc, bone 100 g)
–	Heart, roast (140 g)
–	Kidney, fried (100 g)
–	Leg, roast (120 g)
–	Liver, fried (130 g)
–	Shoulder, roast (120 g)

–	Tongue, stewed (100 g)
.2	Luncheon meat, canned (90 g)
–	Meat pie (180 g)
.9	Moussaka (200 g)
1.3	Pastie (160 g)
–	Pork, chop, ooin, grilled (100 g)
–	Leg, roast (120 g)
–	Sweet and sour (250 g)
1	Pork pie (180 g)
–	Rabbit, stewed (inc. bone 170 g)
.1	Salami, slices (3 = 90 g)
.2	Sausage, liver (60 g)
1.3	Sausage roll (100 g)
.6	Sausages, beef, fried (2 = 120 g)
.6	Grilled (2 = 120 g)
.1	Frankfurter (2 = 100 g)
.5	Pork, fried (2 = 120 g)
.5	Grilled (2 = 120 g)
.4	Saveloy, large (2 = 150 g)
–	Spring roll, fried (200 g)
.7	Steak and kidney pie (180 g)
–	Stewed steak in gravy, canned (100 g)
–	Tongue, canned (100 g)
–	Tripe, stewed (100 g)
–	Turkey, roast (120 g)
–	Veal, cutlet, fried (110 g)
–	Fillet, roast (100 g)
–	Schnitzel (140 g)

Milk and Milk Products

grams per 100 grams	*Milk and Milk Products*
–	Cheese, camembert (25 g)
–	Cheddar (25 g)
–	Cheese spread (10 g)
–	Cottage (25 g)
–	Cream cheese (15 g)
–	Danish blue (25 g)
–	Edam (25 g)
–	Parmesan (10 g)
–	Processed (25 g)
–	Stilton (25 g)
–	Swiss (25 g)
–	Cream, 35% fat (30 g)
–	Sterilized, canned (15 g)
–	Ice cream (60 g)
–	Nondairy (60 g)
–	Milk, cow's, cond, skim, sweet (30 g)
–	Cond, whole, sweet (30 g)
–	Dried, skimmed (12 g)
–	Dried, whole (10 g)
–	Evap, whole, unsweet (30 g)
–	Flavored (230 g)
–	Fresh, skimmed (230 g)
–	Fresh, whole (230 g)
–	Long-life, UHT (230 g)
–	Goat's (230 g)
–	Human (100 g)
–	Milkshake, flavored (340 g)
–	Yoghurt, flavored (200 g)
–	Fruit, low fat (200 g)
–	Natural, low fat (200 g)
–	Plain (200 g)

Nuts

grams per 100 grams	*Nuts*
14.5	Almonds (10 = 15 g)
9	Brazil nuts (5 = 20 g)
–	Cashews, roast (10 = 20 g)
7	Chestnuts (4 = 20 g)
23.5	Coconut, desiccated (15 g)
6	Hazel nuts (10 = 15 g)
–	Macadamia nuts (8 = 20 g)
5.5	Peanuts, raw, in shells (5 = 25 g)
8.1	Roasted, salted (30 = 25 g)
–	Pistachio nuts, shelled (25 = 15 g)
5	Walnuts (5 = 20 g)

Sauces and Condiments

grams per 100 grams	*Sauces and Condiments*
–	Barbecue sauce (10 g)
–	Chilli sauce (–)
2	Chutney, tomato (20 g)
–	Curry powder (–)
0	French dressing (15 g)
–	Ginger (ground) (–)
0	Mayonnaise (20 g)
–	Mustard powder (–)
0	Oxo cubes (–)
–	Pepper (–)
2	Pickles, mustard (20 g)
1.5	Sweet (20 g)
–	Salad cream (25 g)
0	Salt, table (–)
–	Sesame seeds (–)
–	Soy sauce (–)
–	Tartare sauce (20 g)
2	Tomato sauce (25 g)
0	Vinegar (–)
–	Worcestershire sauce (–)

Soups (as served)

grams per 100 grams	*Soups (as served)*
–	Chicken, condensed (230 g)
–	Chicken coodle, dried (230 g)
.5	Minestrone, dried (230 g)
–	Mushroom, canned (230 g)
–	Tomato, condensed (230 g)
.5	Tomato, dried (230 g)
–	Vegetable, canned (230 g)

Sugars, Jams and Spreads

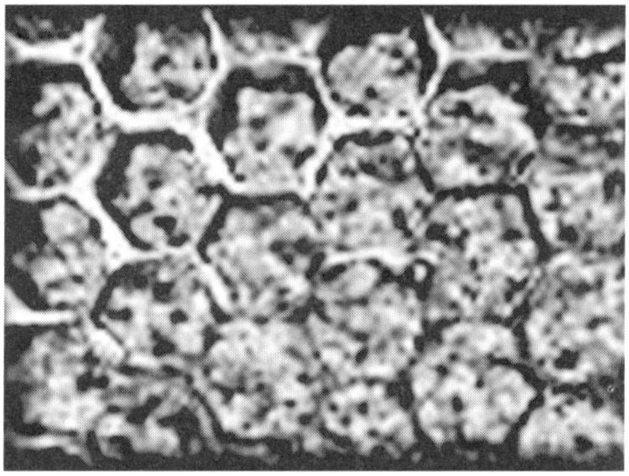

grams per 100 grams	*Sugars, Jams and Spreads*
–	Fish paste (5 g)
–	Honey (30 g)
1	Jam, fruit edible seeds (30 g)
1	Jam, stone fruit (30 g)
.5	Marmalade (30 g)
.1	Meat paste (5 g)
7.5	Peanut butter (20 g)
0	Sugar, white (–)
0	Syrup, golden (30 g)
–	Topping, flavored (40 g)
0	Treacle, black (30 g)
–	Vegemite (3 g)

Sweets

grams per 100 grams	*Sweets*
0	Boiled sweed (5 g)
–	Butterscotch (5 g)
–	Caramel (5 g)
–	Carob bar (75 g)
–	Chocolate square, milk (5 g)
–	Fruit and honey bar (50 g)
–	Jelly bean (5 g)
–	Liquorice allsort (7 g)
–	Pastille (5 g)
0	Peppermint (4 g)
–	Popcorn, plain unsalted (15 g)
–	Sesame bar (50 g)
–	Toffee, mixed (5 g)

Vegetables

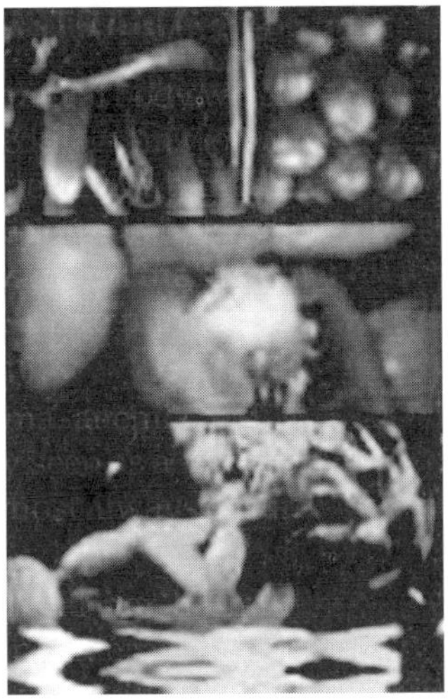

grams per 100 grams	*Vegetables*
–	Artichoke, globe, boiled (100 g)
1	Asparagus, boiled (5 = 100 g)
–	Bamboo shoots (50 g)
3	Beans, french, boiled (100 g)
7.3	Baked, in tomato sauce (125 g)
4	Broad, boiled (100 g)
7.5	Kidney (and haricot), boiled (100 g)
6.5	Mung, cooked dal (100 g)
–	Soya, boiled (100 g)
2.5	Beetroot, slices, boiled (2 = 30 g)
2.8	Canned (2 = 30 g)
4	Broccoli, boiled (100 g)
3	Brussels sprouts, boiled (7 = 70 g)
3	Cabbage, raw (50 g)
2.5	Boiled (100 g)
3	Carrots, raw (50 g)
3	Boiled (50 g)
3.5	Young, canned (50 g)
2	Cauliflower, raw (50 g)
2	Boiled (100 g)
5	Celery, boiled (3 = 60 g)
2	Celery, raw (50 g)
2	Boiled (50 g)
6	Chickpeas, cooked dal (60 g)
.5	Cucumber, slices (5 = 30 g)
–	Egg plant, baked (½ = 100 g)
2	Endive, raw leaves (3 = 15 g)
4	Leeks, boiled (4 = 100 g)
4	Lentils, split, boiled (100 g)
.8	Lettuce, raw leaves (2 = 20 g)
.5	Marrow, boiled (100 g)
2.5	Mushrooms, raw (3 = 30 g)
4	Fried (6 = 60 g)
1.5	Onions, raw (¼ = 20 g)
1.5	Boiled (100 g)
4.5	Fried (70 g)
3	Spring (4 = 20 g)
9	Parsley, sprigs (2 = 5 g)
2.5	Parsnip, boiled (½ = 60 g)
6.5	Peas, canned (60 g)
8	Canned, processed (60 g)
5	Fresh, boiled (60 g)
12	Frozen, boiled (60 g)

5	Split, boiled (60 g)
1	Peppers, green, raw (¼ = 15 g)
1	Boiled (50 g)
2	Potato, baked (inc. skin 120 g)
1	Boiled (120 g)
–	Chips, fresh, fried (12 = 120 g)
3	Chips, frozen, fried (8–14 = 120 g)
3.8	Crisps (10 = 25 g)
1	Mashed (100 g)
3.5	Instant, cooked (100 g)
2	New, boiled (2 = 100 g)
2.5	New, canned (2 = 100 g)
–	Roast (120 g)
2.2	Pumpkin (100 g)
1	Radishes (2 = 20 g)
6.5	Spinach, keaves, boiled (3 = 60 g)
3	Swede, boiled (80 g)
1.7	Sweetcorn, on cob, boiled (150 g)
5.5	Canned kernels (80 g)
2.5	Sweet patato, boiled (100 g)
1.5	Tomato, raw (120 g)
1	Canned (120 g)
3	Fried (120 g)
–	Juice, canned (120 g)
2	Turnip, boiled (80 g)
4	Yam, boiled (100 g)

10 Protein

Protein is an essential part of the diet. It is made-up of various combinations of small organic chemicals called **amino acids**. When we eat food containing protein it is broken down during digestion into its constituent amino acids. These amino acids are absorbed by our bodies and are used to produce new proteins and other necessary substances. Our bodies can make some of the amino acids needed to manufacture proteins, but others must be obtained from the diet; these are the eight so-called 'essential' amino acids. In addition, one other amino acid is needed by infants during early growth and development.

Proteins form part of the structure of the body, so that a continual supply of amino acids is needed. Our bodies are able to put these basic amino acid units together, using different arrangements of amino acids, to produce specific proteins, which can only be produced if all the necessary amino acids are available.

The nutritional value of a protein food can be judged by its ability to provide both the quantity and number of essential amino acids needed by the body. Different food sources contain different groups of proteins, which are made-up of different arrangements and amounts of amino acids. In general, proteins from animal sources are of greater nutritional value because they usually contain all the essential amino acids. Proteins from plant sources, such as cereals and vegetables, may be deficient in one or other of the essential amino acids. For example, the proteins obtained from wheat lack adequate quantities of one essential amino acid, and those from beans are deficient in another.

Because the deficiency is different in each food, when they are eaten together they complement each other and the mixture is of higher nutritional value than the separate foods, and is as good as animal protein. It is important, particularly for strict vegetarians who do not consume dairy or egg products, that a variety of different types of protein foods are eaten.

Cooking can alter the amino acid composition of protein and this usually results in desirable flavor and browning development. Very little nutritional value is lost.

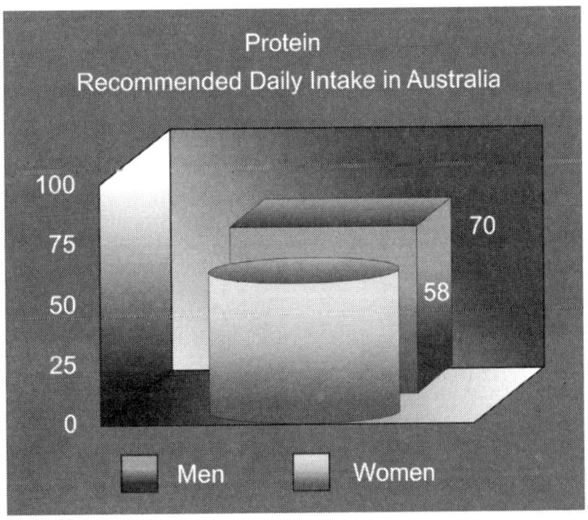

RECOMMENDED DAILY DIETARY INTAKE OF PROTEIN IN AUSTRALIA

The recommended dietary intake (RDI) in Australia is one gram per kilogram of body weight per day. The protein intake for a 70 kilogram man is 70 grams and for a 58 kilogram woman, 58 grams per day. Growing children and pregnant and lactating women have a greater requirement for protein because of the additional needs of these conditions. People who have had severe infections or surgery may require additional protein. Because of the margin of safety in the RDI for protein it is usually not necessary to increase protein intake for additional muscular activity, such as required for heavy work or training.

A deficiency of protein in the diet can lead to muscle wasting, oedema, anemia and, in children, a slowing or stopping of growth. These conditions are usually seen as a result of chronic protein malnutrition. Having an adequate energy intake will almost always ensure an adequate protein intake.

Higher levels of protein consumption appear to be neither beneficial nor harmful. However, it is possible that additional calcium may be required to counterbalance an excessive protein intake. Also there is a higher load of protein breakdown products, which must be excreted by the kidneys.

PROTEIN FOOD CHARTS

Beverages

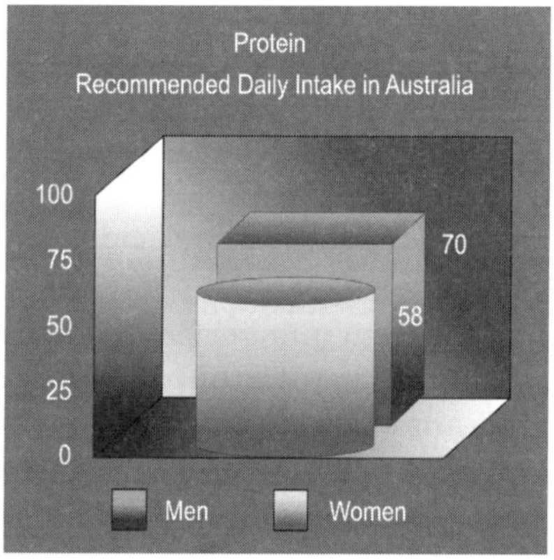

grams per 100 grams	*Beverages*
.3	Beer (240 g)
Tr	Cider, dry alcoholic (180 g)
Tr	Sweet, alcoholic (180 g)
.1	Sweet, nonalcololic (220 g)
19	Cocoa powder (5 g)
.2	Coffee, percolated (230 g)
Tr	Cola-type drinks (240 g)
Tr	Cordial, diluted 1:4 (240 g)
6	Drinking chocolate (10 g)
Tr	Lemonade, carbonated drinks (240 g)
13	Milo (10 g)
13	Ovaltine (10 g)
.1	Port (60 g)
.2	Sherry, dry (60 g)
.1	Medium (60 g)
.3	Sweet (60 g)
Tr	Spirits, e.g. whisky (30 g)
.1	Tea, infusion (230 g)
.2	Wine, red (100 g)
.1	White, dry (100 g)
.1	Medium (100 g)
.3	Sparkling (100 g)
.2	Sweet (100 g)

Cereals, Biscuits, Cakes, Deserts

grams per 100 grams	*Cereals, Biscuits, Cakes, Deserts*
3	Barley, pearl, boiled (–)
6	Biscuit, chocolate (20 g)
5	Cream-filled (20 g)
9	Crispbread, rye (20 g)
45	Wheat, starch-red (11 g)
6	Gingernut (15 g)
7	Semi-sweet (15 g)
6	Short-sweet (15 g)
14	Bran, wheat (8 g)
8	Bread, brown, slice (25 g)
10	Lebanese (pita) (¼ = 25 g)
8	White, slice (25 g)
9	Wholemeal, slice (25 g)
12	Roll, brown (35 g)
44	Starch-reduced (35 g)
12	White (35 g)
5	Cake, fruit (60 g)
5	Plain (60 g)
6	Cake, sponge (60 g)
8	Chapati (60 g)
4	Cheesecake (120 g)
7	Cornflakes (30 g)
8	Crumpet (50 g)
4	Custard (70 g)
6	Custard tart (120 g)
6	Doughnut (40 g)
4	Eclair (50 g)
.4	Flour, corn (–)
11	Plain (–)
11	Self-raising (–)
37	Soya, full-fat (–)
45	Low-fat (–)
12	Wholemeal (–)
4	Fruit pie (150 g)
4	Jam tart (35 g)
1	Jelly, made with water (100 g)
6	Lamington (60 g)
6	Lemon meringue pie (120 g)
5	Meringue (15 g)
4	Milk pudding (e.g. sago) (160 g)
9	Muesli (30 g)
8	Noodles (chow mein) (250 g)
6	Pancake (75 g)

4	Pasta, macaroni, boiled (150 g)
4	Spaghetti, boiled (120 g)
2	Canned in tomato sauce (120 g)
7	Pastry, flaky (–)
7	Short crust (–)
9	Pizza, cheese and tomato (150 g)
1	Porridge (30 g)
2	Rice, boiled (160 g)
6	Fried (120 g)
6	Puffed (25 g)
8	Scone (30 g)
7	Sponge pudding, steamed (100 g)
4	Triffle (100 g)
10	Wheat, breakfast biscuit (35 g)
36	Yeast, dried, baker's (–)

Egg and Cheese Dishes

grams per 100 grams	*Egg and Cheese dishes*
6	Cauliflower, cheese (100 g)
12	Cheese souftle (100 g)
12	Egg, boiled (55 g)
14	Egg, fried (60 g)
11	Omelette (100 g)
12	Poached (55 g)
12	Raw (55 g)
11	Scrambled (70 g)
7	Macaroni cheese (180 g)
15	Ouiche lorraine (150 g)

Fats and Oils

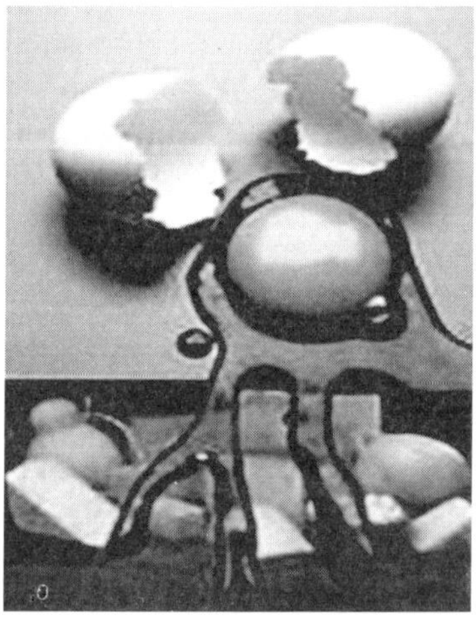

grams per 100 grams	*Fats and Oils*
.4	Butter, salted (10 g)
Tr	Dripping, beef (–)
Tr	Lard (–)
.4	Margarine (10 g)
Tr	Vegetable oils (–)

Fish and Other Seafoods

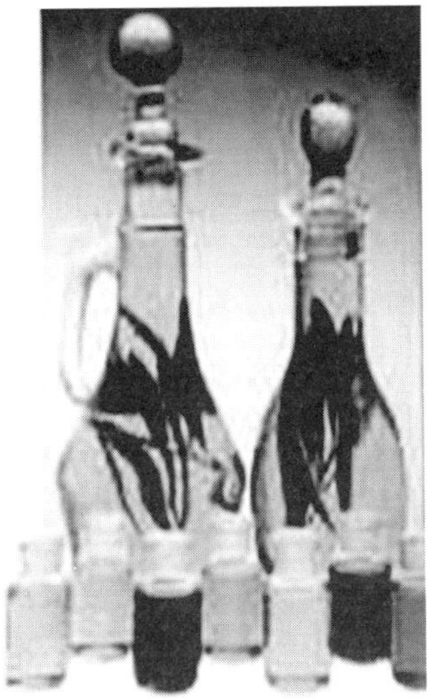

grams per 100 grams	*Fish and Other Seafoods*
18	Bream, steamed (100 g)
21	Cod, baked (100 g)
20	Tried in batter (100 g)
21	Poached (100 g)
19	Steamed (100 g)
20	Crab, boiled (150 g)
18	Canned (90 g)
9	Fish cakes, fried (4 = 100 g)
14	Fingers, fried (5 = 100 g)
14	In batter, fried (120 g)
25	Flounder, baked (100 g)
21	Haddock, fried (100 g)
23	Steamed (100 g)
22	Lobster, boiled (120 g)
17	Mussels, boiled (12 = 120 g)
11	Oysters, raw (12 = 120 g)
23	Prawns, boiled (6 = 120 g)
21	Roe, cod, fried (100 g)
20	Salmon, canned (100 g)
20	Sardines, canned (60 g)
23	Scallops, steamed (10 = 100 g)
23	Tuna, canned in oil (120 g)
18	Whiting, crumbed, fried (100 g)
21	Steamed (100 g)

Fruit

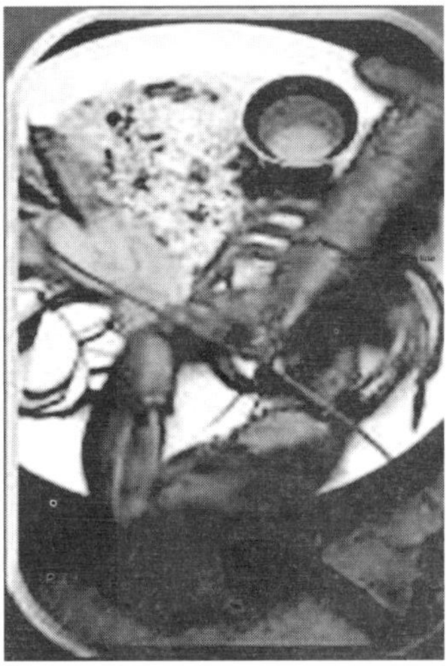

grams per 100 grams	*Fruit*
.2	Apple (inc, skin, core 100 g)
.3	Baked, no sugar (inc. skin 110 g)
.3	Stewed, no sugar (110 g)
.5	Apricots (inc. stones 3 = 100 g)
1	Peach, stewed, no sugar (120 g)
.2	Pear (inc. skin, core 120 g)
.4	Canned (120 g)
.3	Stewed, no sugar (120 g)
.5	Pineapple (80 g)
.3	Canned (80 g)
.4	Juice, canned (120 g)
.5	Plums (inc. stones 3 = 100 g)
.4	Stewed, no sugar (inc. stones 100 g)
2	Prunes (inc. stones 8 = 80 g)
1	Stewed, no sugar (inc. stones 120 g)
.3	Quince, raw (100 g)
1	Raisins, dried (20 g)
.9	Raspberries (100 g)
.6	Canned (100 g)
.9	Stewed, no sugar (100 g)
.6	Rhubarb, stewed, no sugar (120 g)
.6	Strawberries (10 = 100 g)
.4	Canned (100 g)
2	Sultanas, dried (15 g)
.2	Watermelon (260 g)

Meat and Meat Products

grams per 100 grams	*Meat and Meat Products*
24	Bacon rashers, middle, fried (2 = 40 g)
25	Grilled (40 g)
27	Beef, corned, canned (90 g)
28	Fillet steak, grilled (130 g)
23	Mince, stewed (100 g)
29	Rump steak, fried (150 g)
27	Grilled (150 g)
29	Silverside, salted, boiled (120 g)
24	Sirloin, roast (120 g)
31	Stewing steak, stewed (120 g)
27	Topside, roast (120 g)
20	Beefburger, frozen, fried (60 g)
10	Beef stew (250 g)
8	Bolognes sauce (100 g)

29	Chicken, boiled (100 g)
24	Crumbed, no bone (140 g)
23	Roast (130 g)
15	Leg quarter (inc. bone 130 g)
12	Wing quarter (inc. bone 130 g)
21	Chicken livers, fried (130 g)
20	Duck, roast (100 g)
84	Gelatin (–)
27	Ham, canned (90 g)
14	Hamburger (170 g)
11	With cheese (190 g)
5	Lrish stew (250 g)
12	Lamb, brain, boiled (150 g)
18	Chops, loin, grilled (inc. bone 120 g)
15	Cutlets, grilled (inc, bone 100 g)
26	Heart, roast (140 g)
25	Kidney, fried (100 g)
26	Leg, roast (120 g)
23	Liver, fried (130 g)
20	Shoulder, roast (120 g)
18	Tongue, stewed (100 g)
13	Luncheon meat, canned (90 g)
8	Meat pie (180 g)
9	Moussaka (200 g)
8	Pastie (160 g)
22	Pork, chop, ooin, grilled (100 g)
27	Leg, roast (120 g)
7	Sweet and sour (250 g)
10	Pork pie (180 g)
14	Rabbit, stewed (inc. bone 170 g)
19	Salami, slices (3 = 90 g)
13	Sausage, liver (60 g)
8	Sausage roll (100 g)
13	Sausages, beef, fried (2 = 120 g)
13	Grilled (2 = 120 g)
10	Frankfurter (2 = 100 g)
14	Pork, fried (2 = 120 g)
13	Grilled (2 = 120 g)
10	Saveloy, large (2 = 150 g)
5	Spring roll, fried (200 g)
9	Steak and kidney pie (180 g)
15	Stewed steak in gravy, canned (100 g)
16	Tongue, canned (100 g)
15	Tripe, stewed (100 g)
28	Turkey, roast (120 g)
31	Veal, cutlet, fried (110 g)
32	Fillet, roast (100 g)
21	Schnitzel (140 g)

Milk and Milk Products

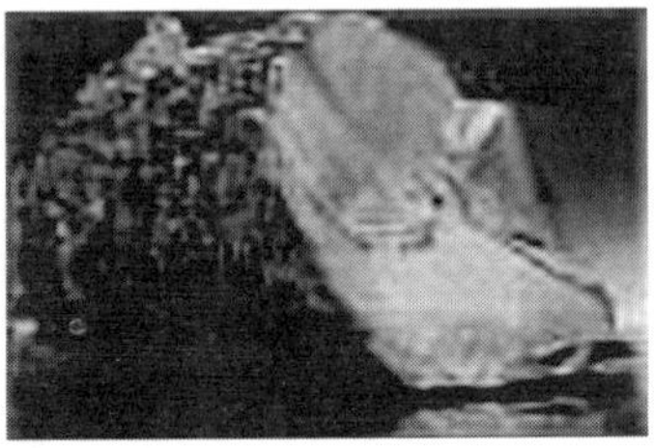

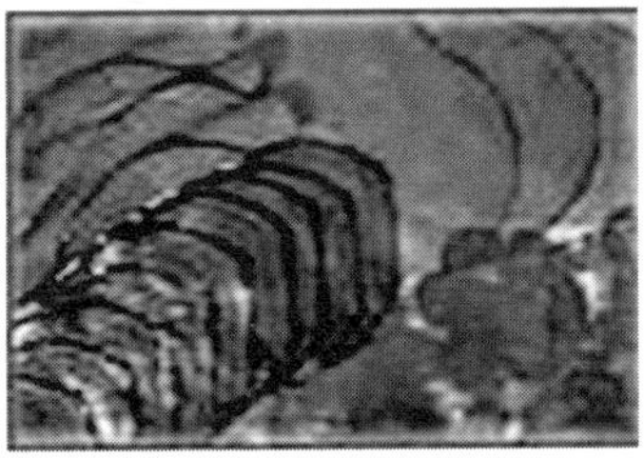

grams per 100 grams	*Milk and Milk Products*
23	Cheese, camembert (25 g)
26	Cheddar (25 g)
18	Cheese spread (10 g)
14	Cottage (25 g)
8	Cream cheese (15 g)
23	Danish blue (25 g)
24	Edam (25 g)
35	Parmesan (10 g)
22	Processed (25 g)
26	Stilton (25 g)
29	Swiss (25 g)
2	Cream, 35% fat (30 g)
3	Sterilized, canned (15 g)
4	Ice cream (60 g)
3	nondairy (60 g)
10	Milk, cow's, cond, skim, sweet (30 g)
8	Cond, whole, sweet (30 g)
36	Dried, skimmed (12 g)
26	Dried, whole (10 g)
9	Evap, whole, unsweet (30 g)
3	Flavored (230 g)
3	Fresh, skimmed (230 g)
3	Fresh, whole (230 g)
3	Longlife, UHT (230 g)
3	Goat's (230 g)
1	Human (100 g)
3	Milkshake, flavored (340 g)
4	Yoghurt, flavored (200 g)
5	Fruit, low fat (200 g)
5	Natural, low fat (200 g)
4	Plain (200 g)

Nuts

grams per 100 grams	*Nuts*
17	Almonds (10 = 15 g)
12	Brazil nuts (5 = 20 g)
18	Cashews, roast (10 = 20 g)
2	Chestnuts (4 = 20 g)
6	Coconut, desiccated (15 g)
8	Hazel nuts (10 = 15 g)
8	Macadamia nuts (8 = 20 g)
24	Peanuts, raw, in shells (5 = 25 g)
17	Roasted, salted (30 = 25 g)
19	Pistachio nuts, shelled (25 = 15 g)
11	Walnuts (5 = 20 g)

Sauces and Condiments

grams per 100 grams	*Sauces and Condiments*
2	Barbecue sauce (10 g)
1	Chilli sauce (–)
1	Chutney, tomato (20 g)
10	Curry powder (–)
.1	French dressing (15 g)
7	Ginger (ground) (–)
2	Mayonnaise (20 g)
29	Mustard powder (–)
38	Oxo cubes (–)
9	Pepper (–)
1	Pickles, mustard (20 g)
.6	Sweet (20 g)
2	Salad cream (25 g)
0	Salt, table (–)
19	Sesame seeds (–)
6	Soy sauce (–)
1	Tartare sauce (20 g)
2	Tomato sauce (25 g)
.4	Vinegar (–)
1	Worcestershire sauce (–)

Soups (as served)

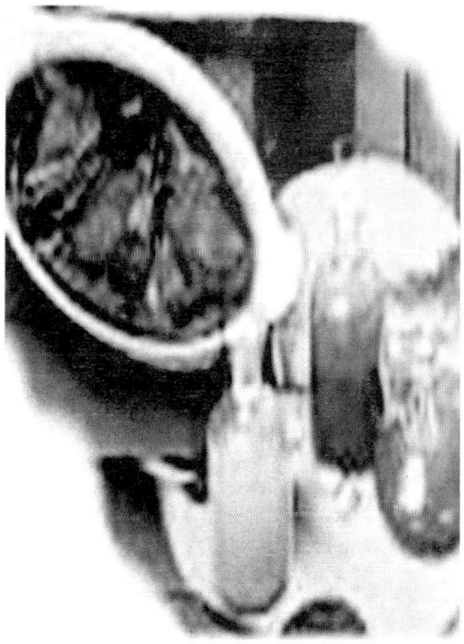

grams per 100 grams	*Soups (as served)*
1	Chicken, condensed (230 g)
.8	Chicken coodle, dried (230 g)
.8	Minestrone, dried (230 g)
1	Mushroom, canned (230 g)
.9	Tomato, condensed (230 g)
.6	Tomato, dried (230 g)
2	Vegetable, canned (230 g)

Sugars, Jams and Spreads

grams per 100 grams	*Sugars, Jams and Spreads*
15	Fish paste (5 g)
.4	Honey (30 g)
.6	Jam, fruit edible seeds (30 g)
.4	Jam, stone fruit (30 g)
.1	Marmalade (30 g)
15	Meat paste (5 g)
23	Peanut butter (20 g)
Tr	Sugar, white (–)
.3	Syrup, golden (30 g)
.1	Topping, flavored (40 g)
1	Treacle, black (30 g)
30	Vegemite (3 g)

Sweets

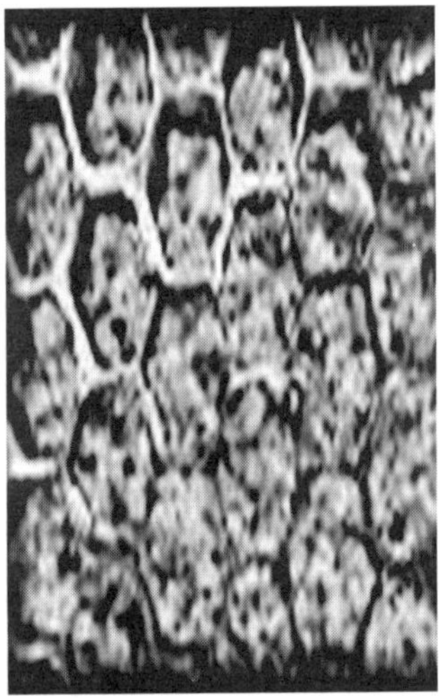

grams per 100 grams	*Sweets*
Tr	Boiled sweed (5 g)
Tr	Butterscotch (5 g)
4	Caramel (5 g)
9	Carob bar (75 g)
8	Chocolate square, milk (5 g)
11	Fruit and honey bar (50 g)
.1	Jelly bean (5 g)
4	Liquorice allsort (7 g)
5	Pastille (5 g)
.5	Peppermint (4 g)
6	Popcorn, plain unsalted (15 g)
11	Sesame bar (50 g)
2	Toffee, mixed (5 g)

Vegetables

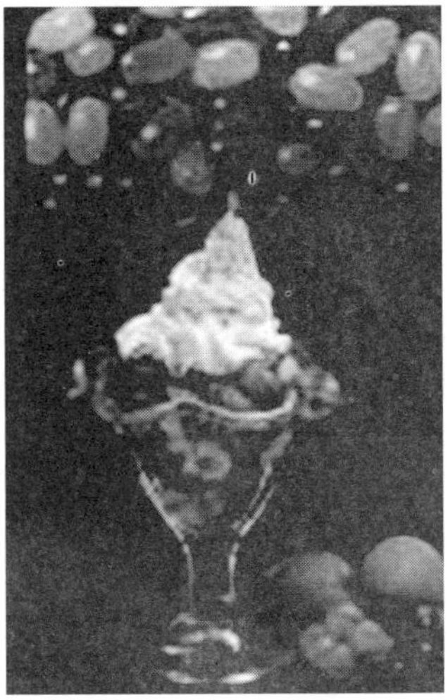

grams per 100 grams	*Vegetables*
.5	Artichoke, globe, boiled (100 g)
2	Asparagus, boiled (5 = 100 g)
3	Bamboo shoots (50 g)
.8	Beans, french, boiled (100 g)
5	Baked, in tomato sauce (125 g)
4	Broad, boiled (100 g)
7	Kidney (and haricot), boiled (100 g)
6	Mung, cooked dal (100 g)
11	Soya, boiled (100 g)
2	Beetroot, slices, boiled (2 = 30 g)
1	Canned (2 = 30 g)
3	Broccoli, boiled (100 g)
3	Brussels sprouts, boiled (7 = 70 g)
3	Cabbage, raw (50 g)
1	Boiled (100 g)
.7	Carrots, raw (50 g)
.6	Boiled (50 g)
.7	Young, canned (50 g)
2	Cauliflower, raw (50 g)
2	Boiled (100 g)
2	Celery, boiled (3 = 60 g)
.9	Celery, raw (50 g)
.6	Boiled (50 g)
8	Chickpeas, cooked dal (60 g)
.6	Cucumber, slices (5 = 30 g)
1	Egg plant, baked (½ = 100 g)
2	Endive, raw leaves (3 = 15 g)
2	Leeks, boiled (4 – 100 g)
8	Lentils, split, boiled (100 g)
1	Lettuce, raw leaves (2 = 20 g)
.5	Marrow, boiled (100 g)
2	Mushrooms, raw (3 = 30 g)
2	Fried (6 = 60 g)
.9	Onions, raw (¼ = 20 g)
.6	Boiled (100 g)
2	Fried (70 g)
.9	Spring (4 = 20 g)
5	Parsley, sprigs (2 = 5 g)
1	Parsnip, boiled (½ = 60 g)
5	Peas, canned (60 g)
6	Canned, processed (60 g)
5	Fresh, boiled (60 g)
5	Frozen, boiled (60 g)

8	Split, boiled (60 g)
.9	Peppers, green, raw (¼ = 15 g)
.9	Boiled (50 g)
2	Potato, baked (inc. skin 120 g)
1	Boiled (120 g)
4	Chips, fresh, fried (12 = 120 g)
3	Chips, frozen, fried (8–14 = 120 g)
6	Crisps (10 = 25 g)
2	Mashed (100 g)
2	Instant, cooked (100 g)
2	New, boiled (2 = 100 g)
1	New, canned (2 = 100 g)
3	Roast (120 g)
.6	Pumpkin (100 g)
1	Radishes (2 = 20 g)
5	Spinach, keaves, boiled (3 = 60 g)
.9	Swede, boiled (80 g)
4	Sweetcorn, on cob, boiled (150 g)
3	Canned kernels (80 g)
1	Sweet potato, boiled (100 g)
.9	Tomato, raw (120 g)
1	Canned (120 g)
1	Fried (120 g)
1	Juice, canned (120 g)
.7	Turnip, boiled (80 g)
2	Yam, boiled (100 g)

11 Sources of Phenylalanine

Based on USDA (US Department of Agriculture) National Nutrient Database Release 22 (SR22). The values are mean nutrient values per 100 grams of the edible portion.

1.	Egg, white, dried	4.736 g
2.	Soy protein isolate	4.593 g
3.	Peanut flour, defatted	2.705 g
4.	Seeds, sesame flour, low-fat	2.658 g
5.	Egg, whole, dried	2.515 g
6.	Soy flour, defatted	2.453 g
7.	Soy meal, defatted, raw	2.346 g
8.	Fish, whitefish, dried (Alaska Native)	2.340 g
9.	Tofu, dried-frozen (koyadofu)	2.334 g
10.	Cheese, parmesan, shredded	2.234 g
11.	Meat extender	2.182 g
12.	Seeds, sesame flour, partially defatted	2.138 g
13.	Soybeans, mature seeds, raw	2.122 g
14.	Cheese, parmesan, grated	2.081 g
15.	Seeds, watermelon seed kernels, dried	2.031 g
16.	Smelt, dried (Alaska Native)	2.010 g
17.	Snacks, pork skins, plain	1.940 g
18.	Cheese, parmesan, hard	1.922 g
19.	Egg mix, USDA commodity	1.903 g
20.	Snacks, pork skins, barbecue-flavor	1.877 g
21.	Pigeon peas (red gram), mature seeds, raw	1.858 g
22.	Soy flour, full-fat, raw	1.802 g
23.	Peanut flour, low fat	1.752 g
24.	Cheese, gruyere	1.743 g
25.	Gelatins, dry powder, unsweetened	1.737 g

(Contd.)

(Contd.)

26.	Milk, dry, nonfat, calcium reduced	1.714 g
27.	Spices, parsley, dried	1.712 g
28.	Cheese, romano	1.710 g
29.	Cheese, swiss	1.662 g
30.	Milk, buttermilk, dried	1.656 g
31.	Seeds, sesame flour, high-fat	1.632 g
32.	Cheese, fontina	1.497 g
33.	Papad	1.491 g
34.	Mungo beans, mature seeds, raw	1.473 g
35.	Egg, yolk, dried	1.463 g
36.	Mung beans, mature seeds, raw	1.443 g
37.	Nuts, butternuts, dried	1.442 g
38.	Lupins, mature seeds, raw	1.435 g
39.	Cheese, edam	1.434 g
40.	Cheese, gouda	1.431 g
41.	Winged beans, mature seeds, raw	1.429 g
42.	Yardlong beans, mature seeds, raw	1.421 g
43.	Mutton, cooked, roasted (Navajo)	1.399 g
44.	Cowpeas, catjang, mature seeds, raw	1.393 g
45.	Snacks, soy chips or crisps, salted	1.371 g
46.	Beans, kidney, royal red, mature seeds, raw	1.370 g
47.	Cheese, tilsit	1.358 g
48.	Peanuts, spanish, raw	1.356 g
49.	Peanuts, all types, raw	1.337 g
50.	Cheese, caraway	1.326 g
51.	Cheese, port de salut	1.323 g
52.	Beans, kidney, california red, mature seeds, raw	1.318 g
53.	Cheese, cheddar	1.311 g
54.	Cracker Barrel, grilled sirloin steak	1.309 g
55.	Peanuts, virginia, raw	1.306 g
56.	Peanuts, valencia, raw	1.300 g
57.	T.G.I. Friday's, classic sirloin steak	1.297 g
58.	Cheese, monterey	1.289 g
59.	Cheese, provolone	1.287 g
60.	Beans, kidney, all types, mature seeds, raw	1.275 g
61.	Milk, dry, whole, with added vitamin D	1.271 g
62.	Cheese, mozzarella, part skim milk	1.266 g
63.	Beans, white, mature seeds, raw	1.263 g

(Contd.)

(Contd.)

64.	Cheese, colby	1.251 g
65.	Beans, cranberry (roman), mature seeds, raw	1.245 g
66.	Cheese, muenster	1.240 g
67.	Lima beans, large, mature seeds, raw	1.236 g
68.	Cheese, brick	1.231 g
69.	Cheese, cheshire	1.231 g
70.	Lentils, pink, raw	1.230 g
71.	Restaurant, family style, sirloin steak	1.223 g
72.	Denny's top sirloin steak	1.221 g
73.	Beans, kidney, red, mature seeds, raw	1.218 g
74.	Cheese, goat, hard type	1.215 g
75.	Hyacinth beans, mature seeds, raw	1.204 g
76.	Cheese, mexican, queso asadero	1.190 g
77.	Beans, yellow, mature seeds, raw	1.190 g
78.	Lima beans, thin seeded (baby), mature seeds, raw	1.188 g
79.	Peanut butter, chunk style, with salt	1.185 g
80.	Beans, great northern, mature seeds, raw	1.182 g

12 Carbohydrate

Carbohydrates can be divided into three main groups:

1. Sugars
2. Starches
3. **Cellulose** and other complex substances that are not digested by humans.

Sugars and starches in food are sources of energy. Australians obtain 20 to 60 percent of their total dietary energy from carbohydrate. Cellulose and some related substances are not used by our bodies as a significant source of energy. Nevertheless, these components are very important as, together with other indigestible substances, they constitute dietary fiber.

Sugars

The main sugars in food are sucrose, glucose, fructose, maltose and lactose. Sucrose is obtained from sugar cane and is usually called 'sugar'. In addition, sucrose (as well as glucose and fructose) is found in fruit, fruit juices and honey. Besides providing energy, sugars also produce the sensation of sweetness. Each sugar contributes the same amount of energy (kilocalories) to our diet regardless of its sweetness. Different sugars are not equally sweet and the degree of sweetness of a food is often not a good indication of the amount of sugars present. For example, maltose is only half as sweet as sucrose.

Sweetness of sugars relative to sucrose

Sugar	*Relative sweetness*	*Other name*
Sucrose	1	Sugar
Glucose	0.7	Grape sugar
Fructose	1.1	Fruit sugar
Lactose	0.4	Milk sugar
Maltose	0.5	Malt sugar
Sorbitol	0.5	–

Sugars are widely distributed in foods, particularly processed foods where their sweetness may sometimes be masked or hidden by other ingredients. Often the list of ingredients on the label will give an indication of the relative amount of sugar present.

The use of non-nutritive or artificial sweeteners can be used to make food and drink sweet without contributing significant amounts of energy. Although there is controversy about their safety, the most widely used artificial sweeteners are saccharin and cyclamate. The label of any food or drink containing these sweeteners must indicate that they are present. An artificial sweetener recently approved by some health authorities is aspartame. It has about the same energy value as sugar but because it is 180 times sweeter, very little needs to be used. The amount of aspartame providing sweetness equivalent to one teaspoon of sugar will only provide one-tenth of a kilocalorie.

Starch

Starch is the main form of carbohydrate in our food. It is present in a variety of cereals, vegetables and fruit, with major contributions from flour, potatoes and legumes (beans, peas). Starchy foods are usually cooked to improve digestibility and give a more desirable texture and flavor. During the ripening of fruit, starch is changed into sugars, which give sweetness to ripe fruits. In contrast to sugars, starch is often accompanied by significant amounts of other nutrients including dietary fiber. Starch has the same energy value as sugars. Health authorities are in agreement that we should increase our consumption of foods containing starch, such as wholegrain bread, cereals, fruits, vegetables and nuts.

Carbohydrate Intake

There is no specific dietary requirement for carbohydrate because energy can also be derived from protein, fat and alcohol. However, a diet that does not contain carbohydrate can lead to muscle breakdown, ketosis and dehydration. This can be prevented by 50 to 100 grams of carbohydrate per day, but levels above this are desirable. Sources of complex carbohydrates, such as starch, are recommended as these often also provide necessary vitamins, elements (minerals) and dietary fiber.

CARBOHYDRATE FOOD CHARTS

Beverages

grams per 100 grams	*Beverages*
2	Beer (240 g)
3	Cider, dry alcoholic (180 g)
4	Sweet, alcoholic (180 g)
12	Sweet, nonalcololic (220 g)
12	Cocoa powder (5 g)
0	Coffee, percolated (230 g)
11	Cola type drinks (240 g)
9	Cordial, diluted 1:4 (240 g)
77	Drinking chocolate (10 g)
10	Lemonade, carbonated drinks (240 g)
68	Milo (10 g)
79	Ovaltine (10 g)
12	Port (60 g)
1	Sherry, dry (60 g)
4	Medium (60 g)

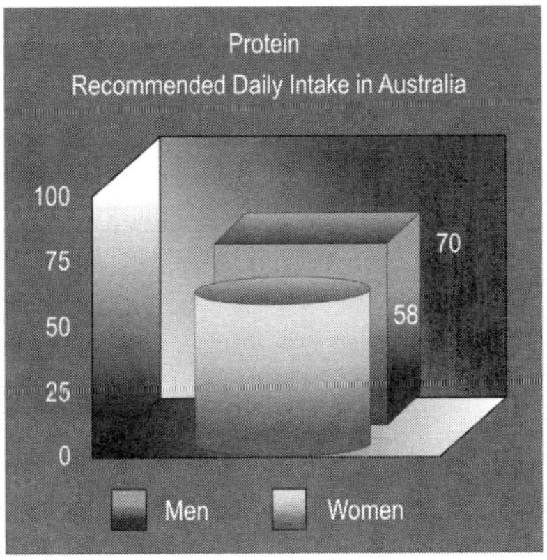

7	Sweet (60 g)
Tr	Spirits, e.g. whisky (30 g)
Tr	Tea, infusion (230 g)
Tr	Wine, red (100 g)
1	White, dry (100 g)
3	Medium (100 g)
1	Sparkling (100 g)
6	Sweet (100 g)

Cereals, Biscuits, Cakes, Deserts

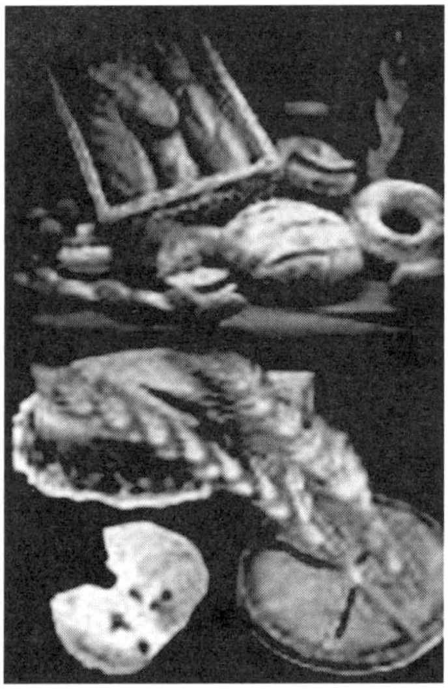

grams per 100 grams	*Cereals, Biscuits, Cakes, Deserts*
28	Barley, pearl, boiled (–)
67	Biscuit, chocolate (20 g)
67	Cream-filled (20 g)
70	Crispbread, rye (20 g)
37	Wheat, starch-red (11 g)
79	Gingernut (15 g)
75	Semi-sweet (15 g)
62	Short-sweet (15 g)
27	Bran, wheat (8 g)
48	Bread, brown, slice (25 g)
53	Lebanese (pita) (¼ = 25 g)
49	White, slice (25 g)
47	Wholemeal, slice (25 g)
57	Roll, brown (35 g)
46	Starch-reduced (35 g)
57	White (35 g)
58	Cake, fruit (60 g)
58	Plain (60 g)
53	Cake, sponge (60 g)
50	Chapati (60 g)
35	Cheesecake (120 g)
87	Cornflakes (30 g)
52	Crumpet (50 g)
4	Custard (70 g)
17	Custard tart (120 g)
49	Doughnut (40 g)
38	Eclair (50 g)
87	Flour, corn (–)
75	Plain (–)
74	Self-raising (–)
24	Soya, full-fat (–)
28	Low-fat (–)
72	Wholemeal (–)
57	Fruit pie (150 g)

63	Jam tart (35 g)
14	Jelly, made with water (100 g)
56	Lamington (60 g)
46	Lemon meringue pie (120 g)
96	Meringue (15 g)
20	Milk pudding (e.g. sago) (160 g)
56	Muesli (30 g)
8	Noodles (chow mein) (250 g)
36	Pancake (75 g)
25	Pasta, macaroni, boiled (150 g)
26	Spaghetti, boiled (120 g)
12	Canned in tomato sauce (120 g)
41	Pastry, flaky (–)
32	Short crust (–)
25	Pizza, cheese and tomato (150 g)
8	Porridge (30 g)
30	Rice, boiled (160 g)
30	Fried (120 g)
88	Puffed (25 g)
56	Scone (30 g)
46	Sponge pudding, steamed (100 g)
24	Triffle (100 g)
75	Wheat, breakfast biscuit (35 g)
4	Yeast, dried, baker's (–)

Egg and Cheese Dishes

grams per 100 grams	*Egg and Cheese dishes*
5	Cauliflower, cheese (100 g)
9	Cheese souftle (100 g)
Tr	Egg, boiled (55 g)
Tr	Egg, fried (60 g)
Tr	Omelette (100 g)
Tr	Poached (55 g)
Tr	Raw (55 g)
Tr	Scrambled (70 g)
15	Macaroni cheese (180 g)
21	Quiche lorraine (150 g)

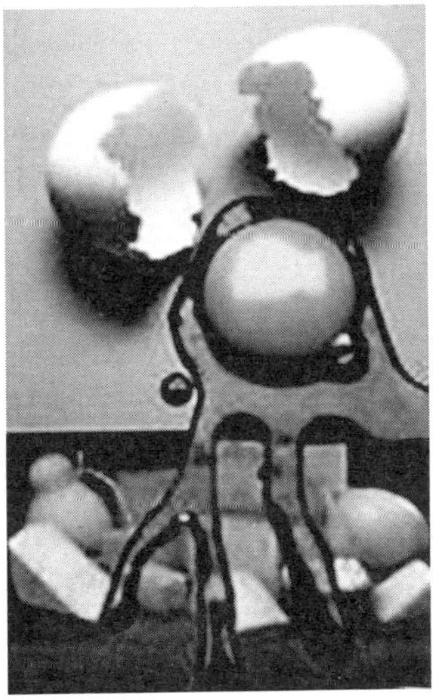

Fats and Oils

grams per 100 grams	*Fats and Oils*
Tr	Butter, salted (10 g)
0	Dripping, beef (–)
0	Lard (–)
Tr	Margarine (10 g)
0	Vegetable oils (–)

Fish and Other Seafoods

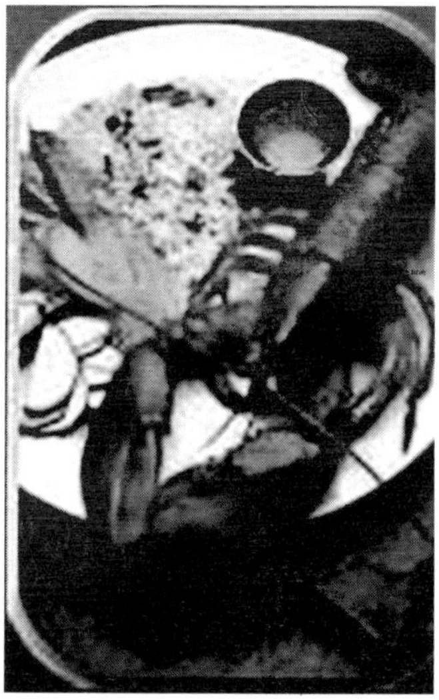

grams per 100 grams	*Fish and Other Seafoods*
0	Bream, steamed (100 g)
0	Cod, baked (100 g)
8	Tried in batter (100 g)
0	Poached (100 g)
0	Steamed (100 g)
0	Crab, boiled (150 g)
0	Canned (90 g)
15	Fish cakes, fried (4 = 100 g)
17	Fingers, fried (5 = 100 g)
14	in batter, fried (120 g)
0	Flounder, baked (100 g)
4	Haddock, fried (100 g)
0	Steamed (100 g)
0	Lobster, boiled (120 g)
Tr	Mussels, boiled (12 = 120 g)
Tr	Oysters, raw (12 = 120 g)
0	Prawns, boiled (6 = 120 g)
3	Roe, cod, fried (100 g)
0	Salmon, canned (100 g)
0	Sardines, canned (60 g)
Tr	Scallops, steamed (10 = 100 g)
0	Tuna, canned in oil (120 g)
7	Whiting, crumbed, fried (100 g)
0	Steamed (100 g)

Fruit

grams per 100 grams	*Fruit*
9	Apple (inc, skin, core 100 g)
8	Baked, no sugar (inc. skin 110 g)
8	Stewed, no sugar (110 g)
6	Apricots (inc. stones 3 = 100 g)
28	Apricots, canned (100 g)
43	Dried (25 g)
5	Stewed, no sugar (inc. stones 110 g)
2	Avocado pear (½ = 150 g)
19	Banana (100 g)
6	Blackberries (100 g)
6	Stewed, no sugar (100 g)
3	Cantaloup (inc. skin 120 g)
10	Cherries (inc. stones 20 = 100 g)
8	Stewed, no sugar (inc. stones 100 g)
7	Currants, black (90 g)
63	Dried (15 g)
4	Red (90 g)
64	Dates, dried (6 = 35 g)
10	Figs (2 = 75 g)
53	Dried (2 = 40 g)
25	Fruit salad, canned (120 g)
13	Grapes, black (20 = 100 g)
15	White (20 = 100 g)
3	Grapefruit, whole (200 g)
16	Canned (100 g)
8	Juice, canned (120 g)
16	Guavas, canned (100 g)
3	Lemon, slices (2 = 15 g)
2	Juice (15 g)
3	Loganberries (100 g)
26	Canned (100 g)
3	Stewed, no sugar (100 g)
18	Lychees, canned (100 g)
11	Mandarins (2 = 100 g)
14	Canned (50 g)
15	Mango (100 g)
20	Canned (100 g)
11	Nectarines (inc. stones 3 = 100 g)
Tr	Olives, in brine (5 = 20 g)
6	Orange, whole (130 g)
9	Juice, fresh (120 g)
9	Canned (120 g)
3	Passionfruit, whole (30 g)

11	Papaw (100 g)
17	Canned (100 g)
8	Peach (inc. stones 120 g)
23	Canned (120 g)
53	Dried (25 g)
20	Peach, stewed, no sugar (120 g)
8	Pear (inc. skin. core 120 g)
20	Canned (120 g)
8	Stewed, no sugar (120 g)
12	Pineapple (80 g)
20	Canned (80 g)
13	Juice, canned (120 g)
9	Plums (inc. stones 3 = 100 g)
7	Stewed, no sugar (inc. stones 100 g)
34	Prunes (inc. stones 8 = 80 g)
19	Stewed, no sugar (inc. stones 120 g)
6	Quince, raw (100 g)
64	Raisins, dried (20 g)
6	Raspberries (100 g)
23	Canned (100 g)
6	Stewed, no sugar (100 g)
1	Rhubarb, stewed, no sugar (120 g)
6	Strawberries (10 = 100 g)
21	Canned (100 g)
65	Sultanas, dried (15 g)
3	Watermelon (260 g)

Meat and Meat Products

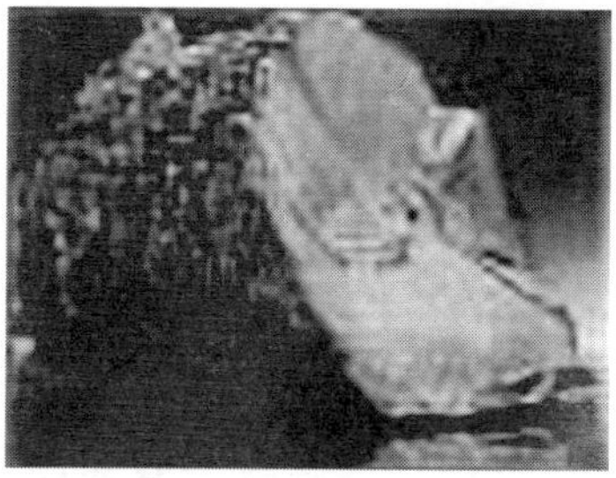

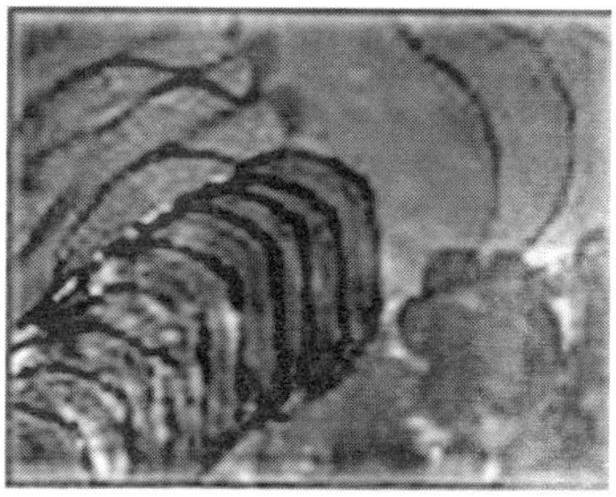

grams per 100 grams	*Meat and Meat Products*
0	Bacon rashers, middle, fried (2 = 40 g)
0	Grilled (40 g)
0	Beef, corned, canned (90 g)
0	Fillet steak, grilled (130 g)
0	Mince, stewed (100 g)
0	Rump steak, fried (150 g)
0	Grilled (150 g)
0	Silverside, salted, boiled (120 g)
0	Sirloin, roast (120 g)
0	Stewing steak, stewed (120 g)
0	Topside, roast (120 g)
7	Beefburger, frozen, fried (60 g)
4	Beef stew (250 g)
3	Bolognes sauce (100 g)
0	Chicken, boiled (100 g)
10	Crumbed, no bone (140 g)
0	Roast (130 g)
0	Leg quarter (inc. bone 130 g)
0	Wing quarter (inc. bone 130 g)
3	Chicken livers, fried (130 g)
0	Duck, roast (100 g)
0	Gelatin (–)
0	Ham, canned (90 g)
22	Hamburger (170 g)
21	With cheese (190 g)
9	Lrish stew (250 g)
0	Lamb, brain, boiled (150 g)
0	Chops, loin, grilled (inc. bone 120 g)
0	Cutlets, grilled (inc, bone 100 g)
0	Heart, roast (140 g)
0	Kidney, fried (100 g)
0	Leg, roast (120 g)
4	Liver, fried (130 g)
0	Shoulder, roast (120 g)
0	Tongue, stewed (100 g)
6	Luncheon meat, canned (90 g)
18	Meat pie (180 g)
10	Moussaka (200 g)
31	Pastie (160 g)
0	Pork, chop, ooin, grilled (100 g)
0	Leg, roast (120 g)
18	Sweet and sour (250 g)
25	Pork pie (180 g)

0	Rabbit, stewed (inc. bone 170 g)
2	Salami, slices (3 = 90 g)
4	Sausage, liver (60 g)
24	Sausage roll (100 g)
15	Sausages, beef, fried (2 = 120 g)
15	Grilled (2 = 120 g)
3	Frankfurter (2 = 100 g)
11	Pork, fried (2 = 120 g)
12	Grilled (2 = 120 g)
10	Saveloy, large (2 = 150 g)
29	Spring roll, fried (200 g)
26	Steak and kidney pie (180 g)
1	Stewed steak in gravy, canned (100 g)
0	Tongue, canned (100 g)
Tr	Tripe, stewed (100 g)
0	Turkey, roast (120 g)
4	Veal, cutlet, fried (110 g)
0	Fillet, roast (100 g)
10	Schnitzel (140 g)

Milk and Milk Products

grams per 100 grams	*Milk and Milk Products*
Tr	Cheese, camembert (25 g)
Tr	Cheddar (25 g)
Tr	Cheese spread (10 g)
1	Cottage (25 g)
Tr	Cream cheese (15 g)
Tr	Danish blue (25 g)
Tr	Edam (25 g)
Tr	Parmesan (10 g)
Tr	Processed (25 g)
Tr	Stilton (25 g)
Tr	Swiss (25 g)
3	Cream, 35% fat (30 g)
3	Sterilized, canned (15 g)
25	Ice cream (60 g)
21	nondairy (60 g)
60	Milk, cow's, cond, skim, sweet (30 g)
56	Cond, whole, sweet (30 g)
53	Dried, skimmed (12 g)
39	Dried, whole (10 g)
11	Evap, whole, unsweet (30 g)
10	Flavored (230 g)
5	Fresh, skimmed (230 g)
5	Fresh, whole (230 g)

5	Long life, UHT (230 g)
5	Goat's (230 g)
7	Human (100 g)
17	Milkshake, flavored (340 g)
11	Yoghurt, flavored (200 g)
18	Fruit, low fat (200 g)
6	Natural, low fat (200 g)
6	Plain (200 g)

Nuts

grams per 100 grams	*Nuts*
4	Almonds (10 = 15 g)
4	Brazil nuts (5 = 20 g)
28	Cashews, roast (10 = 20 g)
37	Chestnuts (4 = 20 g)
6	Coconut, desiccated (15 g)
7	Hazel nuts (10 = 15 g)
14	Macadamia nuts (8 = 20 g)
6	Peanuts, raw, in shells (5 = 25 g)
9	Roasted, salted (30 = 25 g)
19	Pistachio nuts, shelled (25 = 15 g)
5	Walnuts (5 = 20 g)

Sauces and Condiments

grams per 100 grams	*Sauces and Condiments*
8	Barbecue sauce (10 g)
4	Chilli sauce (–)
40	Chutney, tomato (20 g)
26	Curry powder (–)
Tr	French dressing (15 g)
60	Ginger (ground) (–)
Tr	Mayonnaise (20 g)
21	Mustard powder (–)
12	Oxo cubes (–)
68	Pepper (–)
6	Pickles, mustard (20 g)
34	Sweet (20 g)
15	Salad cream (25 g)
0	Salt, table (–)
22	Sesame seeds (–)
10	Soy sauce (–)
6	Tartare sauce (20 g)
8	Tomato sauce (25 g)
1	Vinegar (–)
18	Worcestershire sauce (–)

Soups (as served)

grams per 100 grams	*Soups (as served)*
3	Chicken, condensed (230 g)
4	Chicken coodle, dried (230 g)
4	Minestrone, dried (230 g)
4	Mushroom, canned (230 g)
7	Tomato, condensed (230 g)
6	Tomato, dried (230 g)
7	Vegetable, canned (230 g)

Sugars, Jams and Spreads

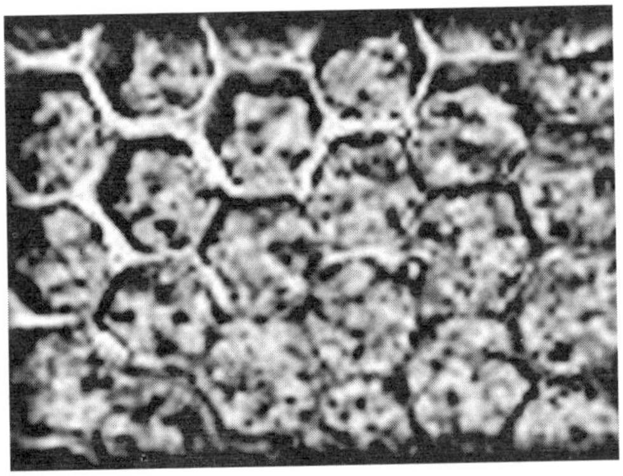

grams per 100 grams	*Sugars, Jams and Spreads*
4	Fish paste (5 g)
76	Honey (30 g)
69	Jam, fruit edible seeds (30 g)
69	Jam, stone fruit (30 g)
70	Marmalade (30 g)
3	Meat paste (5 g)
13	Peanut butter (20 g)
100	Sugar, white (–)
79	Syrup, golden (30 g)
34	Topping, flavored (40 g)
67	Treacle, black (30 g)
13	Vegemite (3 g)

Sweets

grams per 100 grams	*Sweets*
87	Boiled sweed (5 g)
90	Butterscotch (5 g)
77	Caramel (5 g)
37	Carob bar (75 g)
59	Chocolate square, milk (5 g)
25	Fruit and honey bar (50 g)
90	Jelly bean (5 g)
74	Liquorice allsort (7 g)
62	Pastille (5 g)
100	Peppermint (4 g)
85	Popcorn, plain unsalted (15 g)
23	Sesame bar (50 g)
71	Toffee, mixed (5 g)

Vegetables

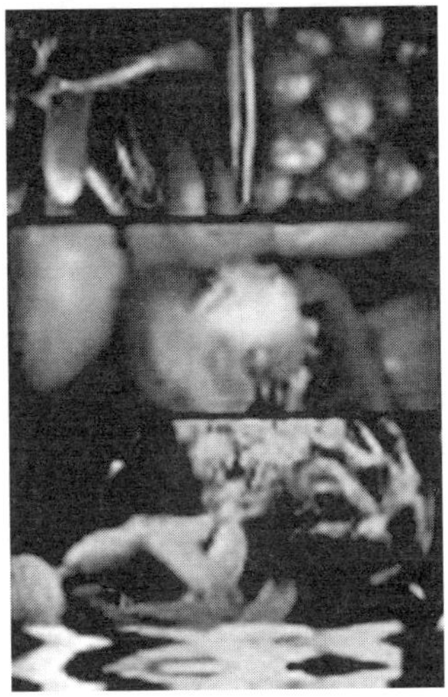

grams per 100 grams	*Vegetables*
1	Artichoke, globe, boiled (100 g)
1	Asparagus, boiled (5 = 100 g)
5	Bamboo shoots (50 g)
1	Beans, french, boiled (100 g)
10	Baked, in tomato sauce (125 g)
7	Broad, boiled (100 g)
17	Kidney (and haricot), boiled (100 g)
11	Mung, cooked dal (100 g)
11	Soya, boiled (100 g)
10	Beetroot, slices, boiled (2 = 30 g)
8	Canned (2 = 30 g)
2	Broccoli, boiled (100 g)
2	Brussels sprouts, boiled (7 = 70 g)
3	Cabbage, raw (50 g)
1	Boiled (100 g)
5	Carrots, raw (50 g)
4	Boiled (50 g)
5	Young, canned (50 g)
2	Cauliflower, raw (50 g)
1	Boiled (100 g)
2	Celery, boiled (3 = 60 g)
1	Celery, raw (50 g)
1	Boiled (50 g)
22	Chickpeas, cooked dal (60 g)
2	Cucumber, slices (5 = 30 g)
4	Egg plant, baked (½ = 100 g)
1	Endive, raw leaves (3 = 15 g)
5	Leeks, boiled (4 = 100 g)
17	Lentils, split, boiled (100 g)
1	Lettuce, raw leaves (2 = 20 g)
1	Marrow, boiled (100 g)
0	Mushrooms, raw (3 = 30 g)
0	Fried (6 = 60 g)
5	Onions, raw (¼ = 20 g)
3	Boiled (100 g)
10	Fried (70 g)
9	Spring (4 = 20 g)
Tr	Parsley, sprigs (2 = 5 g)
14	Parsnip, boiled (½ = 60 g)
7	Peas, conned (60 g)
14	Canned, processed (60 g)
8	Fresh, boiled (60 g)
4	Frozen, boiled (60 g)

22	Split, boiled (60 g)
2	Peppers, green, raw (¼ = 15 g)
2	Boiled (50 g)
20	Potato, baked (inc. skin 120 g)
20	Boiled (120 g)
37	Chips, fresh, fried (12 = 120 g)
29	Chips, frozen, fried (8–14 = 120 g)
49	Crisps (10 = 25 g)
18	Mashed (100 g)
16	Instant, cooked (100 g)
18	New, boiled (2 = 100 g)
13	New, canned (2 = 100 g)
27	Roast (120 g)
3	Pumpkin (100 g)
3	Radishes (2 = 20 g)
1	Spinach, keaves, boiled (3 = 60 g)
4	Swede, boiled (80 g)
23	Sweetcorn, on cob, boiled (150 g)
16	Canned kernels (80 g)
20	Sweet patato, boiled (100 g)
3	Tomato, raw (120 g)
2	Canned (120 g)
3	Fried (120 g)
3	Juice, canned (120 g)
2	Turnip, boiled (80 g)
30	Yam, boiled (100 g)

13 Fat

Fat is also known as lipid and is mainly present in food in a form called 'triglycerides'. Butter and margarine, e.g. are almost entirely made-up of triglycerides. Triglycerides consist of glycerol and three ('tri') fatty acids. The fatty acids can be mainly 'saturated' as in butter or mainly 'polyunsaturated' as in some margarines. There are also monounsaturated fatty acids, which occur in quantity in the triglyceride of olive oil and peanut oil.

Food may contain other fats, such as cholesterol and phospholipids, in addition to triglycerides. Lecithin is a phospholipid, made-up of glycerol, choline and fatty acids, which again may be mainly saturated or polyunsaturated.

Fat is energy dense, having an **at water factor** of 9 kilocalories, or 37 kilojoules per gram. Also, it does not mix with water, so that the food in which it is found tends to be more energy dense because of the relative lack of water. If it is a fat of plant origin, it may be associated with dietary fiber, giving bulk and reducing energy density, as, e.g. with the cereal oats that are relatively high in fat for a cereal, but also relatively high in dietary fiber. If the fat is from animal sources, the energy density will be rather high, not only because of the fat and the low amount of water, but also because there is no dietary fiber. It is important to realize that the fat content of meat, and the polyunsaturated to saturated ratio of the fat, varies considerably depending on the source of the meat, the particular cut and trim, and the method of preparation.

If we are very physically active and in need of energy then fat can be a useful source of the energy. Conversely, if we are physically inactive, too much fat in our diet can lead to overweight.

It is possible to eat very little fat and maintain good health. There are traditional dietary patterns in which the contribution of fat to energy intake is as low as 10 percent. However, in the 'affluent' diet, it may contribute up to 50 percent of energy intake. Nevertheless, it must be remembered that the quality of the fat eaten as well as its quantity is important.

Fat also confers texture and flavor on food, enhancing its palatability. Many flavors are fat soluble; unfortunately it is these desirable properties that encourage overeating.

Fat Intake

The acceptable range for fat intake: About 10–30 percent of energy intake, which for a 35–55 year old man would be 30–80 grams of fat per day, and for a 35–55 year old woman would be 20–60 grams of fat per day.

FAT FOOD CHARTS

Beverages

grams per 100 grams	*Beverages*
Tr	Beer (240 g)
0	Cider, dry alcoholic (180 g)
0	Sweet, alcoholic (180 g)
Tr	Sweet, nonalcoholic (220 g)
22	Cocoa powder (5 g)
Tr	Coffee, percolated (230 g)
0	Cola-type drinks (240 g)
–	Cordial, diluted 1:4 (240 g)
6	Drinking chocolate (10 g)
0	Lemonade, carbonated drinks (240 g)
10	Milo (10 g)
3	Ovaltine (10 g)
0	Port (60 g)
0	Sherry, dry (60 g)
0	Medium (60 g)
0	Sweet (60 g)
0	Spirits, e.g. whisky (30 g)
Tr	Tea, infusion (230 g)
0	Wine, red (100 g)
0	White, dry (100 g)
0	Medium (100 g)
0	Sparkling (100 g)
0	Sweet (100 g)

Cereals, Biscuits, Cakes, Deserts

grams per 100 grams	*Cereals, Biscuits, Cakes, Deserts*
1	Barley, pearl, boiled (–)
28	Biscuit, chocolate (20 g)
25	Cream-filled (20 g)
2	Crispbread, rye (20 g)
8	Wheat, starch-red (11 g)
15	Gingernut (15 g)
17	Semi-sweet (15 g)
23	Short-sweet (15 g)
6	Bran, wheat (8 g)
2	Bread, brown, slice (25 g)
2	Lebanese (pita) (¼ = 25 g)
2	White, slice (25 g)
2	Wholemeal, slice (25 g)

3	Roll, brown (35 g)
4	Starch-reduced (35 g)
3	White (35 g)
13	Cake, fruit (60 g)
17	Plain (60 g)
27	Cake, sponge (60 g)
13	Chapati (60 g)
35	Cheesecake (120 g)
Tr	Cornflakes (30 g)
1	Crumpet (50 g)
4	Custard (70 g)
17	Custard tart (120 g)
16	Doughnut (40 g)
24	Eclair (50 g)
Tr	Flour, corn (–)
2	Plain (–)
2	Self-raising (–)
24	Soya, full-fat (–)
7	Low-fat (–)
3	Wholemeal (–)
16	Fruit pie (150 g)
15	Jam tart (35 g)
0	Jelly, made with water (100 g)
13	Lamington (60 g)
15	Lemon meringue pie (120 g)
0	Meringue (15 g)
4	Milk pudding (e.g. sago) (160 g)
20	Muesli (30 g)
10	Noodles (chow mein) (250 g)
16	Pancake (75 g)
1	Pasta, macaroni, boiled (150 g)
Tr	Spaghetti, boiled (120 g)
1	Canned in tomato sauce (120 g)
41	Pastry, flaky (–)
32	Short crust (–)
12	Pizza, cheese and tomato (150 g)
1	Porridge (30 g)
Tr	Rice, boiled (160 g)
9	Fried (120 g)
Tr	Puffed (25 g)
15	Scone (30 g)
16	Sponge pudding, steamed (100 g)
6	Triffle (100 g)
1	Wheat, breakfast biscuit (35 g)
2	Yeast, dried, baker's (–)

Egg and Cheese Dishes

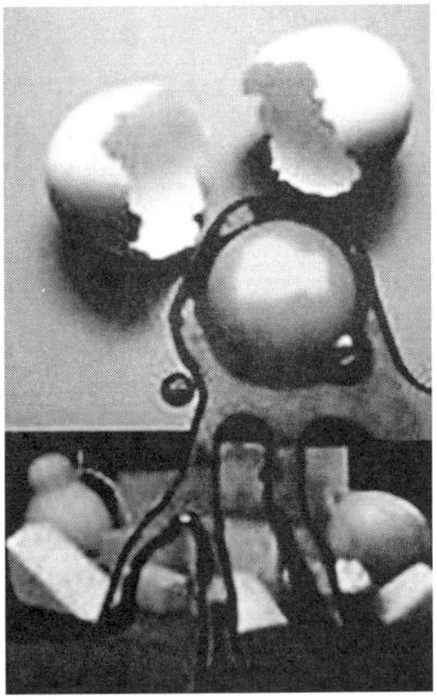

grams per 100 grams	*Egg and Cheese dishes*
8	Cauliflower, cheese (100 g)
19	Cheese souffle (100 g)
11	Egg, boiled (55 g)
20	Egg, fried (60 g)
16	Omelette (100 g)
12	Poached (55 g)
11	Raw (55 g)
23	Scrambled (70 g)
10	Macaroni cheese (180 g)
28	Quiche lorraine (150 g)

Fats and Oils

grams per 100 grams	*Fats and Oils*
81	Butter, salted (10 g)
100	Dripping, beef (–)
100	Lard (–)
80	Margarine (10 g)
100	Vegetable oils (–)

Fish and Other Seafoods

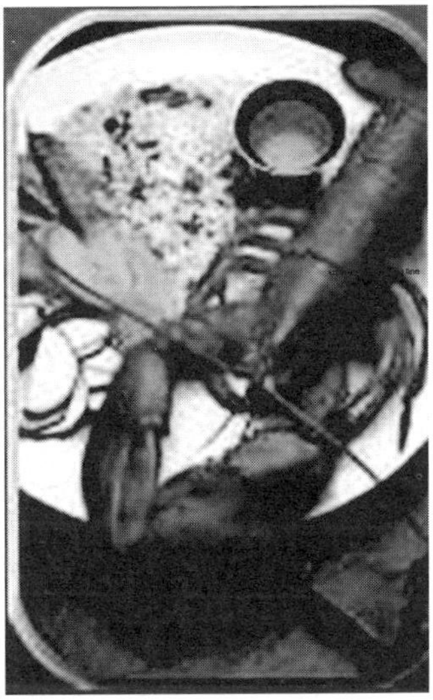

grams per 100 grams	*Fish and Other Seafoods*
3	Bream, steamed (100 g)
1	Cod, baked (100 g)
10	Tried in batter (100 g)
1	Poached (100 g)
1	Steamed (100 g)
5	Crab, boiled (150 g)
1	Canned (90 g)
11	Fish cakes, fried (4 = 100 g)
13	Fingers, fried (5 = 100 g)
16	In batter, fried (120 g)
11	Flounder, baked (100 g)
8	Haddock, fried (100 g)
1	Steamed (100 g)
3	Lobster, boiled (120 g)
2	Mussels, boiled (12 = 120 g)
1	Oysters, raw (12 = 120 g)
2	Prawns, boiled (6 = 120 g)
12	Roe, cod, fried (100 g)
8	Salmon, canned (100 g)
28	Sardines, canned (60 g)
1	Scallops, steamed (10 = 100 g)
22	Tuna, canned in oil (120 g)
10	Whiting, crumbed, fried (100 g)
1	Steamed (100 g)

Fruit

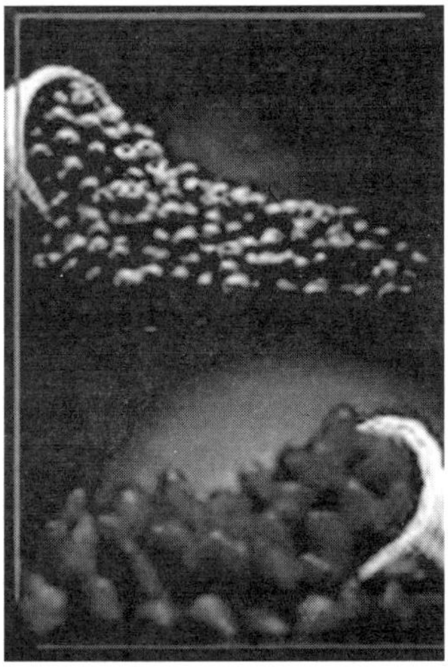

grams per 100 grams	*Fruit*
Tr	Apple (inc, skin, core 100 g)
Tr	Baked, no sugar (inc. skin 110 g)
Tr	Stewed, no sugar (110 g)
Tr	Apricots (inc. stones 3 = 100 g)
Tr	Apricots, canned (100 g)
Tr	Dried (25 g)
Tr	Stewed, no sugar (inc. stones 110 g)
22	Avocado pear (½ = 150 g)
Tr	Banana (100 g)
Tr	Blackberries (100 g)
Tr	Stewed, no sugar (100 g)
Tr	Cantaloup (inc. skin 120 g)
Tr	Cherries (inc. stones 20 = 100 g)
Tr	Stewed, no sugar (inc. stones 100 g)
Tr	Currants, black (90 g)
Tr	Dried (15 g)
Tr	Red (90 g)
Tr	Dates, dried (6 = 35 g)
Tr	Figs (2 = 75 g)
Tr	Dried (2 = 40 g)
Tr	Fruit salad, canned (120 g)
Tr	Grapes, black (20 = 100 g)
Tr	White (20 = 100 g)
Tr	Grapefruit, whole (200 g)
Tr	Canned (100 g)
Tr	Juice, canned (120 g)
Tr	Guavas, canned (100 g)
Tr	Lemon, slices (2 = 15 g)
Tr	Juice (15 g)
Tr	Loganberries (100 g)
Tr	Canned (100 g)
Tr	Stewed, no sugar (100 g)
Tr	Lychees, canned (100 g)
Tr	Mandarins (2 = 100 g)
Tr	Canned (50 g)
Tr	Mango (100 g)
Tr	Canned (100 g)
Tr	Nectarines (inc. stones 3 = 100 g)
9	Olives, in brine (5 = 20 g)
Tr	Orange, whole (130 g)
Tr	Juice, fresh (120 g)
Tr	Canned (120 g)
Tr	Passionfruit, whole (30 g)

Tr	Papaw (100 g)
Tr	Canned (100 g)
Tr	Peach (inc. stones 120 g)
Tr	Canned (120 g)
Tr	Dried (25 g)
Tr	Peach, stewed, no sugar (120 g)
Tr	Pear (inc. skin. core 120 g)
Tr	Canned (120 g)
Tr	Stewed, no sugar (120 g)
Tr	Pineapple (80 g)
Tr	Canned (80 g)
Tr	Juice, canned (120 g)
Tr	Plums (inc. stones 3 = 100 g)
Tr	Stewed, no sugar (inc. stones 100 g)
Tr	Prunes (inc. stones 8 = 80 g)
Tr	Stewed, no sugar (inc. stones 120 g)
Tr	Quince, raw (100 g)
Tr	Raisins, dried (20 g)
Tr	Raspberries (100 g)
Tr	Canned (100 g)
Tr	Stewed, no sugar (100 g)
Tr	Rhubarb, stewed, no sugar (120 g)
Tr	Strawberries (10 = 100 g)
Tr	Canned (100 g)
Tr	Sultanas, dried (15 g)
Tr	Watermelon (260 g)

Meat and Meat Products

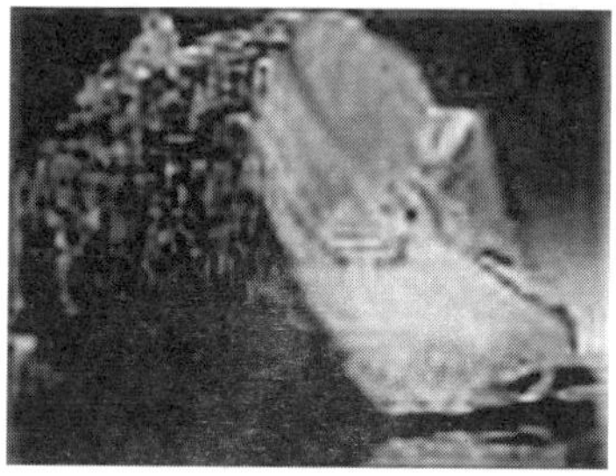

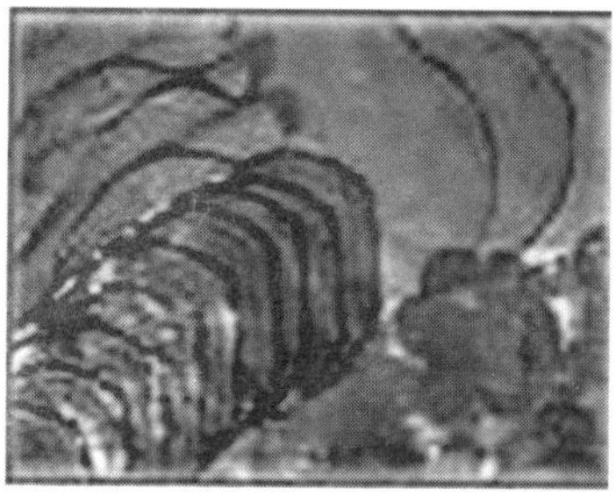

grams per 100 grams	*Meat and Meat Products*
42	Bacon rashers, middle, fried (2 = 40 g)
35	Grilled (40 g)
12	Beef, corned, canned (90 g)
9	Fillet steak, grilled (130 g)
15	Mince, stewed (100 g)
15	Rump steak, fried (150 g)
12	Grilled (150 g)
14	Silverside, salted, boiled (120 g)
21	Sirloin, roast (120 g)
11	Stewing steak, stewed (120 g)
12	Topside, roast (120 g)
17	Beefburger, frozen, fried (60 g)
8	Beef stew (250 g)
11	Bolognes sauce (100 g)
7	Chicken, boiled (100 g)
22	Crumbed, no bone (140 g)
14	Roast (130 g)
3	Leg quarter (inc. bone 130 g)
3	Wing quarter (inc. bone 130 g)
11	Chicken livers, fried (130 g)
29	Duck, roast (100 g)
Tr	Gelatin (–)
5	Ham, canned (90 g)
10	Hamburger (170 g)
13	With cheese (190 g)
7	Lrish stew (250 g)
9	Lamb, brain, boiled (150 g)
23	Chops, loin, grilled (inc. bone 120 g)
20	Cutlets, grilled (inc, bone 100 g)
15	Heart, roast (140 g)
6	Kidney, fried (100 g)
18	Leg, roast (120 g)
14	Liver, fried (130 g)
26	Shoulder, roast (120 g)
24	Tongue, stewed (100 g)
27	Luncheon meat, canned (90 g)
14	Meat pie (180 g)
13	Moussaka (200 g)
20	Pastie (160 g)
19	Pork, chop, ooin, grilled (100 g)
20	Leg, roast (120 g)
9	Sweet and sour (250 g)
27	Pork pie (180 g)

4	Rabbit, stewed (inc. bone 170 g)
45	Salami, slices (3 = 90 g)
27	Sausage, liver (60 g)
18	Sausage roll (100 g)
18	Sausages, beef, fried (2 = 120 g)
17	Grilled (2 = 120 g)
25	Frankfurter (2 = 100 g)
25	Pork, fried (2 = 120 g)
25	Grilled (2 = 120 g)
21	Saveloy, large (2 = 150 g)
22	Spring roll, fried (200 g)
21	Steak and kidney pie (180 g)
13	Stewed steak in gravy, canned (100 g)
17	Tongue, canned (100 g)
5	Tripe, stewed (100 g)
7	Turkey, roast (120 g)
8	Veal, cutlet, fried (110 g)
12	Fillet, roast (100 g)
21	Schnitzel (140 g)

Milk and Milk Products

grams per 100 grams	*Milk and Milk Products*
23	Cheese, camembert (25 g)
34	Cheddar (25 g)
23	Cheese spread (10 g)
4	Cottage (25 g)
47	Cream cheese (15 g)
29	Danish blue (25 g)
23	Edam (25 g)
30	Parmesan (10 g)
25	Processed (25 g)
40	Stilton (25 g)
29	Swiss (25 g)
38	Cream, 35% fat (30 g)
23	Sterilized, canned (15 g)
7	Ice cream (60 g)
8	nondairy (60 g)
Tr	Milk, cow's, cond, skim, sweet (30 g)
9	Cond, whole, sweet (30 g)
1	Dried, skimmed (12 g)
26	Dried, whole (10 g)
9	Evap, whole, unsweet (30 g)
4	Flavored (230 g)
Tr	Fresh, skimmed (230 g)
4	Fresh, whole (230 g)

4	Longlife, UHT (230 g)
5	Goat's (230 g)
4	Human (100 g)
5	Milkshake, flavored (340 g)
4	Yoghurt, flavored (200 g)
1	Fruit, low fat (200 g)
1	Natural, low fat (200 g)
4	Plain (200 g)

Nuts

grams per 100 grams	*Nuts*
54	Almonds (10 = 15 g)
62	Brazil nuts (5 = 20 g)
47	Cashews, roast (10 = 20 g)
3	Chestnuts (4 = 20 g)
62	Coconut, desiccated (15 g)
36	Hazel nuts (10 = 15 g)
74	Macadamia nuts (8 = 20 g)
34	Peanuts, raw, in shells (5 = 25 g)
49	Roasted, salted (30 = 25 g)
54	Pistachio nuts, shelled (25 = 15 g)
52	Walnuts (5 = 20 g)

Sauces and Condiments

grams per 100 grams	*Sauces and Condiments*
7	Barbecue sauce (10 g)
.6	Chilli sauce (–)
Tr	Chutney, tomato (20 g)
10	Curry powder (–)
73	French dressing (15 g)
3	Ginger (ground) (–)
79	Mayonnaise (20 g)
29	Mustard powder (–)
3	Oxo cubes (–)
7	Pepper (–)
1	Pickles, mustard (20 g)
Tr	Sweet (20 g)
27	Salad cream (25 g)
0	Salt, table (–)
49	Sesame seeds (–)
1	Soy sauce (–)
54	Tartare sauce (20 g)
5	Tomato sauce (25 g)
0	Vinegar (–)
0	Worcestershire sauce (–)

Soups (as served)

grams per 100 grams	*Soups (as served)*
4	Chicken, condensed (230 g)
Tr	Chicken coodle, dried (230 g)
1	Minestrone, dried (230 g)
4	Mushroom, canned (230 g)
3	Tomato, condensed (230 g)
1	Tomato, dried (230 g)
1	Vegetable, canned (230 g)

Sugars, Jams and Spreads

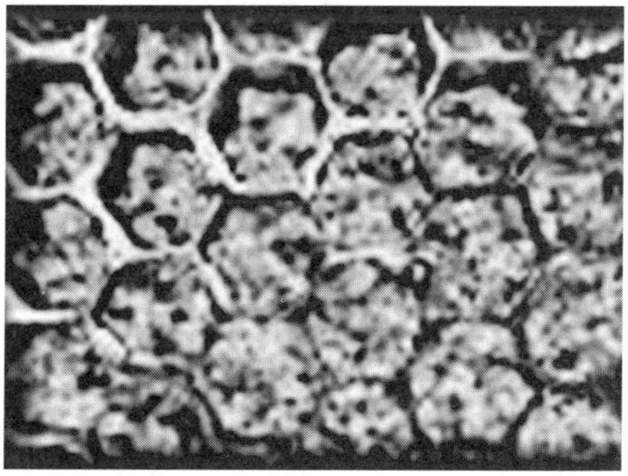

grams per 100 grams	*Sugars, Jams and Spreads*
10	Fish paste (5 g)
Tr	Honey (30 g)
0	Jam, fruit edible seeds (30 g)
0	Jam, stone fruit (30 g)
0	Marmalade (30 g)
11	Meat paste (5 g)
54	Peanut butter (20 g)
0	Sugar, white (–)
0	Syrup, golden (30 g)
Tr	Topping, flavored (40 g)
0	Treacle, black (30 g)
0	Vcgcmitc (3 g)

Sweets

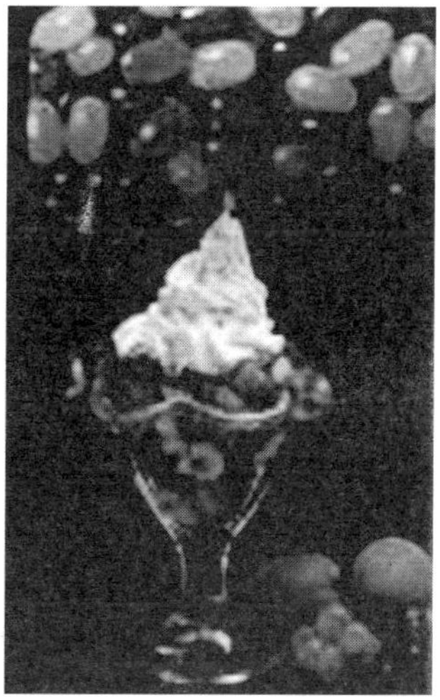

grams per 100 grams	*Sweets*
Tr	Boiled sweed (5 g)
87	Butterscotch (5 g)
11	Caramel (5 g)
27	Carob bar (75 g)
30	Chocolate square, milk (5 g)
31	Fruit and honey bar (50 g)
Tr	Jelly bean (5 g)
2	Liquorice allsort (7 g)
0	Pastille (5 g)
1	Peppermint (4 g)
4	Popcorn, plain unsalted (15 g)
31	Sesame bar (50 g)
17	Toffee, mixed (5 g)

Vegetables

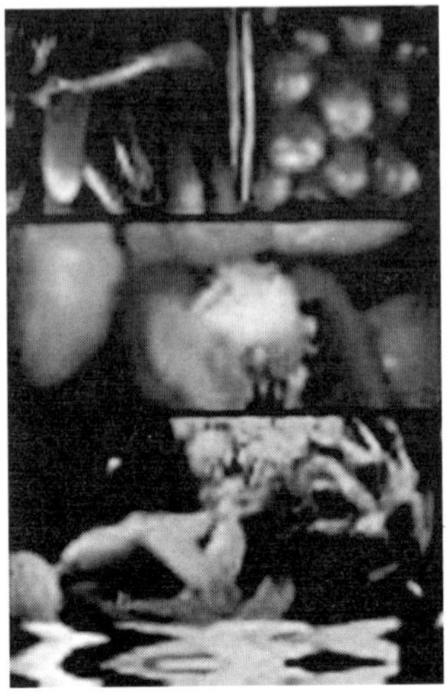

grams per 100 grams	*Vegetables*
Tr	Artichoke, globe, boiled (100 g)
Tr	Asparagus, boiled (5 = 100 g)
Tr	Bamboo shoots (50 g)
Tr	Beans, french, boiled (100 g)
1	Baked, in tomato sauce (125 g)
1	Broad, boiled (100 g)
1	Kidney (and haricot), boiled (100 g)
4	Mung, cooked dal (100 g)
6	Soya, boiled (100 g)
Tr	Beetroot, slices, boiled (2 = 30 g)
Tr	Canned (2 = 30 g)
Tr	Broccoli, boiled (100 g)
Tr	Brussels sprouts, boiled (7 = 70 g)
Tr	Cabbage, raw (50 g)
Tr	Boiled (100 g)
Tr	Carrots, raw (50 g)
Tr	Boiled (50 g)
Tr	Young, canned (50 g)
Tr	Cauliflower, raw (50 g)
Tr	Boiled (100 g)
Tr	Celery, boiled (3 = 60 g)
Tr	Celery, raw (50 g)
Tr	Boiled (50 g)
3	Chickpeas, cooked dal (60 g)
Tr	Cucumber, slices (5 = 30 g)
5	Egg plant, baked (½ = 100 g)
Tr	Endive, raw leaves (3 = 15 g)
Tr	Leeks, boiled (4 = 100 g)
1	Lentils, split, boiled (100 g)
Tr	Lettuce, raw leaves (2 = 20 g)
Tr	Marrow, boiled (100 g)
1	Mushrooms, raw (3 = 30 g)
22	Fried (6 = 60 g)
Tr	Onions, raw (¼ = 20 g)
Tr	Boiled (100 g)
33	Fried (70 g)
Tr	Spring (4 = 20 g)
Tr	Parsley, sprigs (2 = 5 g)
Tr	Parsnip, boiled (½ = 60 g)
Tr	Peas, conned (60 g)
Tr	Canned, processed (60 g)
Tr	Fresh, boiled (60 g)
Tr	Frozen, boiled (60 g)

Tr	Split, boiled (60 g)
Tr	Peppers, green, raw (¼ = 15 g)
Tr	Boiled (50 g)
Tr	Potato, baked (inc. skin 120 g)
Tr	Boiled (120 g)
11	Chips, fresh, fried (12 = 120 g)
19	Chips, frozen, fried (8–14 = 120 g)
36	Crisps (10 = 25 g)
5	Mashed (100 g)
Tr	Instant, cooked (100 g)
Tr	New, boiled (2 = 100 g)
Tr	New, canned (2 = 100 g)
5	Roast (120 g)
Tr	Pumpkin (100 g)
Tr	Radishes (2 = 20 g)
1	Spinach, keaves, boiled (3 = 60 g)
Tr	Swede, boiled (80 g)
2	Sweetcorn, on cob, boiled (150 g)
1	Canned kernels (80 g)
1	Sweet patato, boiled (100 g)
Tr	Tomato, raw (120 g)
Tr	Canned (120 g)
6	Fried (120 g)
Tr	Juice, canned (120 g)
Tr	Turnip, boiled (80 g)
Tr	Yam, boiled (100 g)

14 Cholesterol

There is another type of fat, called sterols. Cholesterol is the sterol found in all animal tissues; in plants, the sterols are of a different kind.

Cholesterol forms a part of all animal cell walls (membranes). It is also used to make hormones like cortisol and to make bile acids.

Unfortunately, it can also accumulate in the inner parts of arteries, leading to progressive reduction in the diameter of blood vessels and in blood flow. This in turn leads to heart attacks, angina, abnormal heart rhythms and heart failure when the vessels affected are the coronary arteries supplying the heart. Arteries supplying blood to the brain, the legs, the kidneys and the gut can also be affected.

The extent to which cholesterol accumulates in arteries depends in part on the level of cholesterol in the blood. When high, this is called hypercholesterolemia. Not only dietary cholesterol, but also dietary saturated fat, elevate the blood cholesterol level. Polyunsaturated fat and certain kinds of dietary fiber lower the blood cholesterol level.

It is worth remembering that the body can make its own cholesterol so that dietary cholesterol is not an essential nutrient.

Note: In seafood, some of the sterols that were once believed to be cholesterol are actually a different kind, so the values shown in the Cholesterol Food Charts for seafood may be less than in some other references.

Cholesterol Intake

The safe range of cholesterol intake is: 200–400 milligrams per day.

CHOLESTEROL FOOD CHARTS

Cereals, Biscuits, Cakes, Deserts

Food	*Cholesterol (milligrams per 100 grams of food)*
Bread	1 (25 g)
Cake, sponge	130 (60 g)
Cornflakes	0 (30 g)
Custard (no egg)	15 (70 g)
Custard tart	60 (120 g)
Eclairs	90 (50 g)
Jelly, made with water	0 (100 g)
Lemon meringue pie	90 (120 g)
Meringues	0 (15 g)
Milk pudding	15 (160 g)
Pancakes	65 (75 g)
Pizza, cheese and tomato	20 (150 g)
Rice, boiled	0 (160 g)
Rice, puffed	0 (25 g)
Scones	5 (30 g)
Sponge pudding, steamed	80 (100 g)
Trifle	50 (100 g)
Wheat flakes	0 (35 g)

Egg and Cheese Dishes

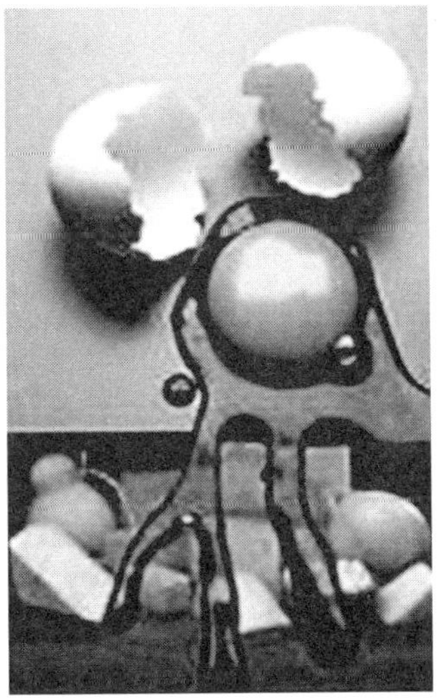

Food	*Cholesterol (milligrams per 100 grams of food)*
Cauliflower cheese	17 (100 g)
Eggs, boiled	450 (55 g)
Eggs, fried	480 (60 g)
Egg omelette	410 (100 g)
Eggs, poached	480 (55 g)
Eggs, scrambled	410 (70 g)
Macaroni cheese	17 (180 g)
Quiche lorraine	130 (150 g)

Fats and Oils

Food	*Cholesterol (milligrams per 100 grams of food)*
Butter, salted	260 (10 g)
Dripping, beef	95 (–)
Lard	95 (–)
Margarine (all vegetable)	0–5 (10 g)

Fish and Other Seafoods

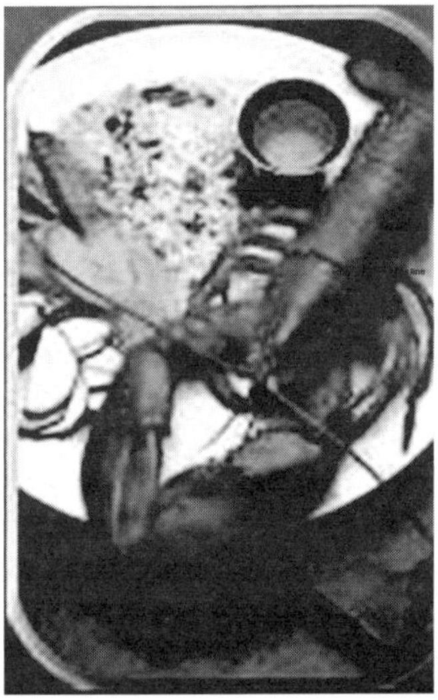

Food	*Cholesterol (milligrams per 100 grams of food)*
Bream	130 (100 g)
Cod, steamed	40 (100 g)
Crab	65 (150 g)
Flathead	60 (100 g)
Fishfingers, fried	50 (5 = 100 g)
Haddock, steamed	75 (100 g)
Lobster	70 (120 g)
Mussels	55 (12 = 120 g)
Oysters, raw	40 (12 = 120 g)
Prawns, boiled	170 (6 = 120 g)
Roe, cod, fried	500 (100 g)
Salmon, canned	90 (100 g)
Sardines, canned	80 (60 g)
Scallops, steamed	30 (10 = 100 g)
Tuna, canned in oil	90 (120 g)
Whiting, steamed	110 (100 g)

Meat and Meat Products

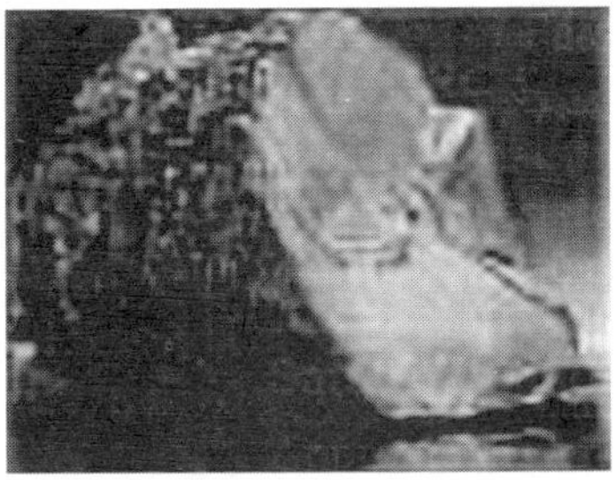

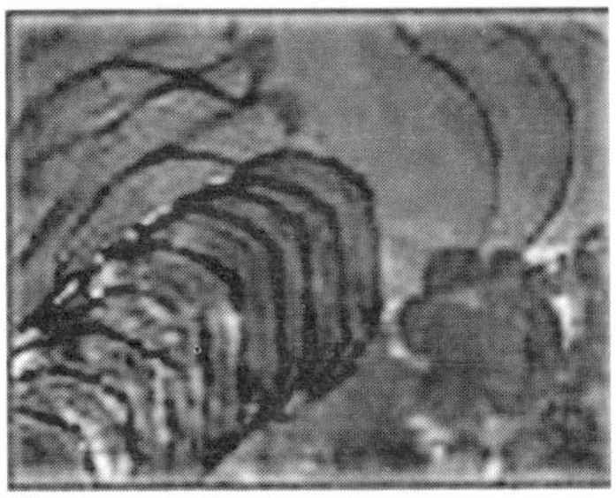

Food	*Cholesterol (milligrams per 100 grams of food)*
Bacon, rashers, fried	80 (2 = 40 g)
Bacon, rashers, grilled	75 (40 g)
Beef, corned, canned	85 (90 g)
Beef, cooked	80 (120 g)
Beefburgers, frozen, fried	70 (60 g)
Beef stew	30 (250 g)
Bolognese sauce	25 (100 g)
Chicken, boiled	90 (100 g)
Chicken, roast	160 (130 g)
Duck, roast	160 (100 g)
Ham, canned	35 (90 g)
Hamburger, cheese	34 (190 g)
Hamburger, plain	20 (170 g)
Irish stew	35 (250 g)
Lamb, brain, boiled	1900 (150 g)
Lamb, cooked	110 (120 g)
Lamb, lddney, fried	550 (100 g)
Lamb, liver, fried	585 (130 g)
Lamb, tongue, stewed	270 (100 g)
Luncheon meat, canned	55 (90 g)
Meat paste	70 (5 g)
Meat pie	20 (180 g)
Moussaka	40 (200 g)
Pastie	50 (160 g)
Pork, cooked	110 (120 g)
Pork, pie	50 (180 g)
Salami, slices	80 (3 = 90 g)
Sausage roll	20 (100 g)
Sausage, liver	120 (60 g)
Sausages, beef, fried	40 (2 = 120 g)
Sausages, beef, grilled	40 (2 = 120 g)
Sausages, pork, fried	55 (2 = 120 g)
Sausages, pork, grilled	55 (2 = 120 g)
Sausages, saveloy	45 (2 = 150 g)
Steak and kidney pie	125 (180 g)
Tongue, canned	110 (100 g)
Tripe, stewed	160 (100 g)
Turkey, roast	80 (120 g)

Milk and Milk Products

Food	*Cholesterol (milligrams per 100 grams of food)*
Cheese, camembert type	70 (25 g)
Cheese, cheddar type	70 (25 g)
Cheese, cottage	15 (25 g)
Cheese, cream	95 (15 g)
Cheese, danish blue type	90 (25 g)
Cheese, edam type	70 (25 g)
Cheese, parmesan	90 (10 g)
Cheese, processed	90 (25 g)
Cheese, spread	70 (10 g)
Cream	100 (30 g)
Cream, sterilized, canned	75 (15 g)
Ice cream	45 (60 g)
Milk, cow's condensed, skimmed, sweetefed	3 (30 g)
Milk, cow's condensed, whole, sweetened	35 (30 g)
Milk, cow's dried, skimmed,	20 (12 g)
Milk, cow's evaporated, whole, unsweetened	35 (30 g)
Milk, cow's fresh, skimmed,	2 (230 g)
Milk, cow's fresh, whole	10 (230 g)
Milk, cow's longlife (UHT treated)	10 (230 g)
Milk, human	15 (100 g)
Yoghurt, low fat, fruit	5 (200 g)
Yoghurt, low fat, plain	5 (200 g)

Sugars, Jams and Spreads

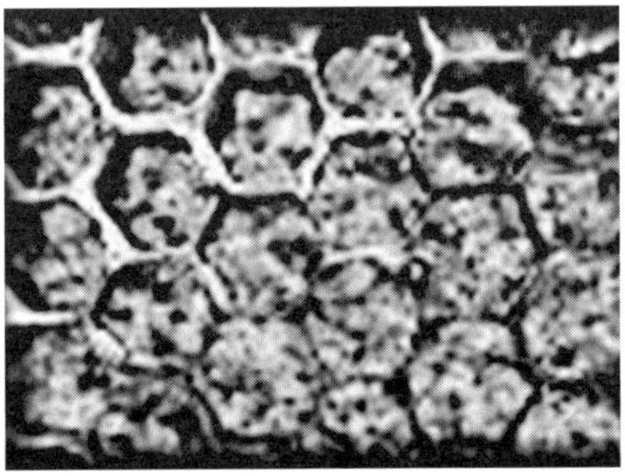

Food	*Cholesterol (milligrams per 100 grams of food)*
Honey	0 (30 g)
Jam	0 (30 g)
Sugar	0 (–)
Syrup, golden	0 (30 g)
Treacle, black	0 (30 g)
Vegemite	0 (3 g)

Sweets

Food	*Cholesterol (milligrams per 100 grams of food)*
Boiled sweets	0 (5 g)
Chocolate, milk	90 (5 g)

* Cholesterol is not found in plant foods—cereals, fruit, nuts, and vegetables. The amount of cholesterol in food depends on the amount of animal produce used.

** Values in parenthesis are average serving sizes.

15 Saturated and Polyunsaturated Fat

There are several types of fats, the chief ones being called triglycerides, cholesterol esters, and phospholipids. They contain fatty acids, which may be saturated, monounsaturated or polyunsaturated.

Some polyunsaturated fatty acids are essential for humans because they cannot be made in our bodies. One group of essential fatty acids comes from plant sources; these fatty acids are found in considerable quantity in polyunsaturated margarine and in vegetable oils. We need about 1 to 2 percent of our energy to come from this type of fatty acid, although a higher intake, up to about 10 percent of energy, may be protective against coronary heart disease. The requirements of another type of essential fatty acid have not been worked out, but they are obtained mainly from seafood and, in a different way, seem protective against coronary heart disease—they reduce the 'stickiness' of the blood. Both kinds of essential fatty acids can lower high levels of blood fats.

Saturated fatty acids come chiefly from ruminant animals, such as sheep and cattle, and from milk and dairy products of these animals. In the stomachs of ruminants the polyunsaturated fatty acids that are present in fodder are broken down to a large extent to saturated fatty acids so that the fatty tissues of animals, such as cattle are mostly saturated. On the other hand, animals with a single stomach (monogastric) absorb the range of fatty acids, saturated and polyunsaturated, present in the diet. Pigs and humans are similar in this respect. Furthermore, domesticated animals have more carcass fat than wild animals so that the advent of animal production for human consumption has led to a great increase in the consumption of saturated fat.

Saturated fat increases the amount of cholesterol in blood. Monounsaturated fat does not increase the blood cholesterol level and may decrease it (olive oil and peanut oil provide monounsaturated fat). Polyunsaturated fat decreases it. Traditional cultures that use olive oil in food preparation or a lot of groundnuts (peanuts) have little coronary heart disease. Cholesterol in food increases the level of cholesterol in blood.

Saturated fat also increases the amount of triglyceride in the blood. Both blood cholesterol and blood triglyceride, when elevated, increase the risk of hardening of the arteries (**atherosclerosis**), with consequent coronary heart disease.

The desirable ratio of polyunsaturated to saturated fat in the diet is: **1:1 (i.e. 50:50).**

Special Polyunsaturated Products

Some novel food products have been developed to decrease the saturated and increase the polyunsaturated fat of the total diet. Foods traditionally high in saturated fat, such as ice cream made with milkfat, are now available made from polyunsaturated vegetable oils. Dairy and beef cattle have been fed polyunsaturated fat protected from digestive breakdown so that the dairy and beef products are more polyunsaturated. Eggs have also had the yolk, rich in cholesterol, removed and replaced with a polyunsaturated oil substitute — hence 'polyunsaturated egg mix', with the main advantage being a low cholesterol content.

Saturated and Polyunsaturated Fat in Margarine and Vegetable Oils

Approximate amounts of saturated and polyunsaturated fat in different types of margarine are shown in Table 15.1, and the amounts in different vegetable oils are shown in Table 15.2.

Table 15.1: Approximate amounts of saturated and polyunsaturated fat in margarines

Type of margarine	Saturated fat (grams per 100 grams of margarine)	Polyunsaturated fat (grams per 100 grams of margarine)
Hard (animal and vegetable oils)	30	14
Hard (vegetable oils only)	30	10
Soft (animal and vegetable oils)	25	16
Soft (vegetable oils only)	26	18
Polyunsaturated	19	60

Table 15.2: Approximate amounts of saturated and polyunsaturated fat in different vegetable oils

Type of oil	Saturated fat (grams per 100 grams of oil)	Polyunsaturated fat (grams per 100 grams of oil)
Coconut oil	85	2
Maize oil	16	49
Olive oil	14	11
Palm oil	45	8
Peanut oil	19	29
Safflower oil	10	72
Soybean oil	14	57
Sunflower oil	13	50

SATURATED AND POLYUNSATURATED FAT FOOD CHARTS

Egg and Cheese Dishes

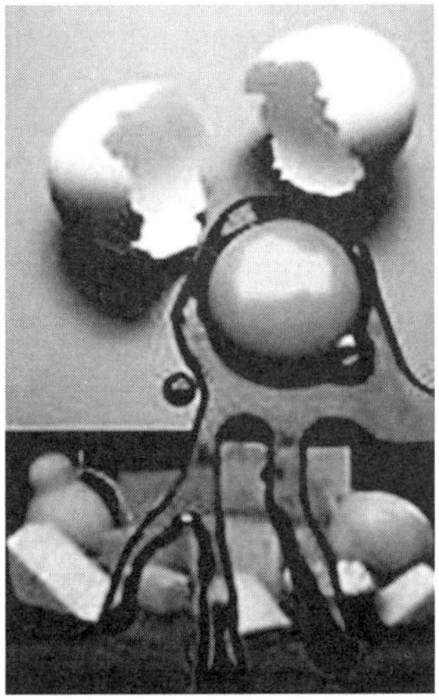

Polynusaturated fat grams per 100 grams	*Saturated fat grams per 100 grams*	*Egg and cheese dishes*
.6	4	Cauliflower cheese (100 g)
2	8	Cheese souffle (100 g)
1	3	Egg, boiled (55 g)
–	–	Egg, tried (60 g)
1	5	Omelette (100 g)
1	4	Poached (55 g)
1	3	Raw (55 g)
1	11	Scrambled (70 g)
.7	5	Macaroni cheese (180 g)
2	13	Quiche lorraine (150 g)

Fats and Oils

Polynusaturated fat grams per 100 grams	*Saturated fat grams per 100 grams*	*Fats and Oils*
2	49	Butter, salted (10 g)
4	43	Dripping, beef (–)
9	42	Lard (–)
–	–	Margarine (10 g)
–	–	Vegetable oils (–)

Fish and Other Seafoods

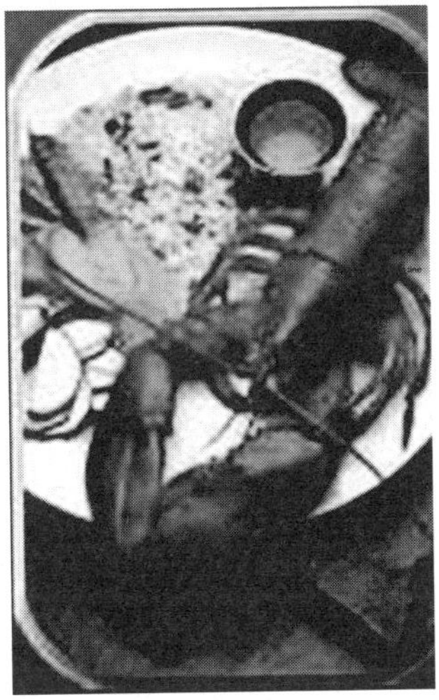

Polynusaturated fat grams per 100 grams	*Saturated fat grams per 100 grams*	*Fish and other seafoods*
–	–	Bream, steamed (100 g)
.1	.5	Cod, baked (100 g)
–	–	Fried in batter (100 g)
.1	.4	Poached (100 g)
.1	.3	Steamed (100 g)
1	2	Crab, boiled (150 g)
.1	.3	Canned (90 g)
–	–	Fish cakes, fried (4 = 100 g)
–	–	Fingers, fried (5 = 100 g)
–	–	In batter, fried (120 g)
–	–	Flounder, baked (100 g)
–	–	Haddock, fried (100 g)
.1	.3	Steamed (100 g)
.7	1	Lobster, boiled (120 g)
.4	.6	Mussels, boiled (12 = 120 g)
.1	.3	Oysters, raw (12 = 120 g)
.3	.7	Prawns, boiled (6 = 120 g)
–	–	Roe, cod, fried (100 g)
3	2	Salmon, canned (100 g)
7	6	Sardines, canned (60 g)
.1	.3	Scallops, steamed (10 = 100 g)
9	8	Tuna, canned in oil (120 g)
–	–	Whiting, crumbed fried (100 g)
.3	.2	Steamed (100 g)

16 Alcohol

The usual alcohol present in food and beverages is called ethanol. It is made by fermentation of carbohydrate. It is virtually never found in freshly collected food. It has an energy value of 7 kilocalories or 29 kilojoules per gram. But, with high alcohol intakes, proportionately less of the alcohol is used to produce useful energy.

There is some evidence that a small amount of ethanol may actually protect against coronary heart disease. However, depending on other lifestyle factors, there may be a trade-off in that any quantity of ethanol increases blood pressure to some extent, which increases the risk of strokes.

Alcohol Intake

When the average intake of ethanol exceeds 80 grams per day, disease of one sort or another is in due course inevitable. This situation is one of alcohol abuse. The adverse effects are seen on brain, liver, heart, muscles, blood, gut, nerves, pancreas (leading to diabetes or pancreatitis) and nutritional status. Alcohol abuse can lead to deficiencies of vitamins, including vitamin B_1, vitamin B_2, niacin, vitamin B_6, folacin and vitamin C, and to element (mineral) deficiencies, which include zinc and magnesium. These deficiencies will arise for various reasons, such as failure to eat food containing these nutrients, decreased absorption or interference with nutrient usage. For some individuals, an average daily alcohol intake of 40 grams per day will adversely affect health. Probably the safest level of alcohol intake is one to two drinks a day, equivalent to 8–20 grams of ethanol.

The safe range of alcohol intake is 8–20 grams of ethanol per day.

Table 16.1: The alcohol content of beverages

Notes: 1 ml of beverage weighs approximately 1 gram. Proof spirit is used to describe the alcohol content of spirits. In Australia and the UK. 100° proof spirit contains 57 percent alcohol by volume, and in the USA 50 percent alcohol.

Beverage	*Average alcohol content*		
	(grams per 100 grams)	*(milliliters per 100 milliliters)*	*(grams per 100 milliliters)*
Beer			
bitter	3.9	4.9	3.9
reduced alcohol (light)	1.6–2.6	2.0–3.3	1.6–2.6

(Contd.)

(Contd.)

Beverage	*Average alcohol content*		
	(grams per 100 grams)	*(millilitres per 100 millilitres)*	*(grams per 100 milliliters)*
Cider			
dry	3.8	4.8	3.7
sweet	3.7	4.6	3.7
Port	15.9	19.6	15.6
Sherry			
Dry	15.7	19.3	15.3
Medium	14.8	18.2	14.4
Sweet	15.6	19.2	15.2
Spirits 700 proof (brandy, gin, whisky, vodka, rum)	31.7	38.1	30.2
Vermouth			
Dry	13.9	17.2	13.7
Sweet	13.0	16.1	12.8
Wine			
White, dry	9.1	11.3	9.0
White, medium	8.8	10.9	8.7
White, sparkling	9.9	12.3	9.8
White, sweet	10.2	12.7	10.1
Red	9.5	11.8	9.4
Rose	8.7	10.8	8.6

The Alcohol Content of Beverages (Standard glasses)

17 Food Ingredients by Companies

TYPES OF FOOD INGREDIENTS

The following summary lists the types of common food ingredients, why they are used, and some examples of the names that can be found on product labels. Some additives are used for more than one purpose.

Types of ingredients	*What they do*	*Examples of uses*	*Names found on product labels*
Preservatives	Prevent food spoilage from bacteria, molds, fungi, or yeast (antimicrobials); slow or prevent changes in color, flavor, or texture and delay rancidity (antioxidants); maintain freshness	Fruit sauces and jellies, beverages, baked goods, cured meats, oils and margarines, cereals, dressings, snack foods, fruits and vegetables	Ascorbic acid, citric acid, sodium benzoate, calcium propionate, sodium erythorbate, sodium nitrite, calcium sorbate, potassium sorbate, BHA, BHT, EDTA, tocopherols (vitamin E)
Sweeteners	Add sweetness with or without the extra calories	Beverages, baked goods, confections, table-top sugar, substitutes, many processed foods	Sucrose (sugar), glucose, fructose, sorbitol, mannitol, corn syrup, high fructose corn syrup, saccharin, aspartame, sucralose, acesulfame potassium (acesulfame-K), neotame
Color additives	Offset color loss due to exposure to light, air, temperature extremes, moisture and storage conditions; correct natural variations in color; enhance colors that occur naturally;	Many processed foods, (candies, snack foods margarine, cheese, soft drinks, jams/jellies, gelatins, pudding and pie fillings)	FD & C Blue Nos. 1 and 2, FD & C Green No. 3, FD & C Red Nos. 3 and 40, FD & C Yellow nos. 5 and 6, orange B, citrus red No. 2, annatto extract, beta-carotene, grape skin extract, cochineal

(Contd.)

(Contd.)

Types of ingredients	*What they do*	*Examples of uses*	*Names found on product labels*
	provide color to colorless and "fun" foods		extract or carmine, paprika oleoresin, caramel color, fruit and vegetable juices, saffron (Note: Exempt color additives are not required to be declared by name on labels but may be declared simply as colorings or color added)
Flavors and spices	Add specific flavors (natural and synthetic)	Pudding and pie fillings, gelatin dessert mixes, cake mixes, salad dressings, candies, soft drinks, ice cream, BBQ sauce	Natural flavoring, artificial flavor, and spices
Flavor enhancers	Enhance flavors already present in foods (without providing their own separate flavor)	Many processed foods	Monosodium glutamate (MSG), hydrolyzed soy protein, autolyzed yeast extract, disodium guanylate or inosinate
Fat replacers (and components of formulations used to replace fats)	Provide expected texture and a creamy "mouth-feel" in reduced-fat foods	Baked goods, dressings, frozen desserts, confections, cake and dessert mixes, dairy products	Olestra, cellulose gel, carrageenan, polydextrose, modified food starch, micro-particulated egg white protein, guar gum, xanthan gum, whey protein concentrate
Nutrients	Replace vitamins and minerals lost in processing (enrichment), add nutrients that may be lacking in the diet (fortification)	Flour, breads, cereals, rice, macaroni, margarine, salt, milk, fruit beverages, energy bars, instant breakfast drinks	Thiamine hydrochloride, riboflavin (vitamin B_2), niacin, niacinamide, folate or folic acid, beta carotene, potassium iodide, iron or ferrous sulfate, alpha tocopherols, ascorbic acid, vitamin D, amino acids (L-tryptophan, L-lysine, L-leucine, L-methionine)
Emulsifiers	Allow smooth mixing of ingredients, prevent	Salad dressings, peanut butter, chocolate, margarine,	Soy lecithin, mono- and diglycerides, egg yolks, polysorbates,

(Contd.)

(Contd.)

Types of ingredients	*What they do*	*Examples of uses*	*Names found on product labels*
	separation	frozen desserts	sorbitan monostearate
	Keep emulsified products stable, reduce stickiness, control crystal-lization, keep ingredients dispersed, and to help products dissolve more easily		
Stabilizers and thickeners, binders, texturizers	Produce uniform texture, improve "mouth-feel"	Frozen desserts, dairy products, cakes, pudding and gelatin mixes, dressings, jams and jellies, sauces	Gelatin, pectin, guar gum, carrageenan, xanthan gum, whey
pH control agents and acidulants	Control acidity and alkalinity, prevent spoilage	Beverages, frozen desserts, chocolate, low acid canned foods, baking powder	Lactic acid, citric acid, ammonium hydroxide, sodium carbonate
Leavening agents	Promote rising of baked goods	Breads and other baked goods	Baking soda, monocalcium phosphate, calcium carbonate
Anti-caking agents	Keep powdered foods free-flowing, prevent moisture absorption	Salt, baking powder, confectioner's sugar	Calcium silicate, iron ammonium citrate, silicon dioxide
Humectants	Retain moisture	Shredded coconut, marshmallows, soft candies, confections	Glycerin, sorbitol
Yeast nutrients	Promote growth of yeast	Breads and other baked goods	Calcium sulfate, ammonium phosphate
Dough Strengtheners and Conditioners	Produce more stable dough	Breads and other baked goods	Ammonium sulfate, azodicarbonamide, L-cysteine
Firming agents	Maintain crispness and firmness	Processed fruits and vegetables	Calcium chloride, calcium lactate
Enzyme preparations	Modify proteins, polysaccharides and fats	Cheese, dairy products, meat	Enzymes, lactase, papain, rennet, chymosin
Gases	Serve as propellant, aerate, or create carbonation	Oil cooking spray, whipped cream, carbonated beverages	Carbon dioxide, nitrous oxide

For centuries, ingredients have served useful functions in a variety of foods. Our ancestors used salt to preserve meats and fish, added herbs and spices to improve the flavor of foods, preserved fruit with sugar, and pickled cucumbers in a vinegar solution. Today, consumers demand and enjoy a food supply that is flavorful, nutritious, safe, convenient, colorful and affordable. Food additives and advances in technology help make that possible.

There are thousands of ingredients used to make foods. The Food and Drug Administration (FDA) maintains a list of over 3000 ingredients in its data base "Everything Added to Food in the United States", many of which we use at home everyday (e.g. sugar, baking soda, salt, vanilla, yeast, spices and colors).

Still, some consumers have concerns about additives because they may see the long, unfamiliar names and think of them as complex chemical compounds. In fact, every food we eat—whether a just-picked strawberry or a homemade cookie is made-up of chemical compounds that determine flavor, color, texture and nutrient value. All food additives are carefully regulated by federal authorities and various international organizations to ensure that foods are safe to eat and are accurately labeled.

The purpose of this brochure is to provide helpful background information about food and color additives: what they are, why they are used in foods and how they are regulated for safe use.

Why are Food and Color Ingredients Added to Food?

See Types of Food Ingredients below.

Additives perform a variety of useful functions in foods that consumers often take for granted. Some additives could be eliminated if we were willing to grow our own food, harvest and grind it, spend many hours cooking and canning, or accept increased risks of food spoilage. But most consumers today rely on the many technological, esthetic and convenient benefits that additives provide.

Following are some reasons why ingredients are added to foods:

1. **To maintain or improve safety and freshness:** Preservatives slow product spoilage caused by mold, air, bacteria, fungi or yeast. In addition to maintaining the quality of the food, they help control contamination that can cause foodborne illness, including life-threatening botulism. One group of preservatives — antioxidants — prevents fats and oils and the foods containing them from becoming rancid or developing an off-

flavor. They also prevent cut fresh fruits, such as apples from turning brown when exposed to air.

2. **To improve or maintain nutritional value:** Vitamins and minerals (and fiber) are added to many foods to make-up for those lacking in a person's diet or lost in processing, or to enhance the nutritional quality of a food. Such fortification and enrichment has helped reduce malnutrition in the US and worldwide. All products containing added nutrients must be appropriately labeled.
3. **Improve taste, texture and appearance:** Spices, natural and artificial flavors, and sweeteners are added to enhance the taste of food. Food colors maintain or improve appearance. Emulsifiers, stabilizers and thickeners give foods the texture and consistency consumers expect. Leavening agents allow baked goods to rise during baking. Some additives help control the acidity and alkalinity of foods, while other ingredients help maintain the taste and appeal of foods with reduced fat content.

What is a Food Additive?

In its broadest sense, a food additive is any substance added to food. Legally, the term refers to "any substance the intended use of which results or may reasonably be expected to result—directly or indirectly—in its becoming a component or otherwise affecting the characteristics of any food." This definition includes any substance used in the production, processing, treatment, packaging, transportation or storage of food. The purpose of the legal definition, however, is to impose a premarket approval requirement. Therefore, this definition excludes ingredients whose use is generally recognized as safe (where government approval is not needed), those ingredients approved for use by FDA or the US Department of Agriculture prior to the food additives provisions of law, and color additives and pesticides where other legal premarket approval requirements apply.

Direct food additives are those that are added to a food for a specific purpose in that food. For example, xanthan gum used in salad dressings, chocolate milk, bakery fillings, puddings and other foods to add texture is a direct additive. Most direct additives are identified on the ingredient label of foods.

Indirect food additives are those that become part of the food in trace amounts due to its packaging, storage or other handling. For instance, minute amounts of packaging substances may find their way into foods during storage. Food packaging manufacturers must prove to the US Food and Drug Administration (FDA) that all materials coming in contact with food are safe before they are permitted for use in such a manner.

What is a Color Additive?

A color additive is any dye, pigment or substance which when added or applied to a food, drug or cosmetic, or to the human body, is capable (alone or through reactions with other substances) of imparting color. FDA is responsible for regulating all color additives to ensure that foods containing color additives are safe to eat, contain only approved ingredients and are accurately labeled.

Color additives are used in foods for many reasons: (1) to offset color loss due to exposure to light, air, temperature extremes, moisture and storage conditions; (2) to correct natural variations in color; (3) to enhance colors that occur naturally; and (4) to provide color to colorless and "fun" foods. Without color additives, colas would not be brown, margarine would not be yellow and mint ice cream would not be green. Color additives are now recognized as an important part of practically all processed foods we eat.

FDA's permitted colors are classified as subject to certification or **exempt from certification**, both of which are subject to rigorous safety standards prior to their approval and listing for use in foods.

- **Certified colors** are synthetically produced (or human made) and used widely because they impart an intense, uniform color, are less expensive, and blend more easily to create a variety of hues. There are nine certified color additives approved for use in the United States. Certified food colors generally do not add undesirable flavors to foods.
- Colors that are **exempt from certification** include pigments derived from natural sources, such as vegetables, minerals or animals. Nature derived color additives are typically more expensive than certified colors and may add unintended flavors to foods. Examples of exempt colors include annatto extract (yellow), dehydrated beets (bluish-red to brown), caramel (yellow to tan), beta-carotene (yellow to orange) and grape skin extract (red, green).

How are Additives Approved for Use in Foods?

Today, food and color additives are more strictly studied, regulated and monitored than at any other time in history. FDA has the primary legal responsibility for determining their safe use. To market a new food or color additive (or before using an additive already approved for one use in another manner not yet approved), a manufacturer or other sponsor must first petition FDA for its approval. These petitions must provide evidence that the substance is safe for the ways in which it will be used. As a result of recent legislation, since 1999, indirect additives have been approved via a premarket notification process requiring the same data as was previously required by petition.

When evaluating the safety of a substance and whether it should be approved, FDA considers: (1) the composition and properties of the substance, (2) the amount that would typically be consumed, (3) immediate and long-term health effects, and (4) various safety factors. The evaluation determines an appropriate level of use that includes a built-in safety margin—a factor that allows for uncertainty about the levels of consumption that are expected to be harmless. In other words, the levels of use that gain approval are much lower than what would be expected to have any adverse effect.

Under the Food Additives Amendment, two groups of ingredients were exempted from the regulation process.

GROUP I: Prior-sanctioned substances are substances that FDA or USDA had determined safe for use in food prior to the 1958 amendment. Examples are sodium nitrite and potassium nitrite used to preserve luncheon meats.

GROUP II: GRAS (generally recognized as safe) ingredients are those that are generally recognized by experts as safe, based on their extensive history of use in food before 1958 or based on published scientific evidence. Among the several hundred GRAS substances are salt, sugar, spices, vitamins and monosodium glutamate (MSG). Manufacturers may also request that FDA review the industry's determination of GRAS status.

Because of inherent limitations of science, FDA can never be absolutely certain of the absence of any risk from the use of any substance. Therefore, FDA must determine-based on the best science available—if there is a reasonable certainty of no harm to consumers when an additive is used as proposed.

If an additive is approved, FDA issues regulations that may include the types of foods in which it can be used, the maximum amounts to be used, and how it should be identified on food labels. In 1999, procedures changed so that FDA now consults with USDA during the review process for ingredients that are proposed for use in meat and poultry products. Federal officials then monitor the extent of Americans' consumption of the new additive and results of any new research on its safety to ensure its use continues to be within safe limits.

If new evidence suggests that a product already in use may be unsafe, or if consumption levels have changed enough to require another look, federal authorities may prohibit its use or conduct further studies to determine if the use can still be considered safe.

Regulations known as Good Manufacturing Practices (GMP) limit the amount of food ingredients used in foods to the amount necessary to achieve the desired effect.

Summary

Food ingredients have been used for many years to preserve, flavor, blend, thicken and color foods, and have played an important role in reducing serious nutritional deficiencies among consumers. These ingredients also help ensure the availability of flavorful, nutritious, safe, convenient, colorful and affordable foods that meet consumer expectations year-round.

Food and color additives are strictly studied, regulated and monitored. Federal regulations require evidence that each substance is safe at its intended level of use before it may be added to foods. Furthermore, all additives are subject to ongoing safety review as scientific understanding and methods of testing continue to improve. Consumers should feel safe about the foods they eat.

QUESTIONS AND ANSWERS ABOUT FOOD AND COLOR ADDITIVES

Q. How are ingredients listed on a product label?

A. Food manufacturers are required to list all ingredients in the food on the label. On a product label, the ingredients are listed in order of predominance, with the ingredients used in the greatest amount first, followed in descending order by those in smaller amounts. The label must list the names of any FDA-certified color additives (e.g. FD & C blue No. 1 or the abbreviated name, blue 1). But some ingredients can be listed collectively as "flavors," "spices," "artificial flavoring," or in the case of color additives exempt from certification, "artificial colors", without naming each one. Declaration of an allergenic ingredient in a collective or single color, flavor, or spice could be accomplished by simply naming the allergenic ingredient in the ingredient list.

Q. What are dyes and lakes in color additives?

A. Certified color additives are categorized as either dyes or lakes. Dyes dissolve in water and are manufactured as powders, granules, liquids or other special-purpose forms. They can be used in beverages, dry mixes, baked goods, confections, dairy products, pet foods and a variety of other products.

Lakes are the water insoluble form of the dye. Lakes are more stable than dyes and are ideal for coloring products containing fats and oils or items lacking sufficient moisture to dissolve dyes. Typical uses include coated tablets, cake and donut mixes, hard candies and chewing gums.

Q. Do additives cause childhood hyperactivity?

A. Although this hypothesis was popularized in the 1970's, results from studies on this issue either have been inconclusive, inconsistent, or difficult to interpret due to inadequacies in study design. A Consensus Development Panel of the National Institutes of Health concluded in 1982 that for some children with Attention Deficit Hyperactivity Disorder (ADHD) and confirmed food allergy, dietary modification has produced some improvement in behavior. Although the panel said that elimination diets should not be used universally to treat childhood hyperactivity, since there is no scientific evidence to predict which children may benefit, the panel recognized that initiation of a trial of dietary treatment or continuation of a diet in patients whose families and physicians perceive benefits may be warranted. However, a 1997 review published in the Journal of the American Academy of Child & Adolescent Psychiatry noted there is minimal evidence of efficacy and extreme difficulty inducing children and adolescents to comply with restricted diets. Thus, dietary treatment should not be recommended, except possibly with a small number of preschool children who may be sensitive to tartrazine, known commonly as FD & C Yellow No.5 (See question below). In 2007, synthetic certified color additives again came under scrutiny following publication of a study commissioned by the UK Food Standards Agency to investigate whether certain color additives cause hyperactivity in children. Both the FDA and the European Food Safety Authority independently reviewed the results from this study and each has concluded that the study does not substantiate a link between the color additives that were tested and behavioral effects.

Q. What is the difference between natural and artificial ingredients? Is a naturally produced ingredient safer than an artificially manufactured ingredient?

A. Natural ingredients are derived from natural sources (e.g. soybeans and corn provide lecithin to maintain product consistency; beets provide beet powder used as food coloring). Other ingredients are not found in nature and therefore must be synthetically produced as artificial ingredients. Also, some ingredients found in nature can be manufactured artificially and produced more economically, with greater purity and more consistent quality, than their natural counterparts. For example, vitamin C or ascorbic acid may be derived from an orange or produced in a laboratory. Food ingredients are subject to the same strict safety standards regardless of whether they are naturally or artificially derived.

Q. Are certain people sensitive to FD & C Yellow No. 5 in foods?

A. FD & C Yellow No. 5, is used to color beverages, dessert powders, candy, ice cream, custards and other foods. FDA's Committee on Hypersensitivity to Food Constituents concluded in 1986 that FD & C yellow No. 5 might cause hives in fewer than one out of 10,000 people. It also concluded that there was no evidence the color additive in food provokes asthma attacks. The law now requires yellow No. 5 to be identified on the ingredient line. This allows the few who may be sensitive to the color to avoid it.

Q. Do low-calorie sweeteners cause adverse reactions?

A. No. Food safety experts generally agree there is no convincing evidence of a cause and effect relationship between these sweeteners and negative health effects in humans. The FDA has monitored consumer complaints of possible adverse reactions for more than 15 years.

For example, in carefully controlled clinical studies, aspartame has not been shown to cause adverse or allergic reactions. However, persons with a rare hereditary disease known as phenylketonuria (PKU) must control their intake of phenylalanine from all sources, including aspartame. Although aspartame contains only a small amount of phenylalanine, labels of aspartame-containing foods and beverages must include a statement advising phenylketonurics of the presence of phenylalanine.

Individuals who have concerns about possible adverse effects from food additives or other substances should contact their physicians.

Q. How do they add vitamins and minerals to fortified cereals?

A. Adding nutrients to a cereal can cause taste and color changes in the product. This is especially true with added minerals. Since no one wants cereal that tastes like a vitamin supplement, a variety of techniques are employed in the fortification process. In general, those nutrients that are heat stable (such as vitamins A and E and various minerals) are incorporated into the cereal itself (they are baked right in). Nutrients that are not stable to heat (such as B vitamins) are applied directly to the cereal after all heating steps are completed. Each cereal is unique — some can handle more nutrients than others can. This is one reason why fortification levels are different across all cereals.

Q. What is the role of modern technology in producing food additives?

A. Many new techniques are being researched that will allow the production of additives in ways not previously possible. One approach is the use of biotechnology, which can use simple organisms to produce food additives. These additives are the same as food components found in nature. In 1990, FDA approved the first bioengineered enzyme, renin, which traditionally had been extracted from calves' stomachs for use in making cheese.

18 Pharmaceutical, Food, Cosmetics Companies

FOOD COMPANIES

Amul

Amul Dairy Road, Anand 388001, Gujarat, India

Tel: 02692-258-506

Flagship brand of the Gujarat Cooperative Milk Marketing Federation (GCMMF), which is India's largest food products marketing organisation; based in Anand, Gujarat; products: milk, butter, sweets, ice cream, etc. site offers online shopping.

Coca-Cola India

Indian arm of the global soft drinks company; based in Gurgaon, Haryana; brands include Coca-Cola, Fanta, Thums Up, Limca, Sprite, Maaza, Kinley and Georgia.

PepsiCo India

Phase-III, Gurgaon 122002, Haryana, India

Tel: 0124-2880699

One of India's leading food and beverage companies, and one of the largest multinational investors in the country; expansive portfolio includes refreshment beverages Pepsi, 7 UP, Mirinda and Mountain Dew, fruit juices, Quaker oats, salty snacks, etc.

GlaxoSmithKline Consumer Healthcare (GSKCH)

One of the largest players in the health food drinks industry in India; brands: Horlicks, Boost, Viva, Maltova, Horlicks Biscuits; also distributes Crocin, Eno and Iodex; headquartered in Gurgaon (Haryana) with facilities at Nabha, Rajamundry and Sonepat.

Nestle India BOM: 500790

Indian subsidiary of Nestle SA, Switzerland; headquartered in Gurgaon, Haryana; makes milk products, confectionery, beverages, etc. brands include Nescafe, Maggi, Milkybar, Milo, Bar-One, Milkmaid, Nestea, Nestle Milk, Nestle Dahi, etc.

Bikanervala

Lawrence Road, New Delhi 110035, India

Tel: 011-47006700

One of the most prominent families of traditional Halwais (sweetmakers) from Bikaner in

Rajasthan; sells traditional Indian sweets, namkeens, fast food, snacks, cookies, etc. and also runs pure vegetarian Angan restaurants.

Al Kabeer

Nariman Point, Mumbai, Maharashtra, India

Tel: 040-4488-5190

Food company that supplies ready meals, meat and poultry, seafood, snacks, vegetables etc; part of the Al Kabeer Group of Companies; products include samosa, spring rolls, parathas, burgers, prawns, fish, mutton, chicken, etc.

KRBL Limited

81-B, Central Avenue, Sainik Farms, New Delhi 110062, India

Tel: 011-43148400

World's largest Basmati rice exporters and India's first integrated rice company with a comprehensive product chain; based in New Delhi; brands include India Gate, Nur Jahan, Doon, Taj mahal Tilla, Indian Farm, Shub Mangal, etc.

Mother Dairy

Noida, Uttar Pradesh 201301, India

Tel: 0120-439-9500

Wholly owned company of the National Dairy Development Board; manufactures, markets and sells milk and milk products under the Mother Dairy brand (milk, cultured products, ice creams, paneer, etc.), Dhara (edible oils), Safal, (fresh fruit and vegetables) etc.

Agro Dutch Industries Ltd

Company that accounts for 85% of India's production and export of mushrooms; runs a fully integrated operation from composting to canmaking; based in Chandigarh.

Agro Tech Foods Limited

Edible oils and branded foods company based in Secunderabad; has a dominant marketshare in the refined oil segment, led by its flagship brand Sundrop; other brands include Healthy World, Rath, ACT II, Crystal, Just Fries, Sudham.

Britannia Industries Ltd BOM:500825

Hungerford Street, Kolkata 700017, West Bengal, India

Tel: 033-2287-0505

Food products company based in Kolkata; makes biscuits, dairy products, etc.; brands: 50–50, Good Day, Little Hearts, Marie Gold, Milk Bikis, Premium Bake, Tiger, etc.

Girnar

Dr B Ambedkar Marg, Parel, Mumbai 400012, India

Tel: 022-4343-7000

Manufacturers and exporters of tea based in Mumbai; has a chain of privilege shops selling instant and grounded coffees, instant tea premixes, ice teas and soups, organic tea masala powder, herbal infusions, etc.

Heritage Foods (India) Limited

Largest private-sector producers of milk and dairy products in south India; based in Hyderabad; founded by former AP chief minister Chandrababu Naidu; products: milk, curd, ghee, buttermilk, flavored milk, skim milk powder, dairy whitener.

Kohinoor Foods Ltd

Food company based in New Delhi; formerly known as Satnam Overseas Ltd; products: Kohinoor basmati rice, heat-and-eat meals (curries, rice and curry combis, etc.) etc.

LT Foods Ltd

Sector 44, Gurgaon 122002, Haryana, India

Tel: 0124-305-5100

Company engaged in milling, processing, and marketing basmati rice, brown rice, white rice, steamed rice, parboiled rice, and organic rice; has over 19 brands (Daawat, Heritage, etc.); exports to 50+ countries; formerly known as LT Overseas Ltd.

Makaibari Tea Estates

Kurseong, West Bengal, India

Tel: 9733-004-577

World's first tea factory established in 1859 in Kurseong, Darjeeling; follows a form of integrated forest management called permaculture where the tea bush is part of a multitier system of trees and plants typical of a sub-tropical rainforest.

MTR Foods Ltd

One of the top 5 processed food manufacturers in India, based in Bangalore; makes and exports ready-to-eat vegetarian curries and rice, gravies, frozen foods, ice cream, instant snacks, dessert mixes, pickles, etc. has kiosks in Bangalore and Chennai.

Ruchi Soya Industries Limited

Manufacturers of edible oils, vanaspati, bakery fats and soya foods based in Indore, Madhya Pradesh; brands include Nutrela (soya chunks, granules), Soyumm (soybean oil), Ruchi Gold (palmolein oil), Sunrich (sunflower oil) and Mandap (mustard oil).

The Global Green Company Ltd

India's largest horticultural company, selling pickled vegetables, peppers and spices around the globe; has units in Bangalore and Hyderabad; sells pickles and fruit conserves under the Tify and Reliable brands; part of the Avantha Group.

Amira Foods India Ltd

Tel: 011-4605-7560

India's largest privately held rice company; also deals in agro-commodities and bulk commodity trading in pulses, sesame seeds, sugar, onion, potatoes, maize, soybean extracts, edible oil, palm oil, wheat, wheat flour, rapeseed, millets and spices.

Balaji Wafers Pvt Ltd

Vajdi (Vad), Rajkot, Gujarat, India

Tel: 0281-278-3755

Company in Rajkot, producing potato wafers and snacks, and selling them across Gujarat, Maharashtra, and Rajasthan; products: aloo sev, gathiya, farali-chevdo, ratlami sev, shing-bhujia, vatana, etc.

Capital Foods

SV Road, Jogeshwari West, Mumbai 400102, India

Tel: 022-6774-0100

Food processors manufacturing products under its own brands and for other companies (private label); offers Chinese, Thai, Italian, Indian and European food products, microwaveable pouched products, frozen entrees, samosas, naans and paranthas, etc.

Dunar Foods Ltd

Karnal, Haryana, India

Tel: 0184-305-5772

One of the largest processors/exporters of Indian basmati rice; offers traditional, pusa, 1121 basmati, and in all forms (brown, milled raw, steamed, par-boiled/sella-white/golden); ISO 22000:2005, HACCP and BRC accredited.

Kashmir Apiaries Exports

GT Road, Doraha, Ludhiana, Punjab, India

Tel: 01628-258-240

Largest exporter of honey from India (to 41 countries) and the largest commercial beekeeping enterprise in India; has more than 50,000 bee colonies, and sells natural, organic, bulk, premium, herb-flavored, and blended honey, beeswax, etc.

Meat Products of India Ltd (MPI)

Koothattukulam-Edayar-Piravom Road, Edayar, Kerala, India

Tel: 0485-225-2365

Public sector undertaking of the government of Kerala, founded to manufacture and market meat and meat products, such as chicken sausages, beef, pork curry, bacon rashers, ham, pork pickle, cutlet mix, etc., based in Koothattukulam in Ernakulam district.

Amrit Banaspati Co Ltd (ABCL)

Rajpura, Punjab 140401, India

Tel: 01762-232-890

Company engaged in the manufacturing and marketing of vanaspati, bakery shortenings, refined and filtered edible oils and other FMCG products, in Rajpura, Punjab; makes pure mustard, palm, groundnut, ricebran oil, soya nuggets, etc.

Continental Coffee

Company in Hyderabad, supplying instant coffee powder made of Arabica and Robusta coffee beans to North America, Europe, the Far East, Australia, Russia, etc., has factory in Duggirala; a division of CCL Products (India) Ltd.

Little Bee Impex (LBI)

GT Road, Doraha, Punjab, India

Tel: 01628-258-240

Largest producer and exporter of natural honey and honey-based products, beeswax, beehives, etc. to 42 countries; also manufactures and exports tomato ketchup, fruit drinks, snacks, and Indian pickles; a 100% export oriented unit, based in Ludhiana.

Lotte India Corporation Limited

Indian arm of the Korean confectionery company; based in Chennai; formed by the divestment of Parrys Confectionery (Murugappa Group); product range: chewing gum (Lotte Xylitol, Lotte Juicy and Fresh, Lotte Spearmint, etc.), candy, biscuits, chocolates.

Ajanta Soya Limited

Manufacturers of vanaspati and refined oil based in Delhi, with its works in Bhiwadi, Rajasthan; has a capacity of 180 tpd; brands include Dhruv and Anchal; supplies vanaspati in tankers to biscuit manufacturers like Parle, Britannia, ITC Foods.

Amalgam Enterprises

The only freeze drying unit in India processing seafood, spices and herbs; comprises 5 companies with 14 factories operating along the Indian coastline; products; frozen food, aquaculture applications and freeze dried products; based in Kochi.

Anik Industries Ltd

Company in Indore formed by the merger of Anik Industries Pvt Ltd and Madhya Pradesh Glychem Industries Ltd (MPGIL); areas of activity include dairy and milk derivative products, wind power, soya protein isolate and concentrate, etc.

AVI's Export

Exporter of buffalo meat (boneless, halal, offal, tail, tongue, liver, kidney, heart), veal, sheep and lamb meat, and egg products; exports 'Al Nazia' and 'Angel' brands to USA, Middle East, Africa, Russia, Europe, etc.

Bagrry's

Lawrence Road, Delhi 110035, India

Tel: 011-2718-3935

Company that manufactures and markets a wide range of high-fiber breakfast cereals and health foods which include oats, muesli, bran, bran added corn flakes, bulk products, etc.

Bambino Agro Industries Ltd

Leading vermicelli producer and pioneers in introducing short-cut vermicelli in India; part of the well known diversified Bambino Group; other products: macaroni, pasta, soups, instant food mixes, blended spices, etc. located in Secunderabad.

Blue Bird Foods

441, Crawford Market, Mumbai 400001, India

Tel: 022-23400153

Manufacturers of food products like baking powder, castor sugar, chocolate mousse, citric acid, corn flour, custard powder, demerara sugar, ice cream mix, pure veg jelly crystals, etc. based in Mumbai, part of United Trading Corporation.

Cadbury India Ltd (Mondelez International)

19, B Desai Road, Mumbai 400026, Maharashtra, India

Tel: 022-4007-3100

Leading confectionery company in Mumbai; has 5 company-owned manufacturing facilities in India; operates in 3 sectors: chocolate confectionery, milk food drinks and candy; has also pioneered the development of cocoa cultivation in India.

Chordia Food Products Ltd

A company of the Chordia Food Park Group in Pune; manufactures and markets high quality, authentic and ethnic Indian processed foods including pickles, spice pastes, instant mixes, ketchup, sauces, milk shakes, custards, syrups, etc.

Flex Foods Ltd BOM: 523672

Flex Group company engaged in the business of agro based food products in Dehradun; offers a wide range of vacuum freeze dried, air-dried, frozen and IQF product range of mushrooms, herbs, spices and fruits/vegetables.

Foods and Inns Ltd

Multinational public limited company in Mumbai; leading manufacturers and exporters of fruit pulp and concentrates in canned and aseptic packing, frozen pulp, vegetables, fruit powders, etc. includes purees, chunks, pickles, snacks, chutneys, etc.

Freshtrop Fruits Ltd

Leading exporter of fresh fruits from India; exports fresh fruits like grapes, pomegranates and mangoes, and vegetables to leading supermarket chains in various parts of Europe; located in Ahmedabad.

Hatsun Agro Product Ltd

Largest private dairy in India located in Chennai; products include Arun ice creams (the largest ice cream brand in south India that offers 70 varieties) and fresh milk (Arokya, Komatha and Santosa).

Himalya International

Shubhkhera Village, Paonta Sahib, Himachal Pradesh 173025, India

Tel: 01704-223-494

Largest mushroom growers of India in the foothills of the Himalayas; product range includes frozen mushrooms, frozen potatoes, frozen vegetables, frozen ethnic dairy products and ready to eat meals; located in Paonta Sahib in Himachal Pradesh.

KS Oils Ltd

One of the leading manufacturers of mustard/rapeseed oil in India; provides all type of cooking media which include edible oils like mustard, refined oils, vanaspati and non edible solvent oil, and DOC; located in Morena, Madhya Pradesh.

Lakshmi Energy and Foods Ltd

One of the largest food grain processing companies and one of the largest producers of non basmati varieties of rice in India promoted by the Uppal family; distributes food grains under the brand name of Lakshmi Foods; located in Chandigarh.

Liberty Oil Mills Ltd

Largest importer and processor of edible oils and vanaspati located in Mumbai; products: edible fats and oils, blended oils and speciality fats; includes refined sunflower oil, refined soybean oil, vegetable oils, etc.; part of the Liberty group.

Lotus Chocolate Company Ltd

Manufacturer of fine chocolate and cocoa products including pure cocoa butter chocolates, and derivatives like cocoa butter and cocoa powder; supplies products to chocolate makers and users across the world; headquartered in Hyderabad.

Mahaan Group

Leading supplier of dairy products in New Delhi; manufactures industrial products in the form of dairy ingredients and FMCG products for household consumption; includes coffee creamers, dairy whiteners, pure ghee, whey powder, milk fat, etc.

Modern Dairies Ltd

ISO:9001-2000 certified company in Chandigarh that manufactures a wide range of milk and milk products for the domestic as well as international markets; includes cheese, skimmed milk powder, pasteurized milk, etc. part of the Modern Business Group.

Ovobel Foods Ltd

Company in Bangalore that manufactures and exports whole egg/yolk/albumen, in powder or frozen form (in collaboration with Ovobel NV, Belgium), which have replaced fresh eggs in industrial food processing applications, baby food, etc.

Riddhi Siddhi Gluco Biols Ltd

Starch and glucose manufacturing company of the Riddhi Siddhi Group based in Ahmedabad; produces maize starch, liquid glucose, dextrose monohydrate, maltodextrin, dextrose syrup, high maltose corn syrup, etc.

Sakthi Sugars Ltd—Soya Division

Leading manufacturer of soya products in Coimbatore; a division of Sakthi Sugars Ltd.; manufactures high protein soya meal, soya flour and soya chunks; owns one of the best plants in Asia with a capacity to process 300 tonnes of soya per day.

SAM Industries Ltd

Leading soybean processing unit in Indore; offers a range of value-added lecithin products extracted from non-GMO soybeans for use in dietary supplements, animal feed, personal care products, industrial applications, etc.

The Ravalgaon Sugar Farm Ltd

Leading sugar and confectionery company that creates sweets with an ethnic flavor; based in Mumbai; products: Mango Mood (with natural mango pulp), Pan Pasand Gold, Kokonut (grated coconut), Cherries (fruit flavors), Mints (menthol and ginger oil) etc.

Umang Dairies Ltd

Milk processing plant in Gajraula (UP); a unit of JK Organisation; has the capacity to process over 300,000 liters of milk per day; products: milk powder, dairy creamers, tea and coffee premixes, pure ghee, fresh cream, etc. based in New Delhi.

Aachi Masala Foods (P) Ltd

34th Street, Anna Nagar West, Chennai, Tamil Nadu 600040, India

Tel: 044-2618-7200

ISO 9001 certified company located in Chennai; produces traditional Chettinad masala famous in south India for its unique cuisine; products include masalas, dals, instant mixes, spices, asafoetida, appalam and pickles.

Adani Wilmar Limited

Manufacturers of edible oils based in Ahmedabad, Gujarat; joint venture between the Adani Group and Wilmar Holdings, Singapore; has a cumulative refining capacity of 3,200 tonnes a day; range: soybean, groundnut, mustard oil, etc. brand: Fortune.

Adarsh Derivatives Ltd

Manufacturers of guar gum powder based in Chandisar, Gujarat; has a production capacity of 4.050 MT.

ADF Foods Ltd (formerly American Dry Fruits Ltd)

Retailers, manufacturers and exporters of ethnic Indian food based in Mumbai; products include pickles, chutneys, frozen vegetables, frozen paranthas, pastes, vegetables in brine, masalas, frozen entrees, ready-to-eat curries, canned mango products, etc.

Alliance Coffee

64A, Ballygunge Circular Road, Kolkata 700019, India

Tel: 033-2290-7162

Marketers of Tata Coffee's spray-dried, freeze-dried and agglomerated instant coffee overseas; joint venture between Tata Coffee Limited and Beeyu Overseas Limited; based in Kolkata; Tata Coffee is Asia's largest integrated coffee company.

Aromco Flavors India (P) Ltd

Joint venture between Aromco UK, an international flavors company, and Synthite, India's leading processor and exporter of natural products; manufactures all types of flavors for food, beverage and allied industries.

Badshah

Ghatkopar East, Mumbai 400077, Maharashtra, India

Tel: 022-2511-7133

Brand of spices marketed by Mumbai-based Jhaveri Industries; has manufacturing unit in Umergaon (Gujarat), and exports about 34 products to USA, UK, South Africa, New Zealand, Hong Kong, Mauritius, the Middle East, Singapore, etc.

Beez India Natural Products

Major supplier of honey in the Indian market dealing in over 1,000 tonnes a year; specializes in various types of honey, such as Brasscia (mustard and Toria), Lychee, Eucalyptus, Karanj and Sunflower; located in Delhi.

Eastern Condiments Private Ltd

4th Floor, Mather Square, Kochi 682018, Kerala, India

Tel: 0484-2393550

Kochi-based company that processes and manufactures spices and blended spice powders; products: turmeric, chilli, coriander, pepper, ginger, kashmiri chilli powders, garam masala, sambar powder, chicken masala, etc.

Fortune Gourmet Specialities Pvt Ltd

Lower Parel, Mumbai 400013, Maharashtra, India

Tel: 022-24950387

Leading specialist food distributor engaged in supplying fine foods to hotels, restaurants, flight kitchens and caterers in Mumbai; supplies a range of chilled, frozen and ambient food including processed meat, seafood, and other specialty products.

Fresh & Honest Ltd (FHCL)

Chennai-based company that deals in coffee-vending machines; claims to have installed 2,300 machines in 22 cities across India; also deals in packaged filter coffee, soya milk and tofu.

Greenage Food Products Ltd

Decars Lane, Kolkata 700069, West Bengal, India

Tel: 033-22319135

Company engaged in manufacturing of spices (meat masala, chat masala, vegetable masala, etc.), filling and packing of milk and oil, and CTC Tea; located in Kolkata, West Bengal.

Haldiram's

Food products company based in Gurgaon; products include namkeens, sweets, sherbets, chips, whoopies, etc. also runs six restaurants.

HMS Agro Proteins Pvt. Ltd

Agro company in New Delhi, producing Sambandh desi ghee, milk and milk products, such as flavored milk, curd, milk powder, paneer, khoya, butter, cheese, milk cake, dodha burfi etc; has plant in Shamli, Uttar Pradesh.

Kitchens of India

Food brand of ITC Hotels, Bangalore; products include ready-to-eat dishes (Bukhara, Dum Pukht, Dakshin, Gharana), curry pastes, biryanis, chutneys, conserves and desserts; site has store locator, Indian recipes, etc.

Mapro Foods Pvt. Ltd

122, Shendurjane, Wai-Surur Road, Wai, Satara 412803, Maharashtra, India

Tel: 02167-222111

Fruit processing company and the largest processor of fresh strawberries in the form of jams, crushes, syrups, squashes and toppings; based in Wai, Maharashtra.

Nadukkara Agro Processing Company Limited

Fruit processing factory in Muvattupuzha, promoted by the Kerala Horticulture Development Programme (KHDP); funded by European Union and government of Kerala; established for the commercial processing of pineapple, mango and other fruits.

Poshtik Milk Products Pvt Ltd

Kailash Colony, New Delhi 110 048, India

Tel: 011-41635891

Leading institutional cheese supplier to major restaurants, fast-food chains and hotels in New Delhi; products include natural cheddar, gouda, feta cheese, processed cheese, parmesan, edam, mozzarella, ricotta, bocconcini, emmental, etc.

Radhakrishna Foodland

Back-end distribution and logistics company that caters to the retail, food service and hospitality industries; based in Thane (near Mumbai); provides a one-stop shop.

Rage Chocolatier

Makers of fine quality home-made chocolates for corporate and personal gifting; based in Bangalore; uses contemporary and traditional culinary methods to handcraft a wide range of chocolates, including plain, dark, crunchy and nut-filled.

Raj Oil Mills Ltd (ROML)

224–230, Bellasis Road, Mumbai 400008, Maharashtra, India

Tel: 022-2302-1996

Producer and supplier of a variety of cooking oils, such as sunflower oil, coconut oil, groundnut oil, til oil, mustard oil, cottonseed oil, soybean oil, etc. brands: Cocoraj, Guinea, Tilraj, Mustaraj, Raj, Khilona, etc. based in Mumbai.

Souza Hatcheries

Highlands, Falnir Road, Mangalore 575002, Karnataka, India

Tel: 0824-2432018

Largest suppliers of day-old chicks and broiler chicken in Mangalore, Udupi and Hassan; products: whole chicken, chicken bone-in cuts, giblets, boneless cuts, etc.

SPAC Tapioca Products (India) Ltd

Company in Erode (Tamil Nadu) that turns out 30,000 tonnes of starch per year; products include super fine tapioca starch, carboxy methyl starch, bio binder, soluble starch, pasting powder, tube pasting powder, dextrin, cross linked starch, etc.

SSS Exports Private Limited

Tel: 04286-285-367

One of the largest exporter of white shell chicken eggs from India; also produces, supplies wholesale, and exports frozen buffalo meat, fresh goat meat, and chickpeas; based in Namakkal, Tamil Nadu.

The Kerala Co-operative Milk Marketing Federation Ltd (KCMMF)

Cooperative organization set up to implement NDDB's Operation Flood program; based in Thiruvananthapuram; comprises of over 2,500 primary milk cooperative societies, and is popularly known as Milma; products: milk, ghee, butter, ice cream, etc.

Vallabhdas Kanji Limited (VKL)

Asia's largest processor of spice and spice ingredients based in Kochi; flagship company of the US $100 million Kanji Moorarji Group; products: spices, seasonings, flavors and fragrances.

Vangili Group

Tel: 04286-221-135

Company in Namakkal, Tamil Nadu, engaged in the poultry business; comprises Vangili Feeds, Gayathri Poultry Farm, Vangili Hatcheries (P) Ltd, Hemanth Poultry Farms Private Ltd, etc. products: Children's Special Eggs, Heart Special Eggs, etc.

WaghBakri

Tea company based in Ahmedabad, Gujarat; products include organic Darjeeling green tea, organic Assam tea, CTC tea, tea bags, etc.

MISCELLANEOUS COMPANIES

Dabur India

FMCG company with interests in healthcare (ayurvedic), personal care and food products; headquartered in Ghaziabad, Uttar Pradesh; brands include Dabur Amla, Dabur Chyawanprash, Vatika, Hajmola and Real.

Personal care products, Food companies, Ayurvedic products

Hindustan Unilever Ltd (HUL) BOM: 500696

India's largest fast-moving consumer goods company and one of the country's largest exporters; headquartered in Mumbai; deals in home and personal care products and foods and beverages; brands: Lifebuoy, Lux, Surf Excel, Rin, Lakme, etc.

Personal care products, Food companies

ITC Limited BOM: 500875

One of India's largest private sector companies with a diversified presence in cigarettes, hotels, paperboards and specialty papers, packaging, agri-business, packaged foods and confectionery, information technology, branded apparel, etc. Kolkata-based.

Business groups, Agricultural companies, Paper, etc.

Tobacco products, Food companies

Tata Tea Ltd BOM: 500800

The world's second-largest global branded tea operation with product and brand presence in 40 countries, and subsidiaries in the UK and USA; headquartered in Kolkata; 86% of its business comes from branded tea.

Agricultural companies, Food companies

Marico

Leading FMCG company based in Mumbai, with products and services in the areas of hair care, skin care and healthy foods; brands include Parachute, Saffola, Sweekar, Hair and Care, Nihar, Shanti, Mediker, Revive, Kaya, Sundari and Aromatic.

Food companies, Personal care products

Keventer Group

2, Clive Ghat Street, Kolkata 700001, India

Tel: 033-2230-4571

Business group in Kolkata, involved in dairy, beverages, real estate, and infrastructure sectors through Keventer Agro Ltd, Keventer Fresh Ltd (KFL), and Keventer Projects; products: Utsav mustard oil, Frooti, Appy, Appy Fizz, Bailey, Metro milk, etc.

Business groups, Food companies, Builders

Godrej Industries Ltd (GIL) BOM: 500164

Leading manufacturers of oleochemicals, with plants in Valia (Gujarat) and Mumbai; formerly called Godrej Soaps; also makes edible oils, vanaspati, bakery fats, and has interests in medical diagnostics and real estate.

Chemicals, Food companies

Karuturi Global Ltd BOM: 531687

11, Crescent Road, Bangalore 560001, Karnataka, India

Tel: 080-4080-9000

Company engaged in floriculture (ranks among one of the largest cut rose producers in the world), food processing (exports bulk and bottled gherkins to international processed food firms and super markets) and information technology; based in Bangalore.

Agricultural companies, Food companies, Internet service providers

Avani Textiles Ltd

Patiala Road, Sangrur 148001, Punjab, India

Tel: 01672-246039

Agro-based textile and food processing industrial unit manufacturing and exporting 100% cotton and organic cotton yarn (knitting, weaving, slub, and compact yarn), edible grade cotton seed oil, and cattle feed; located in Sangrur (Punjab); part of Jindal Group.

Yarn, Food companies, Agricultural

Gujarat Ambuja Exports Ltd (GAEL)

Agro-processing and exporting company based in Ahmedabad, Gujarat; divisions: solvent extraction, wheat milling, cotton yarn, biochemicals, cattle feed, vanaspati, vegetable oil refinery and oil mill.

Food companies, Agricultural companies

Hind Group of Companies

Business group based in Dewas, Madhya Pradesh; comprises Hind Syntex (polyester and viscose yarn, etc.), Hind Filters (cigarette filters), Dewas Soya (soybean oil, soybean meal, etc.).

Yarn, Food companies

IVP Limited

Company that has interests in vanaspati and vegetables oils, foundry chemicals, advanced ceramics and spark plugs; part of the Allana Group; has factories in Bangalore, Ahmedabad, Mumbai, Hyderabad, etc.

Food companies, Chemicals, Miscellaneous supplies

Kaveri's Bio Proteins Pvt Ltd (KBPL)

Tel: 04286-221-218

Biotech animal nutrition and food company in Nanakkal; products and services: white shell eggs, animal feeds, animal health products, organic fertilizers etc; exports these products and maize, jowar, soybean meal, rapeseed de-oiled cakes, etc.

Animal health, Food companies, Agricultural companies

Ponni Group of Companies

Tel: 04286-232-542

Producers, suppliers, and exporters of white and brown shell eggs; engaged in poultry farming, feed manufacturing, etc. also sells day-old layer chicks to farmers across India; comprises Ponne Products Exporters, Ponni Transports, etc. based in Namakkal.

Agricultural companies, Food companies

Sanwaria Group

Business group based in Bhopal, Madhya Pradesh; comprises Sanwaria Energy (power generation and distribution), Sanwaria Agro Oils (soybean processing—edible oil, etc.), Sanwaria Infrastructures (construction) and Sanwaria Foods (flour mill).

Energy, Construction, Food companies

SKM Group

Poultry products company based in Erode, Tamil Nadu; comprises SKM Animal Feeds and Foods (makes layer, broiler and cattle feed), SKM Egg Products (egg, albumen powder), SKM Farm Engineering (poultry farm equipment); also makes siddha medicines, etc.

Agricultural companies, Food companies, Farm equipment

VH Group (Venkateshwara Hatcheries Group)

Largest fully integrated poultry group in Asia; headquartered in Pune; activities: hatcheries (layers, broilers, etc.), processed chicken, eggs, research and breeding, poultry equipment, feed supplements, human biotherapeutics, etc.

Agricultural companies, Farm equipment, Food companies

Alagendran Group of Companies

Business group based in Madurai, Tamil Nadu; has interests in retailing spares for cars, LCVs and two-wheelers, selling motorcycles, 100% cotton yarn, real estate, hire purchase, importing edible oils and pulses, exporting cashew kernels and vegetable oil.

Auto spare parts, Food companies, Yarn, Builders, Auto dealers

Beeyu Overseas Ltd

ISO 9001:2000 company in Kolkata; engaged in the manufacture of CTC and Orthodox tea, packaging and blending of tea, and export of tea and coffee procured from Tata Coffee Ltd.; also exports rice, wheat, sesame seed and other agro-based products.

Food companies, Agricultural companies

Bengal Tea & Fabrics Ltd

Company in Kolkata engaged in the business of tea and textiles; belongs to the BD Kanoria Group; owns a textile mill producing cotton, manmade fiber, blended yarn and fabrics, and tea estates with an annual production of about 1.6 million kg of tea.

Food Companies, Textiles

Eltex Group of Companies

Group with diverse business interests in wheat flour milling, cotton yarn, ferrous castings, sheet metal fabrication, machine building and trading; based in Coimbatore; companies: Eltex Super Castings, McKinnon India, Prokop Eltex, etc.

Jagatjit Industries Ltd

Company that manufactures and markets alcoholic beverages, malt, malt extract, malted milk foods, milk powder, ghee, glass bottles and jars, food grade pet containers etc; located in New Delhi.

Food companies, Liquor

Kriti Industries (India) Ltd

ISO 9001 certified company in Indore with interests in plastics, oil, telecommunications, automotive components, etc.; products includes blow moulded hollow plastic products, cooking oil, MDPE pipes, pipe fittings, telecom ducts, etc.

Plastics, Pipes, etc. Food companies

KSE Ltd

Leader in solvent extraction and ready mixed cattlefeed located in Irinjalakuda, Kerala; earlier known as Kerala Solvent Extractions Ltd; manufactures a range of livestock feed in high volumes, coconut oil from coconut oil cake and refined edible oil.

Food companies, Agricultural companies

Lactose (India) Ltd

Laxmi Industrial Estate, New Link Road, Andheri West, Mumbai 400053, India

Tel: 022-6695-2701

One of India's leading producers of edible and pharmaceutical grade lactose, dairy whitener, dairy calcium, whey powder, casein, caseinate, butter and ghee based in Mumbai; also undertakes contract manufacturing of pharmaceutical products.

Food companies, Pharmaceuticals

Pioneer Group of Industries

Agro-products group based in Pathankot, Punjab; comprises Pioneer Agro Extracts Ltd (hydrogenated vegetable and refined oils) and Pioneer Industries Ltd (vital wheat gluten, starches, liquid glucose, etc.)

Food companies, Agricultural companies

Rajhans Desai-Jain Group

Varachha Road, Surat 395006, Gujarat, India

Tel: 0261-255-1129

Business group involved in real estate, entertainment, textiles, and confectionery sectors; subsidiaries: Rajhans Cine World Ltd, Rajhans Hospitality Pvt Ltd, Rajhans Silk Mills Pvt Ltd, Rajhans Prime Cinema, Rajhans Poly-Prints Pvt Ltd, etc.

Business groups, Builders, Food companies, Hotels, Cinemas, Textiles

Saboo Sodium Chloro Ltd

The first and the largest salt refinery in north India located in Jaipur; manufactures salt under the brand names Surya Salt, Saboo Salt and Tota Salt; also manufactures triple refined free-flowing industrial salt; part of The Saboo Group of Industries.

Sampre Nutritions Ltd

ISO-9002 certified confectionery manufacturer based in Hyderabad; part of the Gurbani group; has been manufacturing a wide range of confectioneries for several leading companies in India.

Food companies, Confectionery

Tata Coffee

Asia's largest integrated coffee company and India's largest coffee producer and exporter with head office in Pollibetta, south Kodagu; range of activities include the growing and curing of coffee and tea, manufacture, marketing, etc.

Agricultural companies, Food companies

Aaranyam Farms

Narayanamangalam, PO Pullut (North), Thrissur 680663, Kerala, India

Tel: 9686-201831

Organic farm located on a seven-acre plot in Kodungallur, 40 km from Cochin International Airport; has 150+ varieties of fruits, vegetables, trees, and medicinal plants; offers farm/home stay facilities.

Bed and breakfast, Food companies

Acres Wild

Coonoor, Tamil Nadu 643101, India

Tel: 094432-32621

Family-run farm in 20 acres in Coonoor, Nilgiris, Tamil Nadu; produces organic soft and hard cheese (Gouda, Romano, Parmasan, Colby, Montery Jack, Cheddar), honey, and farm eggs; offers farmstay accommodation with farm activities.

Food companies, Bed and breakfast

Bhilai Engineering Corporation Ltd

ISO 9002 company that manufactures hi-tech engineering castings, equipment for steel plants, mining, railways, power plants, ports, etc. flagship company of the BEC Group; based in Mumbai; also has fertilizer and food-processing subsidiaries.

Machinery, Food companies, Fertilisers, Miscellaneous supplies

Biotor Industries Ltd

Dr Mascarenhas Road, Mazgaon, Mumbai 400010, India

Tel: 022-6657-2000

Largest fully integrated producer of castor oil and its derivatives in the world; has a manufacturing unit and seed crushing plant at Makarpura and a sebacic acid plant at Ekalbara, both in Vadodara (Gujarat).

Food companies, Chemicals

CavinKare

Personal care and food products company headquartered in Chennai; makes shampoo (Chik, Nyle, Meera, Indica), skin care products (Fairever, Spinz talc), Ruchi Pickles, Chinni's Pickles and Masala, Ruchi Gulab Jamun Mix, etc.

Personal care products, Food companies

Dairy Den

Supplier of fresh ice cream machinery located in Ahmedabad; known internationally for its machines, "Yums" soft ice cream and "Chills, Thrills and Frills" parlour chain serving innovative recipes of fresh ice creams, thick shakes and slush.

Food processing equipment, Food companies

DS Group

Foods and tobacco products company based in Noida (near Delhi); products include chewing tobacco (Baba), pan masala (Rajnigandha), salt and spices, snacks, jaljeera, etc. (Catch); also has interests in the hospitality sector.

Food companies, Tobacco products

Global Rabbit Park

Konaghatta Village, Doddaballapur, Bengaluru, Karnataka 561203, India

Tel: 98868-11007

Producers of rabbits for meat, farming, pets and laboratories; one of the largest meat producers and traders in South India.

Food companies, Agricultural companies

Havmor Group of Companies

ISO certified company in Ahmedabad, engaged in food and ice cream business; has 8 parlours and restaurants in Ahmedabad and Vadodara; also undertakes outdoor catering.

Restaurants, Food companies, Caterers

Hindustan Gum & Chemicals Ltd

Biggest manufacturers of guar gum in the world; based in Bhiwani, Haryana; product range includes refined guar splits, guar gum powder, borated guar, textile thickener, etc.

Chemicals, Food companies

Keggfarms Pvt Ltd

Khandsa, Gurgaon, Haryana 122001, India

Tel: 0124-2373691

Poultry breeding organization in Gurgaon, Haryana; develops genetically-bred rural specific poultry stocks (Kuroiler) and organic eggs (Keggs); produces poultry vaccine, nutritional supplements for poultry feed, etc.

Agricultural companies, Food companies, Animal health

Kwality

Business group with interests in ice cream, bakeries, restaurants, catering services and hotels; based in New Delhi; comprises Kwality Walls Ice Cream, Kwality Restaurants, Kwality Caterers, Village Restaurant Complex, Gaylord Restaurant, etc.

Business groups, Food companies, Restaurants, Food stores

MPS Group

Lake Town, Kolkata 89, West Bengal, India

Tel: 033-25340838

Group engaged in eco-tourism industry, pisciculture, organic agriculture, animal rearing, financial services, production of dairy and dairy products, livestock feed, biogas, processed food products, etc. in Kolkata, West Bengal.

Business groups, Food companies, Agricultural companies

NOL Group

Greams Road, Chennai, Tamil Nadu 600006, India

Tel: 044-2829-0707

Business group based in Chennai; comprises National Oxygen, Pondicherry Agro Foods (flour mill), East Coast Acetylene, Saraf Housing Development, Goodwill International (petrochemical distributors), Sri Ganapati Impex (petrochemicals).

Industrial gases, Petrochemicals, Food companies, Builders, Business groups

Prakriti

Rail Majra, Rupnagar, Punjab 144527, India

Tel: 099-7139-3626

Organic farm in the Shivalik foothills, 7 km from Ropar wetlands and 45 km from Chandigarh; engages in conservation and anti-soil erosion practices; offers farm tours, and accommodation in Swiss cottage tents, safari tents, and mud and thatch cottages.

Bed and breakfast, Food companies

Rasoi Ltd

20, Sir RN Mukherjee Road, Kolkata, West Bengal 700001, India

Tel: 033-2248-7051

Leading vanaspati producers in Eastern India; based in Kolkata; products include vanaspati, salt, edible oils, spices, etc.; group companies include JL Morison (personal care products), Hindustan Composites and Rasoi Express (travel agents).

Food companies, Personal care products, Travel agents, Miscellaneous supplies

19 Herbal and Food Chart

Approximate daily allowance of various food for an executive

Food group	*Number for servings per day at various caloric levels KCAL**				*Approximate size of serving*
Skim or low fat dairy	1200	1500	1800	2000	
	02	02	02	03	1 cup skim or low fat milk or yoghurt/40 gm low fat cheese
Lean meat/fish/ poultry without skin or	01	01	01	02	80–100 gm cooked lean meat, fish/poultry without skin
Pulses and legumes	02	03	03	04	1 katori dal/beans cooked
Vegetables	03	03	03	04	1/2–2/3 cup
Fruits	03	04	04	04	1/2 cup cut-up
Breads/cereals starches	06	08	10	11	1 chapati, 1 slice whole wheat bread or 1/2 cup cooked rice/ pasta/3 tea spoon ready to eat cereal
Fats/oils	05	05	06	06	1 tea spoon oil
Sugar		Not required			as appropriate for caloric
Alcohol		Not required			needs-in moderation only

* kil

Useful health information and diet recommendations

Your blood levels	*Ideally should be*	*Your value*
Total cholesterol	< 190 mg/dl if you do not have CHD < 160 mg/dl if you have CHD	
HDL-C	> 45 mg/dl for men > 55 mg/dl for women	
LDL-C	< 130 mg/dl if you do not have CHD	
VLDL-C	< 28 mg/dl	
Triglycerides	< 130 mg/dl	
Blood sugar		
Fasting mg/dl	< 120	
Postprandial mg/dl	< 160	
Uric acid mg/dl	< 8	
Creatinine mg/dl	< 1.5	
Urea mg/dl	20–40	
Bilirubin: (total) mg/dl	0.2–0.8	
SGOT: Iu/liter	< 40	
SGPT: Iu/liter	< 40	
Serum alkaline		
Phosphatase: KAO-Units	4–13	
Serum albumin gm/dl	4.5–6.0	
Hemoglobin g/dl		
Mal	13–18	
Female	12–16	
Blood pressure (mm/hg)	> 45 years < 140/90	
Male	< 45 years < 130/85–90	
Female	< 140/90	

* CHD-Coronory heart disease

20 Rice Cooking Method

WHAT YOU NEED

1 part Indian basmati rice
1½ parts water (for boiling)
Enough water to cover (for soaking)

WHAT YOU DO

You will also need a timer, a large bowl, and a deep cooking pot with a well-fitting lid. This is not the quickest way to make Basmati rice, but it is foolproof and will give you rice that has nice, long, tender, separate grains like you get in restaurants. It is an especially perfect procedure for when you need to make large quantities of plain rice or pilaf, since there is virtually no way for it to burn or get mushy.

Please note that this recipe works best with Indian Basmati rice. There is a big difference in texture and flavor between Indian Basmati rice, which you can generally find in sacks at Asian food markets, and US-produced Basmatis like Texmati, which is the kind you will find in health food stores. Indian Basmati is aged, so it tends to be more fragrant and flavorful and has a longer, finer, grain. (It is also a lot cheaper, and if you happen to be or know a CostCo member, they have great deals on 20 lb bags.)

Directions

STEP 1: Rinse the rice well. This removes the powdery starches produced by the rice grains rubbing against each other that tend to make rice gummy. Rinse at least three times until the water runs almost clear.

STEP 2: Place washed rice in a good sized bowl, and add enough water to completely cover. Let soak for 15 minutes.

STEP 3: While your rice is soaking, put your cooking water (one and a half times the volume of dry rice) into a large pot and bring it to a boil. (For the mathematically challenged, if you have used 2 cups of dry rice, you will need to boil 3 cups of water).

STEP 4: Drain the soaked rice completely, discarding the soaking water.

STEP 5: Add the drained rice to the boiling water.

STEP 6: Bring the water back up to a boil, then reduce heat to a low simmer and cover. Allow to simmer, covered, exactly 5 minutes, then ...

STEP 7: ... keeping the rice pot covered, remove it from the heat and allow it to sit undisturbed for 15 minutes. (This is when the real cooking happens, so resist the temptation to lift the lid.)

STEP 8: After the 15 minutes is up, check the rice. If it is still a little underdone to your taste, let it sit a while longer. If it looks too dry, you can add a splash of boiling water (not too much). When the rice has the correct texture, transfer it immediately to a serving dish to stop cooking process.

Notes: If you are making a pilaf or other seasoned rice dish, after Step 2, sauté onions and spices or whatever flavoring agents you are using in your cooking pot. Then add the cooking water (same proportions as in the plain rice recipe) and bring it up to a boil as in Step 3, proceeding as directed from there. Lastly, if you are cooking it at a high altitude, you may need a little bit extra water to make this recipe work.

Preparation Time

45 minutes.

21 Roti/Chapati/ Phulka Cooking Method

Use the quantity of water as a guide as flours vary in their capacity to absorb water depending on the humidity. Once you are comfortable with making the basic dough, there is endless scope for experiment by mixing in a variety of other flours, spices like cumin and carom seeds and minced herbs like mint or coriander.

INGREDIENTS

1 cup atta (whole wheat flour)
1/3 to ½ cup water (preferably lukewarm)
¼ tsp salt
Extra flour for rolling
Ghee or oil for cooking (optional)

Method

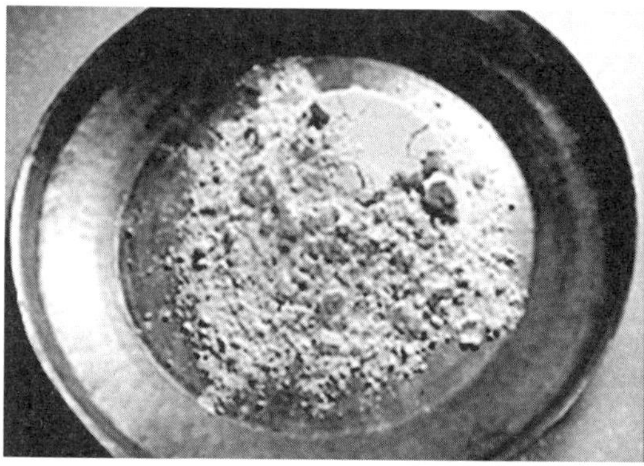

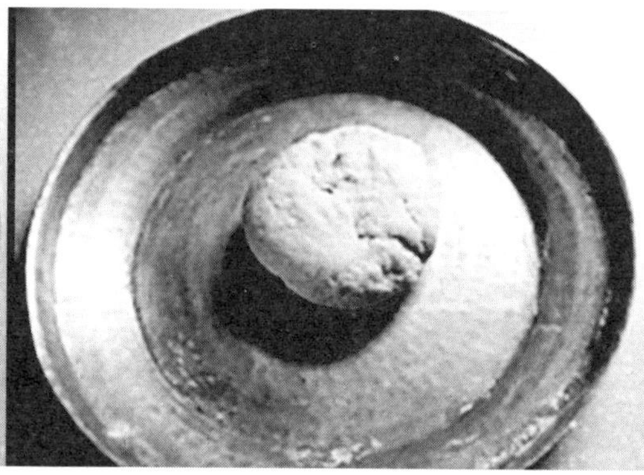

For the dough: Combine the flour and salt in a large bowl or an Indian parath. Pour in the water slowly, gathering the flour together until you get a soft and moist dough. Transfer it to a clean surface or platform (this is not required if using the parath) and knead-the dough for about 5 to 6 minutes until you get a smooth, pliable dough. Cover the dough with a damp cloth and allow to rest for anytime between 10 minutes to ½ an hour. Divide the dough into 6 round balls.

With the help of a food processor: This is super easy and takes only a few minutes to assemble. In a food processor fitted witha metal blade, add the dry ingredients. Process for a few seconds until the dry ingredients are uniform. With the machine running, add water little by little, until he flour begins to form into a mass. If the machine turns slow at any time, turn it off and mix the flour with the water. Turn on the machine and when the ball of dough has formed, process for about 20 to 25 times until it becomes smooth and pliable. Use as required.

To make Rotis: In a small bowl place some atta or whole wheat flour.

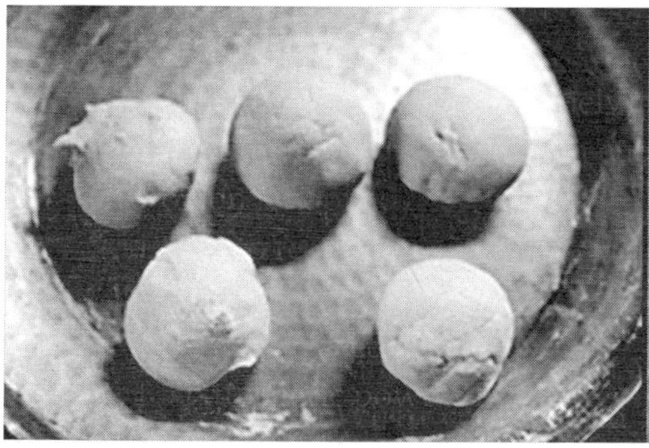

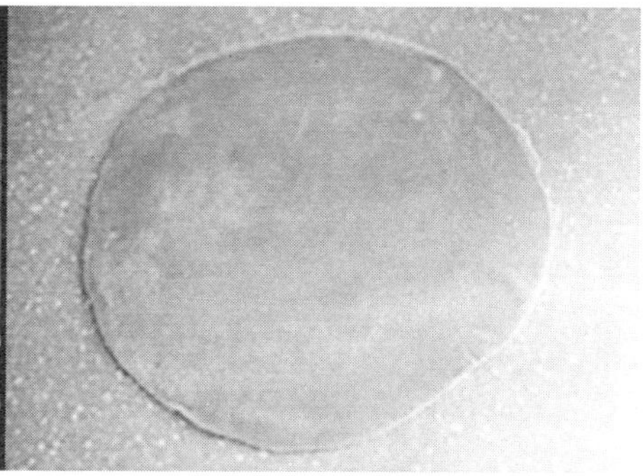

Place a tava or a heavy cast iron griddle over medium heat. On a lightly floured surface, take one ball, dip it into the flour and roll it into a thin circle, about 5 ½″ to 6 ″ in diameter. You can use extra flour while rolling the dough to prevent the dough from sticking to the surface. However, use as little as required, as too much flour will make the roti dry.

Knock the excess flour off the rolled dough by slapping it between your hands and place it on the preheated griddle. When small white bubbles appear on the surface of the roti, turn it over with a pair of tongs and cook until the surface bulges with air pockets. With the help of your tongs, lift the roti and toast on both sides over a direct flame for a few seconds until it puffs up. A well done roti is cooked and has golden brown spots on both sides.

If you don not want to puff your rotis over a direct flame, you can cook the roti by allowing it to stay on the griddle. Turn it over until cooked on both sides. And then gently press the top of the roti with a soft cloth or a flat spatula until the roti puffs up. This requires a little practice.

Brush the rotis with the optional ghee or melted butter and keep them in containers lined with cloth or thick paper towels.

To make Triangle Parathas: Dip the round ball into flour and roll out into a 6" circular disk. Brush the open side lightly with oil.

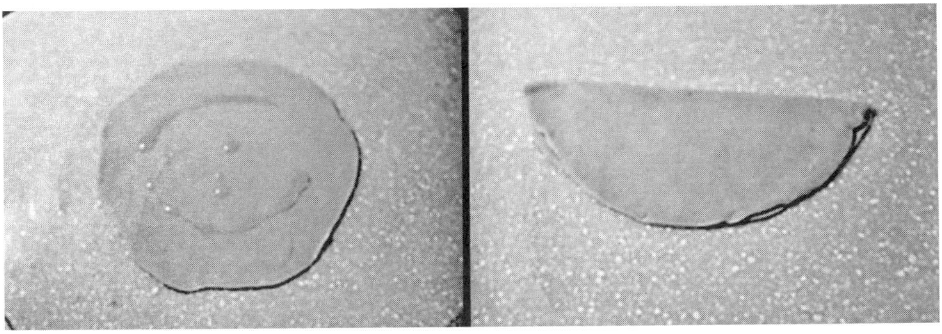

Fold it into half and brush it lightly with oil again.

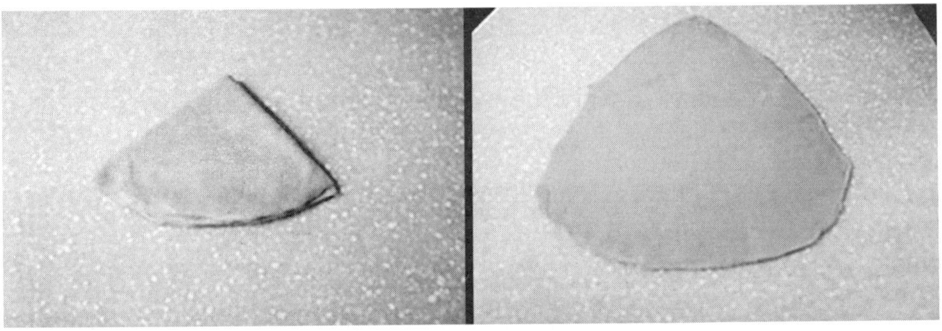

Fold the oiled side again to form a triangle. Dip the triangle into the flour and roll out to about 6". Cook on a griddle by following the instructions given above.

To make Square Parathas: Dip the round ball into flour and roll out into a 6" circular disk. Brush the open side lightly with oil.

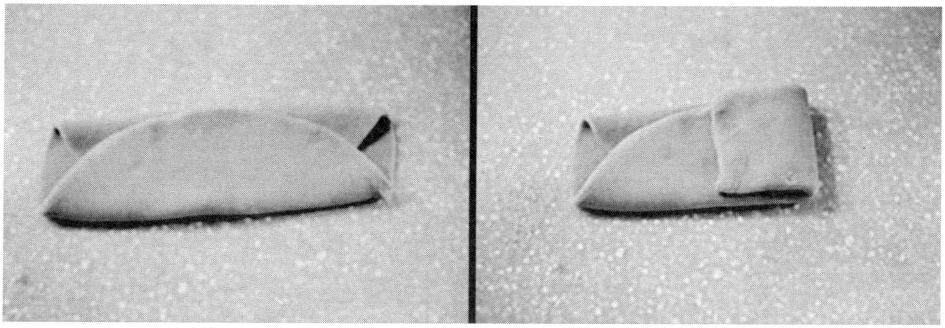

Fold one side of the disk towards the center as shown. Fold the other side over the folded side. Bring the right side towards the center as shown above.

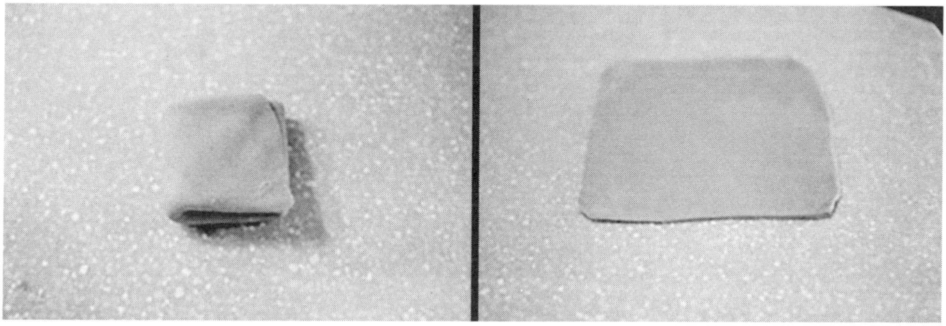

Fold the left side over the right side to form into a square. Roll on all four sides, carefully retaining the square shape.

Cook on a griddle by following the instructions given above.

Makes approximately 6 rotis or parathas.

22 Soups

CHICKEN SHORBA RECIPE

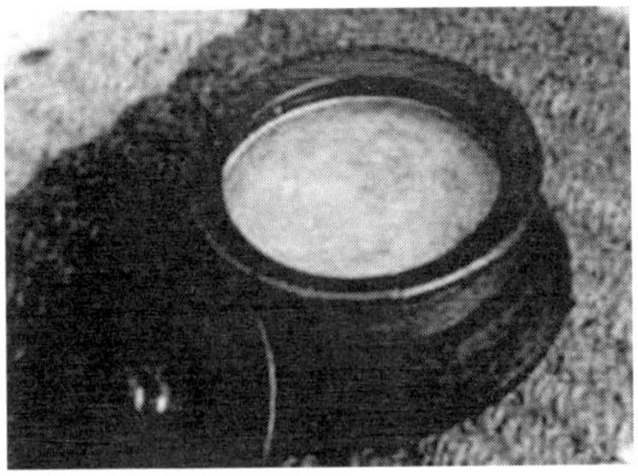

Ingredients

100 gm boneless chicken shredded
500 ml chicken stock
1 tblp garlic finely chopped
1 tsp cumin seeds
1 tblsp white flour
2 tsp butter
1 tblsp oil
Salt and white pepper to taste
1 tsp fresh cream

How to Make Chicken Shorba

- Heat the butter in a pan and fry the shredded chicken pieces till tender.
- Remove and keep aside. In a pan heat oil and let the cumin seeds splutter.
- Add the chopped garlic and saute for a few seconds.
- Add the white flour and fry for 1 min.
- Add the chicken, chicken stock, white pepper powder and salt.
- Cook on medium level for about 4 minutes while stirring all the time. Stir in the fresh cream just before serving.

Note: For 500 ml of chicken stock, cook about 500 grams of chicken bones with one liter of water add chopped onions and garlic till the stock is reduced to half the quantity.

DAL SHORBA RECIPE

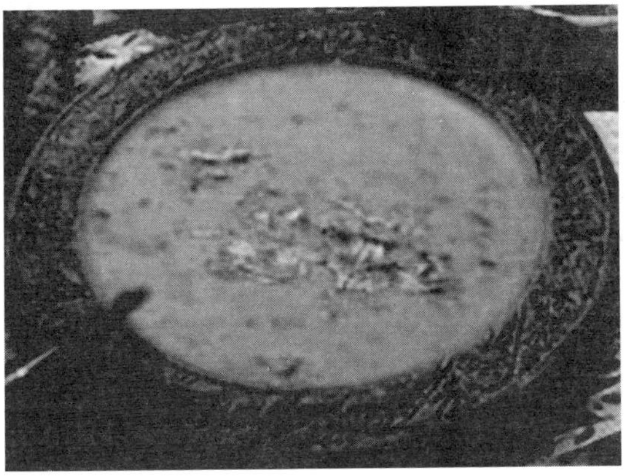

Ingredients

4 eggs (hard boiled)
1 onion
1/2 tomato (pureed)
3–4 flakes of garlic
1/2-inch piece of ginger
1–2 green chilies
2 tbsp chopped coriander leaves
Salt to taste
Red chili powder to taste
3/4th tsp turmeric powder
1/2 tsp coriander powder
3/4 tsp garam masala
2–3 tbsp vegetable oil/ghee
1 cup green peas or 250 gm paneer

Preparation

- Remove the shell of boiled eggs and keep aside. If using Paneer cut into cubes and fry till golden and set aside for later use.
- Make a paste of onion, garlic, ginger and green chilies in a mixer or chopper.
- Heat oil in a kadhi or wok and add onion-garlic paste and fry till golden brown.
- Add all the spices (salt, turmeric, coriander and chili powder) except garam masala and fry for a minute and add tomato puree. Fry till it starts leaving oil.
- Add a cup of water and cook till it dry's.
- Now add the fried paneer cubes or green peas (which ever using) and boiled eggs.
- Add 1 cup of water and bring to boil and reduce the flame.
- Simmer for 10 minutes.
- Garnish with garam masala and coriander leaves and serve dal shorba hot with paratha, roti or rice.

MIX VEGETABLE SOUP RECIPE

Ingredients

1/2 cup carrots (chopped)
1/4 cup french beans (flas beans) (chopped)
1/2 cup peas (matar) (shelled)
1½ cup tomato (tamatar) puree
1 tsp garlic (lasan) paste
1 tsp ginger (adrak) paste
2 tsp coriander leaves (dhania patta) (chopped)
3–4 tsp butter
3 glasses of water
salt (namak) and pepper to taste

for garnishing
cheese granted

How to make mix vegetable soup

- Melt butter, fry ginger and garlic paste, add tomato puree, carrots, French beans, peas and water. Pressure cook for 5–6 minutes.
- Add coriander leaves.
- Boil for 2–3 minutes.
- Garnish with cheese.

Note: If you want thick soup, then add 2 tsp of corn flour mixed in 1/2 cup milk.

HOT AND SOUR SOUP RECIPE

Ingredients

2 tbsp chili sauce or to taste
1½ tbsp corn flour/corn starch
1 tbsp soya sauce

2 tbsp vinegar
2tbsp. capsicum/green bell pepper (chopped)
2tbsp spring onions (chopped)
2 tbsp tomato sauce
2tbsp carrots (chopped)
1/4th cup chopped cabbage
A small block of paneer/organic tofu (thinly sliced), optional
1 tsp black pepper powder or to taste
1/2 tsp sugar
A pinch ajinomoto
Salt to taste
4 cups water

Preparation

- Mix 4 cups of water, chili sauce, soya sauce, vinegar, sugar, salt, pepper powder and ajinomoto and bring to boil.
- Now add all the chopped vegetables except paneer . Cook for a minute on a medium heat.
- Dissolve corn starch in 1/2 cup water and add to the soup stirring constantly till it becomes thick.
- Cook for a minute, add paneer slices.
- Serve hot.
- Hot and sour soup should be prepared just before consuming and should be served fresh, else it will lose the taste.

TOMATO SOUP RECIPE

Ingredients

1½ lbs of ripe tomatoes remove seeds, peeled and chopped
2 tbsp of olive oil
1 onion chopped

1 clove of garlic crushed
1 small red pepper chopped (optional)
4 cup of chicken or vegetable stock
2 oz of tomato paste
1/4 cup of basil

Preparation

- Heat the oil in a heavy pan, cook the onion, garlic and red pepper till soft.
- Add the tomato and cook another 10 minutes.
- Add the tomato paste, salt and pepper to taste.
- Cover and let simmer for 15 minutes.
- Allow to cool slightly and put the mixture in a blender until it is smooth.
- Return to the pan and heat gradually.
- Add the fresh basil to the tomato soup, cook 2 minutes and serve.

POTATO SOUP RECIPE

Ingredients

2 medium-sized potatoes
2 tsp onion (pyaj) paste
1 turnip (shalgam)
1 tomato (tamatar)
2 glasses of water
1/4 tsp garlic (lasan) paste
1/2 tsp ginger (adrak) paste
4 tsp butter
1 tsp cumin seeds

How to make potato soup?

- Boil potato, turnip and tomato till they are tender. Blend and pass through a sieve.
- Melt butter, add cumin seeds, onion, ginger and garlic paste. Fry till it is golden in color.
- Add soup, coriander leaves, salt, pepper and sugar and boil well.

BASIL AND BADAM SOUP RECIPE

Ingredients

50 gm almonds (blanched and minced)
10 basil (tulsi) leaves (chopped)
2 cup water
1 stick cinnamon (tuj/dalchini)
2–3 cloves (lavang)
sant and pepper to taste
2–3 green cardamoms

How to make basil and badam soup?

- Boil minced almonds, water, cinnamon, cloves and green cardamom for 10 minutes.
- Sieve and add salt, pepper and basil leaves to the liquid.
- Boil for 5 minutes.

Note: If you want the soup to be more thick, add 1 tsp of cornflour mixed in 1/4 cup of water

CURRY SOUP RECIPE

Ingredients

50 gm arhar dal
1 tsp ginger (adrak) paste
1 tsp garlic (lasan) paste
50 gm tomato (tamatar) puree
7-8 curry leaves (kari patta)
3 glasses of water
1/4 tsp turmeric (haldi) powder
salt (namak) and pepper to taste
2 tsp butter

for garnishing
1/2 cup boiled rice (chawal)
lemon

How to make curry soup?

- Boil dal well.
- Melt butter, add curry leaves, tomatoes puree, ginger, garlic paste.
- Fry for a while.
- Add salt, turmeric powder and dal.
- Add more water if required.
- Boil well.
- Garnish with boiled rice and lemon ring.

23 Dal Cooking Method

DAL FRY RECIPE

Learn how to make dal fry is one of the most popular recipe in the punjabi menu. It has four different lentils which makes it very nutritive and to enrich its taste it is tempered with various spices. Dal fry tastes best when it is served with jeera rice.

Ingredients

1/4 cup yellow pigeon peas (toor dal)
1/4 cup split yellow peas (yellow moong dal)
1/8 cup bengal gram dal (channa dal)
1/8 cup red split lintels (masoor dal)
4 tbsp clarified butter
2 tsp cumin seed
1/2 tsp asafetida (hing)
1 tsp turmeric powder
1 tsp chili powder
1/2 tsp coriander powder
1/2 tsp garam masala powder
Salt to taste
1 tomato (finely chopped)
1 onion (finely chopped)
1/2 tsp garlic (grated)
1/2 tsp ginger (grated)
1/2 tsp lemon juice
2 tsp coriander leaves (finely chopped)

How to Make Punjabi Dal Fry?

- Mix all the dals together and wash them properly. Soak them in 3 cups of water for 30 minutes before cooking it.
- Pressure cook the dal in 2 cups of water with salt and 1 tsp of turmeric powder till done.
- In a frying pan, heat the ghee and temper it with the cumin seed when the cumin seed starts to crackle add asafetida.

- Stir it and add chopped onions. Fry on medium heat until onions turns pinkish in color. Add garlic, ginger and green chili and cook till they get brown burnt in color.
- To this add the chopped tomatoes and cook for further few minutes till the tomatoes are little soft.
- Now add coriander powder, garam masala, little turmeric powder and cook for another 4–5 minutes adding little water to it to ensure that the mixture does not get burnt.
- Next add cooked dal and mix them well. Add a little more water to it to bring it to the desired consistency. Bring to a boil and simmer at least for 10 to 15 minutes.
- Take out the dal in a serving bowl, add lemon to it and garnish it with the coriander leaves.
- Serve hot with chapattis and jeera rice.

DAL MAKHANI RECIPE (MAA KI DAL)

Ingredients

1 cup whole urad daal (urad sabut)
1 tbsp red kidney beans (Rajma)
1 onion finely chopped
1 tomato finely chopped
1″ ginger piece
2–3 green chilies finely chopped
chopped coriander leaves
4–5 flakes garlic paste
1/2 cup stirred curd
1/2 cup fresh stirred cream (malai)
2 tbsp butter
1 tsp cumin seeds (jeera)
1/2 tsp turmeric powder
1/2 tsp garam masala
Red chili powder to taste
1/2 tsp dhania powder
Salt to taste

How to Make Dal Makhni?

- Soak rajma in water overnight.
- Add water and little salt and pressure-cook rajma and urad dal till soft for about 20–25 minutes. Mash and boil again for 15–20 minutes and add curd and cream to the dal.
- Now in kadhai heat oil, splutter cumin seeds and add garlic paste, fry till light brown. Add onions and fry till golden brown.
- Now add ginger, green chilies and tomatoes and fry till tomatoes soften.
- Now add dry masalas (turmeric powder, chili powder, dhania powder and salt) and fry again for a moment.

- Add dal and stir on medium flame. As soon as it starts boiling remove from the gas.
- Sprinkle garam masala powder and garnish dal makhani with coriander and add butter.
- Serve dal makhani hot. Goes well with laccha paratha, naan or rice.

MASALA DAL

Ingredients

1 cup split red lentil (masoor dal)
5 slit green chili (hari mirch)
1 tblsp chopped coriander leaves (dhania patta)
1/2 tsp turmeric powder (haldi)
1/2 cup grated Coconut
Salt to taste
1 tsp mustard seeds (raai/raee)
1 tsp cumin seed (jeera)
2 chopped tomato (tamatar)
1 tblsp oil
1 meduim sized sliced onion (Pyaj)

How to Make Masala Dal?

- Wash and soak the gram for 30 minutes.
- Grind the grated coconut with a little water to a smooth paste in a blender, keep aside.
- Fry the sliced onions till golden brown, remove and keep aside.
- Cook the gram in a pressure cooker with just sufficient water to cook the dal until soft.
- Remove the lid of the cooker and add the green chilies, turmeric powder tomatoes and salt, cook for 3 minutes.
- When the tomatoes are cooked add the coconut paste. mix thoroughly.
- Cook for a minute and remove from the flame.
- Heat the oil in a pan, add the mustard seeds, when they crackle add the cumin seeds.
- Fry for a few seconds over a low flame, pour over the dal.
- Serve hot garnished with the fried onions and the chopped corriander leaves.

KHATTI MEETHI RECIPE

Here is a delicious recipe of khatti meethi dal or sweet and sour dal. Learn how to make khatti meethi dal?

Ingredients

1 cup bengal gram
100 gm beet root
50 gm groundnut
1 tsp mustard seeds
1/2 tsp cumin seeds

2 dried dates
50 gm jaggery
1/2 cup tamarind juice
1 tsp turmeric powder
2 tsp coriander powder
6–7 curry leaves
1 piece cinnamon
2 tsp cloves
1 tsp clarified butter
1 tblsp chopped coriander
1 tsp salt
a pinch of asafetida
2–3 chilly paste

How to Make Sweet and Sour Dal?

- Rinse bengal garm and add beet root pieces to it and cook in a cooker.
- When cooked add turmeric powder, salt, coriander powder, jaggery, dry dates, tamarind juice, curry leaves, groundnut, chilly paste and boil.
- Prepare the seasoning—heat oil and add asafetida, cloves, butter, cumin seeds, mustard seeds, cinnamon.
- Add to the gram and cook for 5 minutes.
- Garnish with coriander and serve.

CHANA DAL RECIPE

Ingredients

1 cup chana dal
7 cup water
1 tsp salt
1/4 tsp red chilly powder
1/2 tsp turmeric powder
1/2 tsp cumin powder
1/4 tsp garam masala
1 tblsp ghee/clarified butter
1/2 tsp chopped garlic 1 chopped garlic clove

Preparation

- Soak the chana dal in 4 cup water for 2–3 hours then wash and drain.
- Boil 3 cups water, ginger, turmeric and the salt in a pan.
- Add the chana dal, cover the pan and cook over medium flame for 30 min or till the dal is tender and stiring occasionally.

- Stir the dal when cooked.
- For the tempering heat ghee in a pan and when hot add cumin seeds. When the seeds begin to sputter add garlic.
- Stir well and fry till the garlic turns light brown. Add the red chilly powder and stiring it, pour it immediately over the cooked dal and cover the pot.
- Chana dal is ready to be served with rice or bread.

24 Vegetables Cooking Method

BHINDI MASALA RECIPE

Bhindi masala is a popular main course dish made with bhindi cooked in spices and served with chapatis. Learn how to make bhindi masala?

Ingredients

2 pounds bhindi
2 onions (chopped)
1 tblsp ginger garlic paste
1 tblsp coriander powder
1 tsp cumin seeds
1 tsp red chili powder
1 tsp garam masala powder
1 tsp amchur powder
1/4 tsp turmeric powder
Salt to taste
Oil

How to Make Bhindi Masala?

- Wash and cut bhindi in halves.
- Heat oil in a wok or kadai. Add cumin seeds and let it splutter.
- Add chopped onions and ginger garlic paste. Fry till golden brown.

- Now add cut bhindi with rest off the spices and stir well.
- Cook it on medium flame and keep stirring it ocassionaly so it does not stick at bottom.
- Keep feying till bhindis are cooked.
- Serve bhindi masala hot with chapatis.

ALOO PATTA GOBHI RECIPE

Aloo patta gobhi is made by cooking potatoes and cabbage in spices and is an everyday dish made in households. Learn how to prepare aloo patta gobi or Indian cabbage and potato?

Ingredients

1 small cabbage (chopped finely)

1 medium sized potato (cut in cubes)

1 onion (chopped)

1 tomato (chopped)

1 tblsp ginger garlic paste

1 tsp cumin seeds

1 tsp turmeric powder

1 tsp coriander powder

1 tsp red chili powder

Salt to taste

Cooking oil

How to Make Indian Cabbage and Potato?

- Heat oil in a wok or kadai. Add cumin seeds and let it splutter. Then add onions and ginger garlic paste. Fry till golden brown.
- Add chopped tomatoes, turmeric powder and rest of the powdered spices except salt.
- Mix well and cook till oil separates.
- Add cubed potatoes and stir fry for few minutes and then add chopped cabbage and salt, mix well. Cook it covered till the vegetables are done and water evaporates.
- Serve hot with chapatis or parathas.

DUM ALOO RECIPE

Ingredients

900 gm Aloo (potatoes)

$3\frac{3}{4}$ cup water

Salt to taste

Ghee or oil for deep-frying

1 cup ghee

1 large onion (finely chopped)

4 tbsp tomato puree

140 ml curd

4 tbsp hot water

1 green pepper (seeds removed and sliced)

1 tsp garam masala powder

Spices

4 cloves

4 bay leaves

6 black peppercorns

4 green cardamoms

1 brown cardamom

1piece cinnamon stick

Paste

1 large onion (chopped)

12 flakes garlic

2 tbsp ginger

6 black peppercorns

1 tsp poppy seeds

1 tbsp coriander seeds

1 tsp cumin seeds

2 dry red chilies

1 tsp turmeric powder

A pinch of ground mace

A pinch of ground nutmeg

How to Make Kashmiri Dum Aloo?

- Scrape the aloo (potatoes), prick all over with a fork and soak in the water with little salt for 2 hours.
- Dry the potatoes on a cloth and heat the ghee or oil.
- Deep fry the potatoes until golden brown. Drain and set aside.
- Heat the measured ghee in a flameproof pan and fry onions with all the spices until golden.
- Grind the paste ingredients to a fairly smooth paste and stir into the onions.
- Cook for 10 minutes. Stir in the tomato puree, curd and salt.

- Add the aloo (potatoes) and hot water and stir over a low heat for 5 minutes.
- Sprinkle the dum aloo with pepper and garam masala and cook for few minutes.

CHILI PANEER RECIPE

Ingredients

350 gm paneer
2 tsp salt
1 egg
1/2 cup corn flour
1 tsp ginger-garlic paste
2 cups coarsely chopped onions
2 tbsp sliced green chilies
1 tbsp soya sauce
2 tbsp vinegar
1/4 tsp ajinomoto
Oil for frying
Little water

How to Make Chili Paneer?

- Cut the paneer into cubes.
- Mix together the cottage cheese, 1 tsp salt, egg, corn flour, garlic, ginger and water to just coat the paneer pieces with the mixture.
- Heat oil in a pan and fry the paneer pieces caoted with mixture till golden in color.
- Heat 2 tbsp of the oil in a wok and stir fry the onions in it over high heat for half a minute.
- Add the green chilies, salt, soya sauce, vinegar, ajinomoto and the fried paneer cubes.
- Mix well, and garnish the chili paneer with finely cut spring onions and coriander.

SHAHI PANEER RECIPE

Shahi paneer is a typical North Indian dish eaten with roti or naan. Shahi paneer is preparation of paneer pieces in a thick, creamy and spicy gravy prepared in tomato, onion and cashewnuts paste. To give it a little spicy edge green chili and brown cardamoms are added to it along with garam masala. Because of its richness it is usually served in parties, dinners and other occasions which require special menu. Here is a simple and easy recipe to make shahi paneer.

Ingredients

250 gm cottage cheese (cut in cubes)
3 tbsp clarified butter
1 inch piece of ginger (finely chopped)
1 green chili (slit lengthwise)
1 onion (grated)
4 tomatoes (chopped)
2 brown cardamoms (crushed)
1 bay leaf
1/2 cup beaten curd
30 gm melon seeds or 2 tblsp cashew nut paste
1 tsp salt
1/2 tsp cumin powder
1/2 tsp red chili powder
3/4 tsp garam masala
2 tbsp tomato sauce
1/4–1/2 cup milk
1 tsp coriander leaves (finely chopped)

How to Make Shahi Paneer?

- Soak the melon seeds or cashew nuts which ever you are taking for at least 2 hours and then grind them to a smooth paste.
- Heat 2 tbsp of ghee in a kadai, add onion, ginger, green chili and brown cardamoms. Cook till onion turns translucent. Add tomatoes, cover it and cook for 7–8 minute.
- Add curd and cashew nut or melon seeds paste. Cook for 3–4 minute and remove from fire.
- Cool down the above ingredients and put them in a grinder along with 1/2 cup of water. Strain the puree.
- Take a frying pan, add 1 tbsp of ghee and add the above pureed paste and cook for 10 minutes on low flame till oil separates.
- Add salt, red chili powder, cumin powder, garam masala and tomato sauce. Add enough water so that there can be thick gravy.
- Keep on low flame and cook for 5–7 minute. Remove from fire.
- At the time of serving heat the gravy and add paneer pieces.
- Add milk and mix well and cook for 2–3 minutes. **Note:** To make the dish more creamier you can replace milk with 1/4 cup cream.
- Serve hot garnished with coriander leaves.

BAIGAN BHARTA RECIPE

Ingredients

1 medium Baigan (eggplant)
1/2 cup Cooked green peas
1 finely chopped onions
1 finely chopped tomatoes
1 finely chopped green chili
1/2 tsp red chili powder
1/2 tsp garam masala powder
1/4 tsp turmeric powder
3 tbsp vegetable oil
Salt to taste
Chopped green coriander leaves for garnishing

Preparation of Baigan ka Bharta

- Brush baigan (eggplant) with oil and roast it on a gas burner over medium heat.
- Frequently turn the eggplant upside down, until fully roasted.
- Once done, hold it under cold running water or in a bowl full of water. Cool it and peel off the blackened skin.
- Mash the flesh.
- Heat oil in a pan/kadai. Add green chili and onion and fry over medium heat until light golden brown.
- Add red chili powder, turmeric powder, garam masala and salt and stir. Add tomatoes and cook until tender.
- Add green peas and mashed baigan (eggplant). Stir well. Fry the baigan bharta for 5–7 minutes over medium heat.
- Garnish the baigan bharta with green coriander leaves and serve hot.

SHAHI MUSHROOM RECIPE

Here is a scrumptious, spicy recipe with mushrooms. Learn how to make shahi mushroom?

Ingredients

200 gm mushroom
4 onion (pyaj)
7–8 tomato (tamatar)
1 piece ginger (adrak)
2 green chili (hari mirch)
1/2 tsp salt (namak)
1/2 tsp red chili powder (lal mirch)
1/2 tsp spice blend (garam masala)
1 tsp sugar
1 cup cream (malai)
1/2 cup cashew nut (kaju)
3 tbsp clarified butter (ghee)

How to Make Shahi Mushroom?

- Cut mushrooms into 2 pieces.
- Finely chop all the other vegetables.
- Heat ghee in a pan and fry onions until it turns pink.
- Then fry ginger, green chilies and tomato.
- When tomato soften remove it from the flame.
- Grind it in a mixer.
- Then cook in the pan and also add salt, red chili powder, spice blend, sugar, cream and cashew nuts powder.
- Cook for 2–3 minutes and then add mushroom.
- Cook at low flame until mushroom softens.
- Then remove it from the flame and serve hot.

25 Goat Curry Cooking Method

GOAT CURRY

Simple, yet delicious, goat curry or mutton curry is also easy to put together. This is my go to recipe when I want to cook a simple, wholesome nonvegetarian meal for my family. The basic recipe for this dish is my Mother's so I know it is good as I grew up eating it. Mom would cook meat curry with goat meat (also called mutton in India). Goat curry or mutton curry is delicious served with plain rice, a salad and raita. If you thicken the gravy, it tastes just as good with hot, freshly made chapatis.

Prep time: 10 minutes

Cook time: 30 minutes

Total time: 40 minutes

Yield: Serve 4–5 people

Ingredients

1 kg goat leg, cut into suitable bite-sized chunks

4 tbsps vegetable/canola/sunflower cooking oil

2 large onions sliced thin

2 large tomatoes diced

2 tbsps garlic paste

1 tbsp ginger paste

2 tsps coriander powder

1 tsp cumin powder

1/2 tsp turmeric powder

1/2 tsp red chili powder

2 tsps garam masala powder

Salt to taste

Chopped coriander to garnish

Preparation

- Heat the cooking oil in a heavy bottomed pan, on medium heat.
- When hot, add the onions. Sauté till the onions begin to turn a pale golden brown in color. Now remove from the oil with a slotted spoon and drain on paper towels. Turn off heat.

- Grind the onions into a smooth paste (adding very little to no water) in a food processor. Once done, remove into a separate container.
- Now grind the tomatoes, garlic and ginger pastes together, in the food processor, into a smooth paste. Remove into a separate container and keep aside for later use.
- Heat the oil left over from frying the onions, again and add the onion paste. Sauté for 2–3 minutes.
- Now add the tomato paste and all the powered spices, including the garam masala. Mix well.
- Sauté the resulting masala (onion-tomato-spice mixture) unitl the oil begins to separate from it. This can take up to 10 minutes to happen.
- Now add the goat/mutton pieces to the masala, season with salt to taste and stir to fully coat the goat/mutton pieces with the masala. Sauté till the goat/mutton is browned well.
- Add 1/2 a cup of hot water to the pan, stir to mix well, simmer the heat and cover the pan. Cook till the goat/mutton is tender. You will need to keep checking on the goat/mutton as it cooks and adding more water if all the water dries up. Stir often to prevent burning. The dish should have a fairly thick gravy when done.
- When the meat is cooked, garnish with chopped coriander and serve with hot Chapatis (Indian flatbread), naans (tandoor-baked Indian flatbread) or plain boiled rice.

Tip: Use a pressure cooker to cook goat curry or mutton curry and it will be done in half the time it takes to cook in an open pot.

KHEEMA OR MINCE MEAT

Kheema or mince can be made with any meat you prefer. It is extremely versatile and just changing the masala can result in a great new taste each time. Kheema or minced meat can be made with any meat you prefer. It is extremely versatile and just changing the masala when you cook it can result in a great new taste each time. While individual meats taste great on their own when made into kheema, my favorite thing to do is to combine meats and mince them. I have a meat mincer at home which allows me to buy the best (non-fatty) cuts of meat and mince them myself. This allows me to ensure good quality every time. Some meat combinations that taste really good when made into kheema (even though they may not be traditionally Indian) are pork and veal, pork and beef, pork and chicken.... I made the kheema palak in this recipe, using a mixture of equal parts of pork and veal minced together. The resulting dish tastes delicious with chapatis (Indian flatbread) or Parathas (pan fried Indian flatbread).

Prep time: 10 minutes

Cook time: 20 minutes

Total time: 30 minutes

Yield: Serves 4

Ingredients

1/4 kg or 1/2 lb of ground pork

1/4 kg or 1/2 lb of ground veal

3 tbsps vegetable/canola/sunflower cooking oil

1 tsp cumin seeds
2 medium-sized onions chopped fine
1 tbsp garlic paste
1 tbsp ginger paste
2 tbsps coriander powder
1 tbsp cumin powder
1 tbsp garam masala (see link below for recipe to make your own)
Salt to taste
2 medium-sized tomatoes chopped fine
300 gms fresh or frozen chopped spinach
Juice of 1/2 a lime
Chopped coriander leaves to garnish

Preparation

Heat a wok or deep pan, on medium heat. When it is hot, put the cooking oil in and let it heat.

- When the oil is hot, add the cumin seeds and fry until the seeds stop spluttering. They will give off a lovely aroma!
- Add the onions now. Fry, stirring often to prevent burning, till they turn a pale golden color.
- Add the ginger and garlic pastes and fry for a minute. Another sign that the ginger and garlic are sufficiently fried, is that they will stop spluttering.
- Now add both the minced meats and all the powdered spices -coriander, cumin, garam masala and salt to taste. Use your stirring spoon to 'mash' any lumps in the minced meat. These become harder to break as the mince cooks.
- Continue to brown the minced meats, stirring often to prevent burning. This should take about 5–7 minutes.
- Add the chopped tomatoes, the chopped spinach, stir and cook till the tomatoes are soft. The mince will be fully cooked by this time.
- Turn the fire off, add the lime juice and stir.
- Garnish with chopped coriander leaves and serve with hot chapatis or parathas.

BIRYANI

Biryani nicely made, is a pleasure to behold and eat! Fragrant long-grained rice is layered with meat or vegetables that have been cooked in a mixture of spices. This has to be one of my favorite foods! With biryani, it is not just the taste that has me going ga-ga! I love how it is a meal in one dish! Serve my biryani with a yogurt raita and kachumbar salad. My biryani can be made with chicken, mutton, goat meat or mixed vegetables! My personal favorite however, is goat meat so I've used it in this recipe. Follow the same instructions for chicken or mutton if you choose to use them instead. This recipe serves 6.

Prep time: 30 minutes

Cook time: 2 hours

Total time: 2 hours, 30 minutes

Ingredients

1 kg goat meat (I always use leg and get the butcher to cut it into bite-sized chunks)

2 tbsps garlic paste

2 tbsps ginger paste

3 tbsps sunflower/canola/vegetable cooking oil

2 large red onions, chopped fine

30–40 curry leaves

2 green chilies (optional)

2 tbsps coriander powder

1 tbsp cumin powder

1/2 tsp turmeric powder

1 tbsp garam masala

1 tsp salt (this is how much I use, you can add salt to suit your taste)

1 cup hot water

50 g ball of tamarind

700 gms basmati rice

1 tsp salt

2 drops orange food color (optional but it makes the Biryani look very pretty)

2 drops green food color (optional)

To garnish:

2 large onions sliced thin

3 tbsps sunflower/canola/vegetable cooking oil

Preparation

I make biryani in a large vessel called a handi (basically a deep pot with a nicely fitting lid). The latter part of the cooking process involves putting the Biryani under 'Dum' or pressure. I do this by sealing the dish (see how below) and putting it under the hood of our pre-heated barbecue. I leave it there for about 20 minutes. You could even do this in your oven.

- Put the goat meat, garlic and ginger pastes in a large bowl and mix well to coat the meat with the pastes. Keep aside for 20 minutes.
- While the meat is marinating, heat (on medium temperature) the cooking oil (3 tbsps) in a large, deep pot/pan. Add the finely chopped onions and fry till translucent.

- Add the curry leaves and green chilies fry for 1 minute.
- Now add the powdered spices - coriander, cumin, turmeric, and garam masala powders. Mix well and cook for 2–3 minutes. Stir often to prevent burning.
- Add the marinated meat now. Stir well and often and cook till the meat is browned.
- Add 1½ cups of hot water, stir, cover, simmer heat and cook till meat is tender. Keep checking for this stage as you do not want the meat overcooked and soft.
- While the meat is cooking, make the tamarind puree: Put the tamarind in a plastic or glass bowl and pour 1/2 cup of hot water over it. Allow to stand for 5–10 minutes. Now strain the tamarind and water mixture through a sieve (do not use a very fine sieve) into a bowl to get tamarind puree. Add this to the curry when you feel the meat is almost done. Stir well. Once the meat is cooked, keep it aside and prepare the rice.
- Put the rice in a sieve and wash under running water till the water runs clear. Now put it into a large deep cooking pot (preferably one with handles).
- Add enough water to fully cover the rice-at least 4″ over the surface of the rice. Add 1 tsp of salt to taste. Set the rice up to boil. Cook till almost done. To determine when it has reached that stage, remove a few grains from the pot and press between your thumb and forefinger. The rice should mostly mash but will have a firm whitish core. Turn off the fire. Strain through a colander and keep aside.
- Heat 3 tbsps of oil in a pan and fry 2 of the onions till caramalized-golden brown. Drain and keep aside on paper towels for later use.
- If you are using the food coloring, divide the rice into 3 equal portions and put into separate dishes. Add the orange food coloring to one portion of the rice and the green food coloring to another portion of the rice. Leave the third portion white. With each portion, mix the rice till all the grains are well colored. Keep aside for 10 minutes after which you can mix all 3 portions of rice together in a bowl for use in the next step.
- Grease a deep dish or pot (which has a nicely fitting cover). Now evenly layer the cooked rice, meat (and its gravy) in the dish/pot, to form at least 2 sets of layers (rice-meat-rice-meat-rice). Garnish with the previously caramalized onions. Cover the dish tightly. If your dish does not have a cover use 2 layers of aluminium foil (shiny side of both layers pointing down towards the rice) and secure onto dish with baking string. Since I use a Handi (a deep pot with a nicely fitting lid) which has a flat rim, I seal it by making a firm dough with flour and water and pressing this over the joint of the Handi's rim and cover.
- Now put the dish/pot in a pre-heated oven set at 350°F/180°C/gas mark 4 for 20 minutes. As I said earlier, I have even done this stage of the cooking on our barbecue. Just preheat the griddle section, set the Handi on it when it is hot and close the hood. Keep for 20 minutes.
- Turn off the oven/barbecue and let the dish sit in the oven/barbecue till you are ready to eat. Only open when you are ready to eat.
- The way to serve biryani is to gently dig in with a spoon so you get through the layers.
- I serve my biryani with raita and kachumbar salad.

BEEF

This beef Stroganoff recipe is based on the classic Russian dish, but is served on buttered noodles. Beef Stroganoff is also great made ahead of time and reheat before your dinner.

Makes 4–6 portions Beef Stroganoff

Ingredients

2 pounds beef chuck roast, cut into 1/2-inch thick strips
salt and pepper to taste
1 tbsp vegetable oil
1 tbsp butter
1/2 onion, sliced or diced
8 oz sliced mushrooms
2 cloves garlic
1 1/2 tbsp flour
1/2 cup white wine
2 cup beef broth, divided
3/4 cup creme fraiche or sour cream
1 tbsp fresh sliced chives
1 lb wide egg noodles, prepared, tossed in butter

Preparation

Season the beef generously with salt and fresh ground black pepper to taste. In a large hot skillet, brown the beef thoroughly in the oil, over high heat. Reserve the beef in a bowl, and return the pan to the stove over medium heat. Add the butter, mushrooms, and onions. Saute for 5–6 minutes, or until the mushrooms begin to brown.

Add the garlic, and cook for 1 minute. Add the flour, and cook stirring for 2 minutes. Whisk in the wine and half the beef broth. Stir and bring up to a simmer. Add the beefback in, and the rest of the beef broth. Bring to a simmer, turn the heat to low, cover tightly and braise for about 1 hour, or until the meat is tender. Stir occasionally. Add more broth or water if the mixture gets too dry. When ready, stir in the crème fraiche or sour cream, and the chives. Once heated through, taste for seasoning, and serve immediately, spooned over the buttered noodles.

KOFTA CURRY RECIPE

Ingredients

1 kg mutton, boneless
2 pyaj
Oil (tel) for frying
6 green chilies finely cut
2½ tblsp besan roasted
Salt (namak) to taste
1 egg
1 tsp red chili powder
2 inch piece ginger (adrak) finely cut

for the curry

2 tsps coriander leaves (dhania patta)
1 tsp haldi powder
3 pyaj
1 tsp garam masala
3–5 garlic (lasan)
1 cup. tomatoes, boiled and skinned
salt (namak) to taste
1½" ginger (adrak)
1 tsp red chili powder

How to Make Kofta Curry?

- To make the koftas, grind the meat with all the other ingredients.
- Make small balls with this mixture.
- Deep fry these balls till golden brown and keep aside.
- For the curry, stir fry the onions, garlic and ginger till golden brown.
- Mix in the rest of the curry ingredients with enough water to make a gravy.
- Bring it to a boil, mix in the fried koftas and simmer (boil slowly at low temperature) for 45 mins.
- Decorate with cut coriander leaves before serving.
- Serve hot.

SHAMI KABAB RECIPE

Ingredients

500 gm minced mutton
2 eggs
1 meduim sized chopped onion (pyaj)
5 green chili (hari mirch) chopped

100 gm bengal gram (chana) soaked overnight
10 pods garlic (lasan/lahsun)
1 tsp cumin seed (jeera)
4 cardamoms
1″ long piece cinnamon (tuj/dalchini)
1″ long piece ginger (adarak)
6 Pepper corns (kalimirchi)
4 Red chilies
Clarified butter (ghee)

How to Make Shami Habab

- Boil minced meat in 3 cups of water and a teaspoonful of salt till water is absorbed and meat is tender.
- Grind meat into a fine paste.
- Take garlic, cumin seeds, cardamoms, cinnamon, ginger, peppercorns, red chilies and soaked gram dal and grind into a fine paste.
- Mix both the pastes well.
- Now mix well beaten eggs and prepare a uniform dough.
- Add finely chopped green chilies and onion to dough and mix well.
- Shape the dough into small round flattened balls or kababs.
- Heat ghee and deep fry kababs till golden brown and serve hot with sauce or chutney.

SHAHI ROGAN JOSH RECIPE

Ingredients

250 gm minced mutton
2 meduim sized sliced onion (pyaj)
1 tsp garam masala
4 chopped green chili (hari mirch)
3 skinned and chopped tomato (tamatar)
1 cup fresh curd (dahi)
A big pinch of saffron (kesar) oaked in lukewarm milk
15 cashewnut (kaju)
4 tblsp clarified butter (ghee)
1 ″ long piece ginger (adarak)
1 tblsp coriander seeds powder (dhania powder)
1 tblsp turmeric (haldi)
6 Red chilies
1 tblsp cumin seed (jeera)
6 cloves garlic (lasun)

How to Make Shahi Rogan Josh?

- First grind ginger, corainder seeds, turmeric powder, red chilies, cumin seeds, garlic with adequate quantity of salt to a thick paste.
- Now heat ghee.
- Fry onions, green chilies, tomatoes till brown and ghee begins to separate.
- Add masala paste and simmer for 3 minutes.
- Add keema and simmer.
- Add beaten curd and a cup of water.
- Cook till meat is tender and gravy is thick.
- Add garam masala, soaked saffron and cashewnuts.
- Cover it with a lid for few minutes.
- Serve hot garnished with chopped coriander leaves.

26 Fish Cooking Method

DEEP FRIED FISH

Ingredients

700 gm steaks with bone fish
Salt to taste
1 tbsp lemon juice
1 1/4 cup fresh green coriander
6 green chilies
4–6 cloves garlic peeled
3/4 cup plain yoghurt
Oil for deep frying

How to Make Deep Fried Fish?

- Cut fillets into pieces that are about 5–6.5 cm long and 4 cm wide.
- Spread the pieces out in a single layer in a large plate and sprinkle with about 1/3 tsp of salt and 1 tbs of lemon juice.
- Turn the pieces over and repeat with another 1/3 tsp of salt and 1 tbs of lemon juice. Set the plate at a tilt and leave it tilted for 2–3 hours.
- As water accumulates at one end, discard it. Put the green coriander, green chilies, garlic, 1/4 tsp of salt and tbsp of water into the blender.
- Blend until you have a paste. Empty the paste into a deep dish or shallow bowl. Put the yoghurt into another deep dish or shallow bowl.
- Add 1/4 tsp of salt to the yoghurt and mix it in. Set the oil to heat in a wok, kadai or frying pan over a medium flame.
- When very hot, dip 2 or 3 pieces of fish, first in the yoghurt and then in the green paste to cover thoroughly and then put them in the hot oil.
- Fry for about 5 minutes, turning the pieces over once, until the fish is cooked through. Remove with a slotted spoon.
- Fry all the pieces of fish this way.
- Serve the fried fish hot with green chutney.

INDIAN FISH CURRY

Ingredients

700 gm/11/2 lb white fish fillet
2 medium onions
4 cloves garlic (paste)
1 tbsp ginger (paste)
4 tbsp tomato puree
2/3rd cup water
Salt to taste
1/2 cup ghee

Spices

1 tsp white cumin seeds
1 tsp turmeric powder
1 tsp garam masala powder

How to Make Curry Fish?

- Cut the fish into medium-sized pieces.
- Heat the ghee in a frying pan and fry the fish pieces gently for 5 minutes. Drain the fish on absorbent kitchen paper and set aside.
- Chop one onion finely and grind the other one.
- Add the chopped onion to the ghee in the pan and fry until golden.
- Add all spices and cook stirring for 10 seconds.
- Now add the grinded onion, garlic, ginger and tomato puree. Fry the mixture until the ghee starts to separate.
- Add the water and salt. Bring the mixture to the boil. Add fried fish pieces. Reduce the heat and simmer for about 10 minutes.
- Serve the Indian fish curry hot with rice or roti.

FISH KOFTA CURRY

Ingredients

1 kg white fleshed fish
250 gm tomatoes blanched and diced
2 tbsp beaten curd
1 inch piece ginger
6 flakes garlic
2 cloves
1/2 tsp turmeric powder
Small piece cinnamon bark
1 tsp garam masala powder

2 cardamom
1 onion
Few mint leaves
1 slice bread soaked and squeezed dry
1 tsp cumin seeds
1 tsp coriander seeds
8 green chilies
small bunch coriander leaves
1 tsp chili powder
3 tbsp oil
Oil to fry
Salt to taste

How to make Indian Fish Kofta Curry?

- Boil the fish and remove the bones nicely.
- Mince the small onion, 4 green chilies, mint, coriander leaves and blend with the fish along with bread, salt and garam masala powder.
- Knead to a smooth mixture, form into small balls and deep fry to a golden brown color. Drain and set aside. Pound together the remaining spices to a fine powder.
- Grind onion, ginger and garlic to a paste. Heat 3 table spoons of ghee and fry the ground paste to a golden brown color.
- Put in spices and fry for a couple of seconds, then put in tomatoes and curd.
- Cook till the ghee floats to the top. Put in 2 cups of water, mix nicely and cook over a low fire till all the liquid dries. Mash to a smooth paste with the help of a wooden spoon and then pour in 2 more cups of water.
- Bring to a rolling boil, reduce heat and simmer gently for 5 minutes.
- Put in the fish balls and simmer for 5 more minutes.
- Serve fish kofta curry hot garnished with coriander leaves.

FISH KORMA RECIPE

Ingredients

1 kg fish
1/2 cup curd
1/2 cup onion paste
2 tsp ginger paste
1 tsp garlic paste
1 tbsp coriander paste
6 cardamom
1 inch cinnamon
2 tsp salt
3/4 cup ghee or oil

6 green chili
2 tbsp kewra
1 tbsp sugar
1 tbsp lemon juice

Preparation

- Use large fish for korma.
- Do not cut the fish into too small pieces.
- Carp is great for Korma.
- Except for the green chilies and kewra, add all the rest of stuff into the cooking dish. Mix well. Heat covered in low heat.
- Turn over the fish once (be careful).
- When the water has almost dried up, add the green chili and the kewra heat for another half hour in very low heat.
- When the oil begins to float on top, you are done.
- Serve fish korma hot with tandoori roti or rice.

FISH PAKORA

Ingredients

4 white fish fillets (steamed and cut into pieces)
2 eggs
A large pinch of salt
A pinch of red chili powder
2 tbsp corn flour
2 tbsp lemon juice
1 tsp chopped coriander leaves
Oil for deep-frying pakora

Preparation

- Beat the eggs, salt, chili powder, lemon juice and coriander leaves together to make a batter. Add corn flour and mix well to form a smooth batter.
- Heat oil in a kadai or deep-frying pan.
- Dip each fish piece into the batter and fry in batches till golden and crisp all over.
- Serve the fish pakora hot with your favorite chutney or ketchup.

INDIAN TANDOORI FISH

Ingredients

2 lbs of any white fish fillets (cut into 2–3 inch pieces)
1 tbsp chopped fresh ginger
4 cloves garlic
1/3 cup vinegar

Salt to taste
1 tbsp ground coriander seeds
1 tbsp ground cumin seeds
1 tsp ground cayenne pepper
1/2 cup vegetable oil

How to Make Barbecued Fish?

- Blend together ginger, garlic, vinegar, salt, coriander, cumin, cayenne and oil in the blender to form a fine paste.
- Marinate the fish pieces into the paste for about 4 hours in the refrigerator.
- Preheat the oven on maximum heat at broil.
- Cover the oven tray with foil to avoid mess.
- Place the marinated fish pieces on the tray and broil for about 8–10 minutes.
- Turn over and broil for about 8 minutes again.
- Keep a constant check. Broiling time may vary depending on the thickness of fish pieces.
- Serve the tandoori fish hot with your favorite chutney.

YOGHURT FISH

Ingredients

500 gm fish
2 cups curd blended smooth
4 tbsp mustard oil
a little flour
1 bay leaf
1 cinnamon
1 cardomom
2 ginger grounded to paste
1 onion grounded to paste
2 tsp red chili powder
1 tsp turmeric powder
1 tsp cummin powder
1 tsp sugar
Salt to taste

How to Make Masala Fish Curry?

- Cut fish onto cubes, or as traditional cross-section.
- Roll pieces separately in flour.
- Heat 2 Tbsp oil.
- Fry fish till pale golden.
- Drain and keep aside.

- Add remaining oil and fry bay leaf, cardamom and cinnamon.
- Add ginger, onion, chili powder turmeric and cummin.
- A little water may be added if it becomes too dry.
- Fry for a while.
- Add blended curd.
- Simmer on slow fire till oil comes up on top.
- Add fish with a little water, salt and sugar.
- Simmer till gravy is thick golden.
- Serve yoghurt fish with plain rice.

27 Chicken Cooking Method

BUTTER CHICKEN RECIPE

Indian butter chicken is slightly sweet and sour. Butter chicken curry is tomato based with marinated chicken pieces garnished with butter. Learn how to make butter chicken?

Ingredients

300 gms chicken breast boneless

Marinate

1–2 tsp hung thick curd

1 tsp salt

1/2 tsp red chili powder

1 tsp tandoori masala

1/4 tsp tandoori color

Curry

2 tbsp butter

2 tsp garlic paste

1 green chili sliced
1/2 tsp cumin powder
1/2 tsp red chili powder
1 tsp salt
6 or 1/2 kg tomato
10 cashewnuts
1 big tblsp tomato ketchup
1/2 tsp sugar
1/4 cup water
1/2 cup milk
2 tbsp Cream
1/4 tsp garam masala
1 tsp fenugreek crushed
Finely chopped coriander leaves

How to Make Butter Chicken Curry?

- In a bowl take all the ingredients under the marinate head and the chicken pieces. The chicken pieces should be 1" (inch) in size. Mix well and keep aside for at least 2–3 hours.
- Blanch, peel and puree the tomatoes. Keep aside.
- Soak the cashewnuts for 2–3 hours in hot water and then strain and grind the cashewnuts into a fine paste.
- For the curry heat the pan and add butter and immediately add the garlic paste.
- Now add the sliced green chilly. Also add cumin powder, red chilly powder and salt. Add 1 tbsp water and mix well.
- Add the tomato puree and cook till the gravy leaves the side.
- Lower the flame and add the cashewnut paste and stir constantly.
- Now add the tomato ketchup, sugar and 1/4 cup water.
- Meanwhile in a separate pan shallow fry the marinated chicken pieces for 4–5 minutes. If overcooked then the chicken will get hard and stiff. Keep aside.
- Once the gravy comes to a boil add the chicken pieces. And cook for a minute.
- Now lower the flame add the milk and stir well. Cook for another minute and then add the cream. Mix well.
- Now add the garam masala and crushed fenugreek leaves. Mix well.
- Transfer the chicken to a serving bowl and garnish with chopped coriander leaves, crushed fenugreek leaves and swirls of cream.
- Indian butter chicken is ready to be served with any Indian bread. Relish it.

Note:
1. Milk should be at room temperature before adding to the gravy.
2. Add milk and cream at low flame only.
3. Add the garam masala only at the end.

CHICKEN BIRYANI

Ingredients

2 cups basmati rice
3/4 kg chicken pieces
1/2 cup milk
1 cup yoghurt (curd)
3 sliced onion
1 tsp ginger paste
1/2 tsp garlic paste
1 tsp green chili paste
1/2 cup tomato puree
2 tsp red chili powder
1 tsp turmeric powder
1 tsp roasted cumin powder
2 tsp garam masala powder
1/2 tsp green cardamom powder
Saffron a pinch
1 tsp coriander powder
2 tbsp green coriander leaves
Salt to taste
7 tbsp oil

Preparation

- Mix tomato puree, yogurt, ginger garlic paste, green chili paste, red chili powder, turmeric powder, roasted cumin powder, garam masala, coriander powder and salt. Stir well.
- Marinate the chicken with this mixture and keep aside for 3–4 hours.
- Heat oil in a pan. Fry the onions until golden brown.
- Add the marinated chicken and cook for 10 minutes.
- Add 4 cups of water to the rice. Mix saffron in milk and add to it.
- Add cardamom powder. Add the chicken pieces.
- Pressure cook the rice. Mix gently.
- Garnish with green coriander leaves and serve hot.

CHICKEN CURRY

Ingredients

1 tbsp butter
1 cup chopped apple
1 cup sliced celery
1 clove garlic, minced
1/2 cup chopped onion
2 tbsp cornstarch
2 to 3 tsp curry powder
3/4 cup cold chicken stock
2 cups milk
2 cups cooked chicken, diced
1 (3 ounce) can mushrooms, drained
Salt to taste

Rice Ring

1/4 cup butter
1/2 cup chopped onion
1/4 cup slivered almonds
1/2 cup light raisins
6 cups hot cooked rice
6½ cup ring mold

How to Make Curry Chicken?

- Melt butter in saucepan; add apple, celery, garlic and onion. Cook until onion is tender. Combine cornstarch, curry powder, 3/4 teaspoon salt and broth.

- Stir into onion mixture; add milk. Cook until thickened, stirring constantly. Add chicken and mushrooms; stir and heat through. Serve over rice ring.
- **Rice ring:** Melt butter in skillet; add onion and almonds (until golden). Add raisins; heat until plump. Add all to rice and mix.
- Press mixture into greased mold. Unmold at once on platter and fill with indian chicken curry.

CHICKEN KORMA

Indian Chicken korma recipe is a muglai speciality. Chicken korma curry has pieces of boneless chicken cooked with almond sauce and spices and garnished with roasted almonds.

Ingredients

400 gms chicken breasts, chopped in big pieces
1 tblsp ground almonds
1 tblsp lemon juice
1/2 tsp black pepper powder
1 tsp garlic paste
2–3 oil or clarified butter (ghee)
1 medium size onion, chopped finely
1/4 tsp turmeric (haldi) powder
150 ml curd (dahi)
2 green chilies
4 pods cardamom
3 cloves
2 medium size cinnamon sticks
1 bay leaf
1/2 tsp garam masala
1 tblsp chopped green coriander
1/2 tblsp roasted chopped almonds
Salt to taste

How to Make Chicken Korma

- Marinate the chicken pieces with lemon juice, pinch of salt, black pepper and garlic paste. Rub the mixture thoroughly to the pieces and keep it aside for 1/2 an hour.
- In a heavy bottom pan, heat the oil/ghee and when it is medium hot add the chopped onions and turmeric.
- Fry till the onions are golden and then take them out and keep aside. Leave the oil behind for further use.
- In a mixer make a fine paste of fried onions, curd, almonds, green chilies. Pour this mixture on the marinated chicken pieces.
- Now reheat the oil in the pan on medium flame and then add cardamom, cloves, cinnamon and bay leaf. Stir them for 30 secs and then add the marinated chicken along with leftover paste.

- Let the chicken cook on low flame while stirring occasionally till it boils. Then cover the pan with a lid and let it simmer till the chicken is cooked properly.
- Finally add garam masala and chopped green coriander.
- Add the salt according to taste and garnish with roasted almonds.

CHILI CHICKEN RECIPE

Ingredients

250 gm boneless chicken breast (cut into 1 inch cubes)
1 egg white
1 tsp salt
4 tsp red chili sauce
2–3 tsp cornflour
1 tblsp soy sauce
2 tblsp tomato ketchup
1 tsp white vinegar
2 tblsp oil
1/2 tsp ginger paste
1 tsp garlic paste
1 big onion sliced long
1/2 cup capsicum (cut into big cubes)
1–2 green chilies
Green corainder and green onion for garnish
Oil for frying

How to Make Chili Chicken?

- Marinate the chicken pieces in egg white, 1 tsp salt, 2 tsp red chili sauce and 2–3 tsp cornflour. Mix well and keep for 10–15 minutes.
- In a bowl mix 2 tsp red chilly sauce, soy sauce, tomato ketchup and white vinegar. Keep aside for later use.

- Now heat oil for frying in a kadai/wok and fry the chicken pieces separately for 2–3 minutes. Do not over fry otherwise the chicken will get hard. Take them out on a paper tissue.
- In a separate pan heat 2 tblsp oil and add garlic and ginger paste. Fry till golden color and then add sliced big onion and capsicum cubes and slit green chilies. Stir fry on high flame for 2–3 minutes. Do not over cook the vegetables. The vegetables should be crunchy.
- Now lower the flame and add the sauce mixture and 1/4 cup of water. Mix well.
- When slightly thick and dry, shut the flame and move it in a serving platter.
- Garnish with green chopped coriander and green onion. Serve hot.

Note:

1. Be careful with salt as the soy sauce also has salt.
2. Cook the vegetables on high flame to keep their crunchiness.

28 Eggs Cooking Method

BOILED EGG

Ingredients

1 to 4 eggs

Water (enough to cover the eggs by 1 inch)

High saucepan with cover (large enough to completely cover eggs)

Preparation

- Place the eggs in the pan with the help of a spoon and add cold water enough to cover the eggs by 1 inch.
- Bring the water to boil and then remove from heat. Cover the pan, and let sit for 15–20 minutes.
- Later transfer the eggs to a pan of ice cubes and water.
- Chill the eggs for 2 minutes. At the same time boil the water again in which the eggs were boiled earlier.
- Transfer the chilled eggs from the ice bowl to the boiling water pan and bring to the boil again. Let them boil for 10 seconds.
- Remove the eggs and place them back into the ice cold water. Placing them in the ice water agian prevents dark lines from forming. After 5–10 minutes take them out and use them accordingly.

EGG BIRYANI

Ingredients

1/2 cup ghee/oil

8 large eggs (hard boiled)

1 large onion (finely chopped)

2 flakes garlic (curshed)

2 bay leaves
1 inch cinnamon stick
1 brown cardamom (badi elaichi)
4 green cardamom pods (chhoti elaichi)
1/2 tsp turmeric powder
1/2 tsp chili powder or to taste
2 cups basmati (long grain) rice
2½ cups warm water
Salt to taste
1 tsp garam masala powder
1 tbsp chopped coriander leaves
3–4 tomatoes (thickly sliced) to garnish

Preparation

- Heat the oil/ghee in a deep sauce pan and fry onions and garlic together with the bay leaves, cinnamon and cardamoms, until golden.
- Carefully prick the eggs with a fork and add to the pan.
- Stir in turmeric, chili powder and fry for about 5 minutes.
- Add presoaked rice and stir slowly and carefully for 2 minutes.
- Pour in water and salt to taste, and cook over a modeate heat until the rice is tender and water is absorbed.
- Sprinkle garam masala powder over it.
- Garnish egg biryani with chopped coriander and tomato slices, serve hot.

EGG CURRY

Ingredients

4 eggs (hard boiled)
1 onion
1/2 tomato (pureed)
3–4 flakes of garlic
1/2 inch piece of ginger
1–2 green chilies
2 tbsp chopped coriander leaves
Salt to taste
Red chili powder to taste
3/4th tsp turmeric powder
1/2 tsp coriander powder
3/4 tsp garam masala
2–3 tbsp vegetable oil/ghee
1 cup green peas or 250 gms paneer

Preparation

- Remove the shell of boiled eggs and keep aside. If using paneer cut into cubes and fry till golden and set aside for later use.
- Make a paste of onion, garlic, ginger and green chilies in a mixer or chopper.
- Heat oil in a kadai or wok and add onion-garlic paste and fry till golden brown.
- Add all the spices (salt, turmeric, coriander and chili powder) except garam masala and fry for a minute and add tomato puree. Fry till it starts leaving oil.
- Add a cup of water and cook till it dry's.
- Now add the fried paneer cubes or green peas (which ever using) and boiled eggs.
- Add 1 cup of water and bring to boil and reduce the flame.
- Simmer for 10 minutes.
- Garnish egg curry with garam masala and coriander leaves and serve hot with paratha, roti or rice.

EGG PAKORA

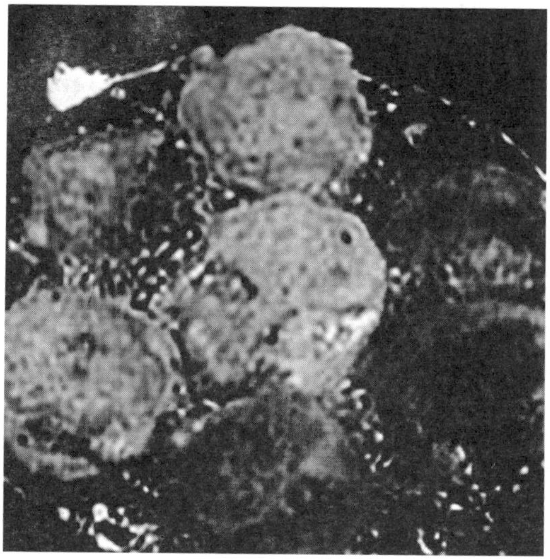

Ingredients

4 eggs (hard boiled)
3 tbsp gram flour (besan)
Salt to taste
Red chili powder to taste
Little black pepper powder
Oil to fry

Preparation

- Peel and cut boiled egg into two halves.
- Sprinkle little salt and pepper on eggs.
- In a bowl take gram flour salt, chili powder and make a thick batter using water.
- Heat oil in a kadai.
- Dip each egg piece in the batter and deep fry till golden brown on medium flame.
- Serve egg pakora hot.

EGG OMELETTE

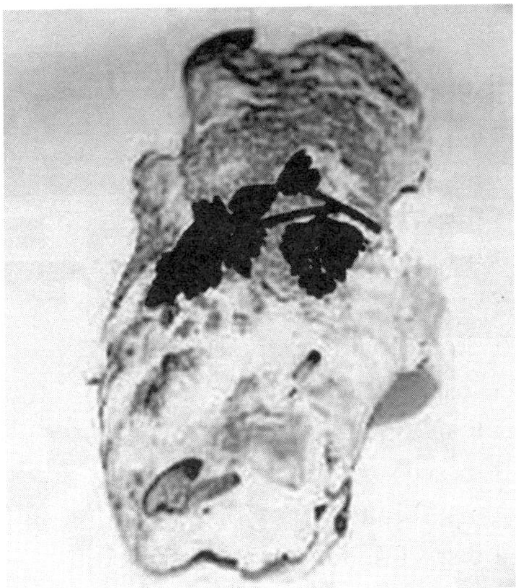

Ingredients

2 eggs
1/4th onion (finely chopped)
1–2 green chilies (finely chopped)
1/4th tomato (chopped), optional
2 tbsp chopped coriander leaves
Salt to taste
1/4th tsp red chili powder or to taste
1 tbsp milk
Oil to fry

How to Make an Egg Omelette?

- Beat the eggs and add milk, chopped onions, tomatoes, green chilies, coriander, salt and chili powder.
- Beat the mixture until foamed.
- Heat oil in a frying pan and add the mixture. Cook over low heat till mixture is firm and flip it and fry the other side.
- Serve hot with bread or paratha.

EGG TOAST

Ingredients

2 eggs
2-3 slices of bread
1/2 onion (finely chopped)
1/2 tomato (finely chopped)
1–2 green chilies (finely chopped)
2 tbsp chopped coriander leaves
Salt to taste
1 tbsp milk
1/2 tsp red chili powder or to taste
Oil to fry

Preparation

- Beat the eggs and add milk, chopped onions, tomatoes, green chilies, coriander, salt and chili powder.
- Beat the mixture until foamed.
- Heat oil in a frying-pan or griddle.
- Dip bread slice in the mixture and coat it evenly and fry over low flame.
- Fry on both sides until done. Repeat the same for other slices.
- Serve egg toast hot with ketchup.

STUFFED EGGS

Ingredients

4 eggs (hard boiled)
1 tbsp ghee/oil
1 tbsp chopped onions
3 tbsp cooked ground/minced meat
Salt to taste
1 green chili (chopped)
1/2 tsp ginger (grated)
1 tbsp tomato paste
1 tbsp corn flour/corn starch
1 egg (beaten)
1 tbsp coriander leaves (chopped)
1 lemon juice
breadcrumbs for coating
12 pieces of liver (fried) for garnishing
Oil for deep-frying

Preparation

- Heat the oil/ghee in a frying pan and fry the onions till golden.
- Add the meat, salt, chili, coriander, ginger, tomato paste and lemon juice and fry for about 5 minutes.
- Peel the shell and cut the hard boiled eggs into half lengthways.
- Take out the yolks and add to the frying mixture.
- Cook for another 5 minutes and remove from the heat and allow to cool.
- Stir the corn flour into the beaten egg, making a batter.
- Place the breadcrumbs on a flat dish.
- Fill the meat mixture into the yolk cavity (hole from where yolk is separated) of each egg half, cover with another half to make complete egg shapes.
- Dip the stuffed egg into the egg and corn flour batter and roll over the breadcrumbs.
- Heat oil in a kadai/deep-frying pan over a moderate heat and fry the stuffed eggs until golden all over.
- Remove and drain on a paper towel.
- Serve garnished with fried liver, coriander leaves and with chutney or sauce.

29

Salads and Raitas

EGG SALAD

Ingredients

6 eggs (fully boiled)
2 boiled potatoes
1 capsicum 1 onion (thinly sliced into rings)
1 tomato (thinly sliced into rings)
2 tsp lemon juice
Salt to taste
Black pepper to taste
Finely chopped coriander leaves

Preparation

- Cut eggs into halves.
- Take out the yolk and mash with boiled potatoes.
- Mix salt, pepper, lemon juice and chopped coriander.
- Fill eggs whites with the mixture.
- Serve the egg salad in a tray garnished with onion, tomatoes, chopped capsicum and coriander.

FRUIT SALAD

Ingredients

3 bananas
1 apple
2 orange
1 ripe mango
1 bunch green grapes
1/4th cup pomegranate seeds
Few canned cherries
1 guava

1/2 cup sugar (or to taste)
1 lemon juice

Preparation

- Peel and cut all fruits into banana and apple in the end to avoid browns.
- Pour lemon juice immediately on fruits.
- In a little water add sugar and half melt it on heat.
- Mix melted sugar to the fruits. Refrigerate it and serve the fruit salad chilled.

Note: Salt and chaat masala can also be used

MIXED VEGETABLE SALAD

Ingredients

50 gms french beans
3–4 carrots
1 small cabbage
100 gms broccoli (cut into florets)
1 capsicum
Salt to taste
1 tomato (cut into thin rings)
2 green chilies (slit vertically)
Finely chopped coriander leaves
1 lemon juice
Black pepper powder to taste

Preparation

- Cut and steam the vegetables.
- Add tomatoes, green chilies salt, pepper powder and lemon juice, and mix well.
- Garnish with coriander leaves.

FRUIT AND NUT SALAD

This is a very popular fruit and nut salad recipe. It is liked by one and all.

Ingredients

1/2 cup paneer (mashed)
1/4 cup mayonnaise
6-7 pieces dated (stone removed)
6 pieces canned peach (aadoo)
1/4 cup cashewnut (kaju) (roasted)
1/4 bunch lettuce (kasmisaag) (chopped)
1 tomato (tamatar) (sliced)

2 tsp green chutney
1 tsp tomato (tamatar) chutney

How to Make Fruit and Nut Salad?

- Mix paneer, mayonnaise, lettuce and green chutney and make a layer of it in a flat bowl.
- Mix dates, tomato chutney, peaches, cashewnuts and place it over the 1st layer.
- Garnish with tomato slices.

POTATO SALAD

This a simple recipe for making potato (aloo) salad in sour curd.

Ingredients

4 potato (aloo) (boil ed)
2 tblsp coriander leaves (dhania patta) (chopped)
1/2 cup peas (matar) (boiled)
1/2 cup cream (malai)(sour)
1 green chili (chopped)
1/2 tsp mustard powder
Salt (namak) to taste
1 tsp sour curd (dahi) (if not available, then lime juice)

How to Make Potato Salad?

- Cut potatoes into cubes. Mix all the other ingredients with it in a bowl. Mix well.

VEGETABLE YOGHURT SALAD

Very easy and simple to make vegetable yoghurt salad recipe.

Ingredients

2 tomato (tamatar) (chopped)
1/4 cucumber (kheera) (chopped)
1 spring onion (pyaj) (chopped)
1/2 raddish (chopped)
1 cup yoghurt a pinch of salt (namak)
1 dry red chili (lal mirch) (chopped)

How to Make Vegetable Yoghurt Salad?

Mix all ingredients in a bowl.

ALOO RAITA

Aloo raita is made by mixing boiled potatoes, curd, green chilly and garnished with chopped coriander. This raita is very delicious and can be tried with rice, dal or with currries. Here is a simple recipe of how to make aloo ka raita.

Cooking time: 20 minutes
Serves: 3 people

Ingredients

2 cup beaten dahi/curd
2 potatoes (boiled, peeled and cubed)
1 green chili (finely chopped)
1 tsp roasted cumin seed powder
1/4 tsp red chili powder
1/2 tsp finely chopped coriander leaves

How to Make Aloo ka Raita?

- Beat the yoghurt till smooth and thick.
- Add salt, red chili powder, green chili and cumin powder.
- Add potato cubes and stir gently, so that potato pieces do not break up.
- Garnish it with coriander leaves, red chili powder, cumin powder and green chili.
- Serve cold with naan or rice and dal.

Note: To add a new twist to the recipe pour in 1 tsp of sweet imli chutney.

BAIGAN KA RAITA

Here is a tempting, tasty baigan ka raita recipe for baigan lovers. Learn how to make eggplant raita.

Ingredients

250 gm curd (dahi)
1 brinjal (baigan)
A pinch asafetida (hing)
1 tsp oil
1/2 tsp salt (namak)
1/2 tsp black pepper powder (kali mirch)
1/2 tsp roasted cumin powder (bhuna jeera powder)

How to make baigan ka raita?

- Beat curd and keep aside.
- Grease oil on brinjal and pierce a hole with a knife. Sprinkle hing in the hole. Fry baigan on a gas until cooked well.
- When it cools, peel the outer layer and mash properly.
- Mix it with curd along with salt, kali mirch and jeera powder.
- Serve baigan ka raita chilled.

BOONDI RAITA (CURD PREPARATION)

Ingredients

2 cup curd (yoghurt)
100 gm gram flour (besan)
1/2 tsp roasted cumin (jeera) powder
Salt to taste
Red chili powder to taste
very little garam masala
Finely chopped coriander leaves
Oil to fry

Preparation

- Add water to gram flour and mix well to spreading consistency.
- Add salt and beat till becomes light. Heat oil and pass the paste through draining spoon. Fry till golden and crisp.
- Stir the curd with hand mixer (mathani).
- Add boondi and mix gently. If it becomes thick add little milk and mix it.
- Now add salt, cumin powder and chili powder, mix well.
- Sprinkle garam masala and garnish with chopped coriander.
- Keep in refrigerator for an hour or so.
- Serve boondi raita chilled.

CAPSICUM RAITA

Capsicum raita recipe is very easy to make and a quick side dish for rice or roti. Shimla mirch ka raita is made with sauted capsicum and curd; seasoned with mustard seeds. Learn how to make capsicum raita by following this easy recipe.

Cooking time: 15 minutes
Serves: 2–3 people

Ingredients

2 cup curd
1/2 cup capsicum (cut into 1 inch cubes and remove the seeds)
1/2 tsp mustard seed
1/2 tsp jeera
Salt to taste
2 dried red chilly
1/2 tsp sugar

How to Make Capsicum Raita

- Heat oil in a small frying pan, add mustard seed adder and fry till it turns translucent.
- When it starts to splutter; add broken red chilies and then add the chopped capsicum and fry till it becomes soft but is crunchy.

- Beat the curd in a bowl and add sugar, salt and chili powder. Mix well.
- Finally add fried capsicum and mix it well.
- Serve it chill.

MIXED FRUIT RAITA

Ingredients

2 cup curd (yoghurt)
3 bananas
1 small pineapple
2 apples
1 ripe mango
1 cup pomegranate seeds
Chopped coriander leaves
Sugar to taste
Salt to taste
Black pepper powder to taste

How to Make Fruit Raita?

- Whisk the curd with hand mixer (mathni) properly and mix salt, sugar, and curd is thick add little milk or water.
- Cup all fruits in small cubes and add to the curd.
- Garnish mixed fruit raita with chopped coriander and pomegranate.

GHIYA RAITA (CURD PREPARATION)

Ingredients

2 cups curd (yoghurt)
1 cup grated ghiya (lauki)
1tsp cumin (jeera) powder
Salt to taste
Red chili powder to taste

How to Make Ghiya (lauki) Raita?

- Boil grated ghiya till soft, drain and cool it.
- Stir the curd with hand mixer.
- Add ghiya and mix well. If curd is thick mix little milk or water.
- Now add salt, cumin powder and chili powder, mix well.
- Keep in refrigerator for an hour or so.
- Serve ghiya raita chilled.

ONION RAITA (CURD PREPARATION)

Ingredients

1/2 kg curd
2 onion (finely chopped)
1 green chili (finely chopped)
1 ginger (finely chopped)
few coriander leaves (finely chopped)
1 tsp oil for tadka
1/4 mustard seeds (small)
1 tsp salt

How to Make Onion Raita?

- Beat curd.
- Add onion, salt, green chili and coriander leaves.
- Heat oil in a large spoon. Add mustard seeds.
- Add it to the raita. Mix well.
- Refrigerate for 1–2 hours before serving.
- Serve the onion raita with imli rice.

TOMATO ONION RAITA

Tomato onion raita is deliciously made with curd, tomato and onions seasoned with a tempering of mustard and cumin seeds, fresh curry leaves and spiced with some green chilies. Pyaz tamatar ka raita is generally served with rice and roties. Learn how to make tomato onion raita.

Cooking time: 15 minutes
Serves: 2–3 people

Ingredients

2 cup plain curd/dahi BR > 1 cup tomatoes and onions (finely chopped)
1 tsp ginger (grated)
1/2 tsp coriander leaves (finely chopped)
Salt to taste
Pinch of sugar
2 tsp oil
1/2 tsp split black gram
1/4 tsp cumin seed, mustard seed
1 chili (finely chopped)
2–3 curry leaves

How to Make Tomato Onion Raita?

- Mix the tomatoes, onion and ginger. Add some salt and sugar to it and mix it well.
- Heat oil in frying pan, add curry leaves to it after that add split black gram fry it for few minute. As the dal turns brown add cumin seed and mustard seeds. When they start to pop add the green chili and fry for few seconds.
- Pour the above seasoning over tomato and onion mixture.
- Add the yogurt and mix it well.
- Serve it with roti or rice.

30 Desserts

APPLE JAM

Ingredients

1 kg cooking apples (seb)
750 gram sugar (cheeni)
2 cup water
2 teaspoon lemon (nimbu) juice or 1/2 teaspoon citric acid

How to Make Apple Jam

- Peel, core and cut the apples into slices, cook in water until tender.
- Add sugar and lemon juice or citric acid and stir on a hot fire until jam sets when tested.
- Cool a little and pour into sterilized jars and cork tightly.
- Serve after one day.

LEMON JELLY

Ingredients

1/2 kg lemons (nimbu)
1/2 cup (3 pints) water
Sugar (cheeni)

How to Make Lemon Jelly?

- Wash and dry the lemons.
- Remove the skin, then cut them into quarters and take out the pips.
- Put the lemon pieces in a bowl, cover with water, and keep for 24 hours.
- Boil the lemon pieces in the same water, strain through a muslin cloth.
- Measure the juice and allow 1/2 kg sugar for each pint of the liquid.
- Heat the juice, add sugar and stir till it is dissolved.
- Cook on a hot fire until the syrup sets quickly or falls in drops when tested on a plate.
- Cool and pour into jars and close the lid tightly.

GUAVA JELLY

Ingredients

1½ kgs guavas (amrood)
6 cup water
1/2 tsp citric acid
Sugar (cheeni)

How to Make Guava Jelly?

- Wash and cut guava into thin slices and cook with water until very soft.
- Put this mixture in a coarse cloth and allow the juice to drip through into a bowl.
- Underneath and leave it for 12 hours.
- Do not squeeze the bag.
- Use the mixture in the bag for guava cheese.
- Measure the juice and add 3 cups of sugar to each pint of juice.
- Heat the sugar, guava juice and stir until it is dissolved.
- Strain the juice, add lemon juice and cook on a hot fire until setting point is reached.
- Cool and pour into airtight jars.

APPLE JELLY

Ingredients

1½ kgs cooking apples (Seb)
1½ pints water (6 teacups)
2 cloves (lavang)
Sugar (cheeni)
Juice of half lemon (nimbu)

How to Make Apple Jelly?

- Cut the apples in quarters and boil them in water with cloves till they become soft.
- Drain through a muslin cloth.
- Measure the juice and allow 2 cups sugar to each pint of juice.
- Heat the juice, add the sugar and lemon juice and stir till dissolved.
- Boil on a hot fire until the syrup sets quickly when tested on a cold plate.
- Cool and pour into clean and dry jars.

APRICOT AND PINEAPPLE JAM

Ingredients

250 gram dried apricots (khumani)
5 cup sugar (cheeni)
5 cup water
500 gram tin of pineapple (ananas) slices

How to Make Spricot and Pineapple Jam?

- Stone the apricots and cut into slices.
- Wash them and soak in water for 24 hours.
- Put apricots along with the water in a pan and cook until tender.
- Cut pineapples into thin slices.
- Cook pineapple slices with its syrup and sugar and the cooked apricots and stir until.
- Sugar is dissolved.
- Cook on a hot fire till the syrup thickens.
- Pour one teaspoon of the jam on a cold plate; if it sets, remove from the fire.
- Pour hot into a clean jar and cork tightly.

MANGO JAM (serve after two days)

Ingredients

2½ cup mango (aam) pulp
250 gram sugar (cheeni)
1/4 teaspoon citric acid
l teaspoon pectin
1/4 teaspoon potassium metabisulfite

How to Make Mango Jam?

- Cook mango pulp and sugar until a little thick and sets on the plate when tested.
- Dissolve citric acid, pectin and potassium metabisulfite in 1/4 cup of hot water and mix it in the jam.
- Pour the hot jam in sterilized jars, seal when cool and cork tightly.

RASPBERRY JAM

Ingredients

1/2 kg raspberries
2 cup water
2½ cup sugar
Juice of one lemon (nimbu) or 1/2 tsp citric acid

How to Make Raspberry Jam?

- Clean the fruit and cook with water on a low fire until tender, thin mash.
- Add sugar and lemon juice and stir on a hot fire until it thickens.
- Put a little on a cold plate; if it sets, it is ready.
- Cool a little, then pour into jars and seal immediately.

PUDDING

BANANA BREAD PUDDING RECIPE

Ingredients

1 loaf french bread
2 tblsp vanilla extract
4 bananas, mashed
4 cups milk
3 eggs
1 cup sugar
1 cup raisins
1 tsp freshly ground nutmeg
1 tsp cinnamon
Splash of rum (optional)

How to Make Banana Bread Pudding?

- Cut the lof in small cubes.
- Put the cubed loaf in a bowl.
- Now pour the milk on it and keep it aside for a hour.
- Preheat oven to 325 degrees.
- Grease 9 × 13 inch baking dish.
- In a separate bowl mix the eggs, sugar and vanilla essence.
- Pour this mixture onto the bread mixture and then spread the mashed bananas and raisins.
- Add rum, cinnamom and nutmeg powder.
- Pour this mixture on the baking dish.
- Bake in the oven for 1 hour and then let it cool.

CHOCOLATE BREAD PUDDING

Ingredients

300 ml milk
4–5 tblsp sugar
4 slices brown bread
3 eggs
2 tblsp drinking chocolate or cocoa powder
1/2 tsp vanilla essence
250 ml thick sweetened cream

How to Make Chocolate Pudding with Cream?

- Cut the bread into pieces. Beat the eggs and add the essence.
- Warm the milk and mix in the sugar. Gently mix in the cooca powder.
- Put off the flame and add the beaten eggs and the breadcrumbs. Mix well.
- Grease pudding mould and pour the mixture into the mould.
- Cover lossely with foil and steam in a rice cooker or pressure cooker without whistle for 30–40 minutes or until the pudding is spongy.
- Allow the pudding to shrink before unmoulding.
- Then put it in the fridge for 1 hour before serving with fresh, thick and sweetened cream.

FRUIT CUSTARD PUDDING

Here is a delicious pudding recipe with lots of fruits. Learn how to make fruit custard pudding?

Ingredients

1 small cake
1 tin cocktail fruits
2 cup fresh cream
4 cup milk (doodh)
4 tbsp custard powder
1 cup sugar
1/2 packet strawberry jelly
1 apple (seb)
1 orange (santra)
1 cup grapes (angoor)
4–5 cherries

How to Make Fruit Custard Pudding?

- Cut cake in the center into two halves.
- Prepare jelly according to the instructions.
- Beat cream until it thickens.
- Peel all the fruits and cut into small pieces.
- Mix custard in a little milk.
- Boil the remaining milk and then add sugar and dissolved custard.
- Stir continuously until it thickens. Remove it from the flame.
- Put one cake slice in a dish and then spread some of the custard and cocktail fruits and some fresh fruits over it.
- Then put jelly and place another cake slice over it.
- Garnish with remaining custard and fruits.
- Spread cream on the top.
- Put jelly on the sides and garnish with cherries.
- Refrigerate it for setting and then serve chilled.

MILK PUDDING

Ingredients

2 oz rice sago
1 tbsp sugar
1/2 oz butter
1 pint milk
Pinch of salt

How to Make Milk Pudding?

- Just cover the cereal with water and let it stand for 5 minutes.
- Strain off water, and put the cereal in a greased pie dish with the sugar, butter, salt and milk.
- Let it soak for about 1 hour.
- Then stir it well and cook slowly in a cool oven for 2 hours, stirring well after 1/2 hours.
- The above recipe makes a pudding of medium thickness; more or less cereal should be used to vary the consistency according to taste.
- An egg can be added if desired, in which case the cereal should be boiled in the milk first and the egg added when cool.
- Then bake in the oven for 20 minutes.

FRUIT COCKTAIL PUDDING

Here is a delicious pudding recipe that can be served chilled anytime. Learn how to make fruit cocktail pudding?

Ingredients

1 tsp coffee
1 packet lemon jelly (nimbu ki jelly)
2 cup fresh cream
3 tbsp sugar

How to Make Fruit Cocktail Jelly Pudding?

- Boil 2 cup water and dissolve jelly in it.
- When it mixes properly, remove it from the flame. Let it cool.
- Place some of the jelly in the tin and refrigerate for sometime.
- Mix coffee in the remaining jelly and refrigerate it separately.
- Grind sugar and blend with cream.
- Now add coffee jelly mixture to the above.
- Now spread this over the lemon jelly already set in the tin and again refrigerate it for setting.
- Serve it chilled once it sets properly.

31 Beverages

AAM PANNA RECIPE

Aam panna is a popular tangy summer cooler. Here is a simple recipe for how to make aam panna? Green mango panna or aam panna is a great remedy for heat stroke and dehydration. It is packed with vitamins too.

Serves: 10

Cooking time: 20 mins

Ingredients

3 medium size green raw mangoes

1 cup sugar

1 tblsp roasted cumin powder

Black salt to taste, salt to taste

2 cup water

1 tblsp mint leaves (pudina patta)

Ice crushed

How to Make Aam Panna?

- Place the mangoes along with water in a sauce-pan and bring to a boil. Simmer for 10 minutes. Then remove from fire.
- Alternately you can pressure cook the mangoes with water till soft.
- Let them cool and then peel the mangoes and get the pulp with the help of a spoon. Grind mango pulp along with water to a smooth paste.
- In a pan take the pulpy mixture, add sugar and let it cook on flame till the sugar dissolves completely. Stir continously lest you burn the mixture.
- Remove from fire and add roasted cumin powder, black salt and salt.
- Let this mixture cool down properly.
- To make the drink: Take a tall glass pour 1–2 tblsp of the mango mixture and pour in chilled water till 3/4 th. Now add finely chopped mint and crushed ice.
- Garnish with mint leaves and serve immediately.

Note:

1. You can increase or decrease the quantity of sugar as per your desire.
2. You can use jaggery instead of sugar.
3. This mixture can stay in refrigerator for up to a week.

ANGOOR SHARBAT

Ingredients

1/2 × 3-inch piece of orange zest
1/4 tsp cardamom seeds (elaichi)
4 whole cloves (lavang)
6 cup grape juice (angoor ka raas)
1/4th cup honey (shahad)
3-inch piece of cinnamon (tuj/dalchini) stick
2 cup sparkling water

How to Make Angoor Sharbat?

- Tie the zest, cardamom seeds and cloves in a small piece of cheese cloth.
- Place the juice and honey in a large stainless steel pan and bring it to near the boiling point over moderate heat.
- Remove the pan from the heat, add the spice bag and cinnamon stick, cover, and set aside until the juice has cooled to tepid.
- Remove the spice bag and cinnamon stick and chill.
- Add the water before serving.

BANANA LASSI

Ingredients

1 cup curd (dahi, plain non-fat yoghurt)
1 peeled and sliced ripe banana (kela)
2 tblsp sugar (cheeni) or to taste
1/4th tsp cardamom powder (elaichi powder) (optional)
Few ice cubes

How to Make Banana Lassi?

- Combine all ingredients and blend until smooth in a blender.
- Pour in glasses and serve chilled.

BANANA SHAKE

Ingredients

2 cup milk (doodh)
1 firm ripe banana (kela)

2 tblsp sugar (cheeni)
1/4 tsp ground nutmeg (jaiphal)

How to Make Banana Shake?

- Place the milk in a heavy-bottomed pan over a high heat.
- Bring it to boil, stirring constantly, then reduce the heat and simmer for 2 minutes.
- While the milk is simmering, place a banana, sugar and nutmeg in a blender and process until pureed.
- Pour 1 cup milk into the blender and process for another minute.
- Add the remaining milk and process for 1/2 minute.
- Pour the milk in warmed mugs or cups and serve immediately.

APPLE MILK SHAKE

Here is a yummy apple shake recipe. Learn how to make it?

Ingredients

2 apple (seb)
2 glass milk (doodh)
2 tbsp sugar
4 green cardamom (hari elaichi)
Ice as required

How to Make Apple Milkshake?

- Peel apple and cut in small pieces.
- Now blend milk, sugar and apple in a mixer.
- Grind elaichi to a powder and mix in the shake.
- Now pour shake in the glasses.
- Put some crushed ice and serve it chilled.

COLA SHAKE

Ingredients

200 ml any chilled cola
1 scoop vanilla ice cream
50 ml sweetened milk (doodh)
2 ice cubes

How to Make Cola Shake?

- In a tall thin glass add a scoop of ice cream.
- Pour the sweetened milk over it and add ice cubes.
- Now very carefully pour the cola in the glass.
- See it does not flow out.
- Serve with a spoon.

GULAB SHARBAT

Ingredients

1½ cup freshly picked rose petals (gulab ke patti)
3/4 cup boiling water
1/4th tsp cardamom seeds
3/4th cup sugar (cheeni)
1/4th cup strained fresh lemon juice (nimbu ka raas)
2/3rd cup pomegranate juice
5 cup cold water

How to Make Gulab Sharbat?

- Crush the rose petals with mortar and pestle and place them in a large bowl.
- Add the boiling water, then pour the mixture to a metal container and add cardamom seeds. set aside for 8 hours or overnight.
- Pour the rose-cardamom water through a muslin lined strainer set over a bowl.
- Add the sugar, and float the bowl over a hot water filled sink until the sugar dissolves.
- Remove from the hot water and filter it again.
- Cool it to room temperature.
- Combine all the ingredients in a pitcher and stir well.
- Serve in a glass half filled with crushed ice.

JEERA LASSI

Ingredients

3 cup curd (dahi, plain yoghurt)
2 tblsp cream (malai) (optional)
2 tblsp lemon juice (nimbu ka raas) (optional)
1/3rd cup ice water
To taste salt (namak)
6 ice cubes
1/2 tblsp dry-roasted cumin seed powder (jeera powder)

How to Make Jeera Lassi?

- Place the curd, cream, lemon juice, ice water and salt in a blender.
- Process for 2 minutes.
- Add ice cubes and blend for another minute.
- Add all but few pinches of cumin powder and process for 5 seconds.

NIMBU PANI

Ingredients

4 juicy lemon (nimbu)
8 cup water
10 pitted and halves dates (khajoor)
1/3rd cup honey (shahad)

How to Make Nimbu Pani?

- Cut the lemons in halves crosswise, remove the zest from 6 of the halves and squeeze out the juice.
- Slice the remaining lemons into thin rounds.
- Place the water and the dates in a sauce pan and gently boil for ten minutes.
- Add the zest and boil for another 2–3 minutes.
- Remove the pan from the heat, stir in the honey, lemon juice and lemon slices, and set aside, loosely covered, for 8–12 hours.
- Strain through a muslin lined sieve.
- Served chilled.

SPICED TEA

Ingredients

2½ cup water
2 cloves (lavang)
1 brown cardamom (badi elaichi)
4 black pepper corns (kalimirchi)
1 cinnamon stick (tuj/dalchini)
2 tsp tea leaves (chai patti)
1¼ cup milk (doodh)
2 tblsp sugar (cheeni) or as desired

How to Make Spiced Tea?

- Place the water, cloves, cardamom, peppercorns and cinnamon in a saucepan and bring to boil.
- Stir in the tea leaves and continue to cook over a moderate heat for 2 minutes.
- Add the milk and sugar and boil, remove from the heat.
- Strain and serve piping hot.

32 Desi Ghee

I love to make desi ghee and I learned this recipe from my mother . You can easily make it at home with the cream/malai of milk. What I do is that I collect the cream of fresh milk whole month and then I make ghee out of it. So guys here is the 100% authentic recipe of making desi ghee at home. It has no smell and it tastes so great.

(this is the picture of butter which we get from milk cream)

(This is pure ghee which we get after heating above butter)

Ingredients of Desi/Pure Ghee

1 large bowl of milk cream/malai

2 tbsp yoghurt

2 glass of cold water

Method of Desi/Pure Ghee

- Place all the cream of milk in a thick base pan. Add yoghurt in it and mix it well. Leave it for overnight.
- In the morning add cold water in it and whisk it with hand beater. Now butter will start coming on surface and white liquid will be separated. Take out the butter. Do not throw that liquid because its a lassi and you can drink it after adding some salt in it.
- Now put that butter on low flame. It will take one hour and ghee will start coming out of the butter. Stir it occasionally.
- The foam curdles and settle at the bottom. Strain the ghee and pour it in some airtight container. You can use it for months on room temperature.

Tip: If you are making this ghee in summers then use cold water and if you are making it in winter then use hot water.

33 Noodles

SPRING ROLL

Ingredients

Cover

250 gm. All purpose flour (maida)
1 egg
Little salt
Water to make batter

Filling

2–3 carrots grated
1 cup leeks shredded and well washed (white section only)(optional)
1/2 tsp ginger minced
1/2 tsp garlic minced
100 gm cabbage shredded
50 gm mushrooms chopped
75 gm sprouted beans
3 green chilies chopped)
Salt to taste
2 tbsp soya sauce
1/2 tbsp white pepper powder

How to Make Spring Roll?

- Sift the flour and add salt, egg and water and make a smooth batter.
- Heat little oil in a flat nonstick pan and add enough batter so that it covers the base of the pan.
- Cook both sides of the pancake till golden. Repeat the same till whole batter is utilized.
- To make the filling heat 2–3 tbsp oil in a wok, add ginger, garlic and mushrooms, stir fry for 10–15 seconds.
- Add leeks (if available) and stir fry for about 1 minute, then add carrots, cabbage and cook tossing the vegetables until they are crisp-tender.

- Add the bean sprouts, salt, pepper and soya sauce, cook stirring for 2 minutes. Set aside the filling to cool.
- To make the spring rolls place 2–3 tbsp of the filling in the center of each pancake.
- Fold in the sides and form a tight roll, sealing the edge with a little flour and water paste.
- Deep fry in hot oil until golden.
- Serve the vegetarian spring roll hot.

VEGETABLE CHOW MEIN

Ingredients

1 packet noodles
1 onion sliced
1 capsicum sliced
1 cabbage shredded
1 carrot sliced
1/2 cup beans chopped
2 tbsp soya sauce
1 tbsp vinegar
1 tbsp chili sauce
Salt to taste
1/4 tsp pepper powder
2 tbsp oil

Preparation of Vegetable Chow mein

- Boil noodles in enough water.
- Take care do not overcook.
- Strain noodles through cold water 2–3 times and drain water and set aside, add few drops of oil to the noodles to avoid sticking.
- Heat oil in a wok and add sliced onions and stir fry for 20–30 seconds, add all other vegetables and stir fry for 2 minutes.
- Add salt and pepper and mix well. Now add boiled noodles and mix well (take care that noodles do not break).
- Add vinegar, chili sauce and soya sauce and stir fry for a minute.
- Serve the vegetable chow mein hot.

Note: According to taste vinegar, soya sauce and chili sauce can be increased or decreased.

HOT AND SOUR SOUP

Ingredients

2 tbsp chili sauce
1½ tbsp corn flour/corn starch

1 tbsp soya sauce
2 tbsp vinegar
2 tbsp capsicum chopped
2 tbsp spring onions chopped
2 tbsp tomato sauce
2 tbsp carrots chopped
1/4 cup chopped cabbage
1 tsp black pepper powder
1/2 tsp sugar
A pinch ajinomoto
Salt to taste
4 cups water

Preparation for Hot and Sour Soup

- Mix 4 cups of water, chili sauce, soya sauce, vinegar, sugar, salt, pepper powder and ajinomoto and bring to boil.
- Now add all the chopped vegetables except paneer.
- Cook for a minute on a medium heat. Dissolve corn starch in 1/2 cup water and add to the soup stirring constantly till it becomes thick.
- Cook for a minute, add paneer slices. Serve hot.

Note: Soup should be prepared just before consuming and should be served fresh, else it will lose the taste.

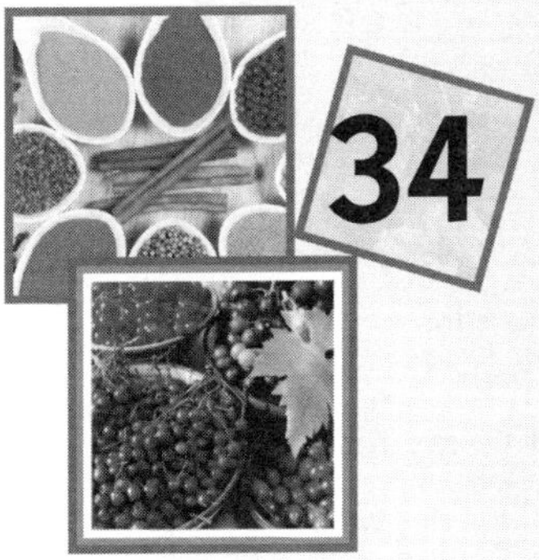

34 Pickles

AAM KA MITHA ACHAR

Ingredients

675 gm/11/2 lb. green aam (mangoes)
575 gm/11/4lb sugar
2 tsp salt
1 tbsp white cumin seeds
2 tsp brown cardamom seeds
1 tbsp poppy seeds
1 tsp red chili powder

How to Make Mango Pickle (Aam ka Mitha Achar)?

- Wash, peel and grate the aam (mangoes). There should be about 450 gm/1 lb of flesh.
- Add sugar and salt and mix well in a large bowl.
- Roast cumin seeds, cardamom seeds and poppy seeds, stir in chili powder and mix with the sweetened mango.
- Turn the mango pickle into a sterilized jar, cover with a clean cloth and leave out in the sun or in warm, light place for about a week.
- Shake the jar at least once a day.

AMLA (GOOSEBERRY) PICKLE

Ingredients

1/2 kg amla
125 gm green chilies (slit)
125 gm oil
50 gm salt
1/2 tsp jeera
1/2 tsp mustard seeds
2 tblsp roasted and powdered sesame seeds
1 small lemon

How to Make Amla Achar?

- Wash and dry amla and keep aside.
- Heat oil in a pan and fry green chilies for 2 minutes.
- Remove the chilies from the pan add jeera and mustard seeds.
- Then add aamla and fry for few minutes.
- Sprinkle some water and cover the pan with a lid and let it stay for 6 minutes.
- Turn the flame to medium and stir regularly.

DRY DATES PICKLE

Ingredients

250 gram dry dates (khajoor)
1 tsp red chili pepper (lal mirchi)
5 tsp coriander (dhania) powder
5 tsp aniseed powder
2 tsp white cumin powder
3/4 or 1 cup lemon (nimbu) juice
Salt (namak) to taste

How to Make Dry Dates Pickle?

- Boil the dates until a little tender.
- Remove the stones and keep them whole.
- Dry with a clean cloth.
- Mix all the ground ingredients together with a little salt and fill in the dates.
- Keep the dates in clean jar.
- Mix a little salt with lemon juice and pour over the dates, taking care that dates must be covered with lemon juice.
- Keep aside for 7 days.
- Shake the jar every other day and serve after one week.

CARROT PICKLE (GAAJAR KA ACHAR)

Ingredients

3 cup water
230 gm carrots (scraped and cut into 2″ long sticks)
1½ tbsp mustard seeds
1/2 tsp chili powder
1/8th tsp each ground mace, cloves and cardamom
2 tsp salt
1/4 th cup shredded jaggery (gur)
1/3rd cup mustard oil

Preparation

- Boil the water in 2-liter saucepan. Add carrots and blanch for a minute.
- Drain the water and then spread carrots on a clean cloth and sundry (or spread them on a towel lined cookie tray and air dry in an oven (200 °F) for an hour).
- In a bowl mix the mace, cloves, cardamom, salt and jaggery.
- Add the carrots and toss to mix. Transfer to a sterilized glass jar.
- Pour the mustard oil into a small saucepan and place it over a moderate heat. As soon as oil begins to smoke remove it from the heat and cool it for 4 minutes, then pour it into the jar and cover it with a clean cloth.
- Set the jar in sunlight for 13–14 days, bringing it indoor every night. Shake the jar two or three times daily.

HOT LEMON PICKLE

Ingredients

1 kg lemons (nimbu)
250 gram salt (namak)
2 tsp turmeric (haldi)
3 tsp red chili pepper (lal mirchi)
125 gram ginger (adarak), scraped and sliced
1 cup vinegar (sirka)
125 gram green chilies (hari mirch) (slit)
4 tsp fenugreek
4 tsp mustard seeds (rai/sarson)
2 level tsp asafoetida
1½ cups mustard oil (sarson ka tel)

How to Make Hot Lemon Pickle?

- Cut each lemon into eight pieces.
- Mix salt with lemons, keep in the sun for 15 days in the jar and shake it daily.
- Heat oil till smokes.
- Remove it from the fire and cool a little.
- In it fry asafoetida, fenugreek and mustard seeds.
- Mix vinegar, ginger.
- Green chilies, chili powder and lemon with its juice.
- Keep 15 days in the sun.

LEMON PICKLE IN OIL

Ingredients

1 kg lemons (nimbu)
240 gram salt (namak)

1/2 liter mustard oil (sarson ka tel)
2 big pieces of asafoetida
4 tsp red chili pepper (lal mirchi)
1/2 kg ginger (adarak)
30 gram mustard seeds (rai/sarson)
120 gram whole fresh red chillies (lal mirchi)
60 gram methi seeds
juice of two galgals or 1 cup lemon (nimbu) juice
1 tblsp salt (namak) for lime juice

How to Make Lemon Pickle in Oil?

- Wash and dry the lemons with a cloth.
- In each lemon make four cuts and pack the salt inside and rub a little salt outside also till tender.
- Heat the oil till smoky.
- Remove from the fire, add asafoetida and when it swells up, crush it with a spoon.
- Add chili powder and stir till red color appears.
- Remove from the fire, add mustard seeds and stir for a little while.
- Now stir in lemons, fresh red chilies and ginger and cook until a little tender.
- Roast methi seeds and powder.
- Mix methi seed powder and the juice of galgal or lime mixed with one tablespoon salt cook for 5 minutes.
- Remove from the fire, pour the lemons with the juice into a clean jar, and cork tightly.

SPICY ONION PICKLE

Ingredients

1/2 Kg button onions (pyaj) (very small onions)
2 cups white vinegar (sirka)
1 cinnamon (dalchini)
4 Cloves (lavang)
16 peppercorns
16 green chilies, slit in the middle
1/3 cup salt (namak)

How to Make Spicy Onion Pickle?

- Peel the onions, rub salt on them and keep for one day.
- Drain the salt water.
- Boil the vinegar with spices and in it cook onions and green chili to boiling.
- Cool and put in ajar; cork it tightly.
- Keep for 4 days before using.

35 Cakes

APPLE CAKE

Try an attempt at baking this apple cake made of cinnamon, nutmeg and glazed with brown sugar and vanilla essence.

Ingredients

1 cup oil
2 cup sugar
3 cup flour
1 tsp salt
1 tsp nutmeg
1 tsp cinnamon powder
1 tsp baking powder
3 eggs
1 tsp vanilla extract
1 cup chopped nuts
1 tsp cloves
1 cup baking soda
4 cup chopped apples

Glaze

2 tblsp milk
1/2 tsp vanilla essence
1/2 stick butter
1/2 cup brown sugar

How to Make Apple Cake?

- In a bowl mix the oil, eggs and vanilla extract together.
- In a separate bowl sift the dry ingredients together and add this mixture to the oil and egg mixture and mix well.
- Add in the apples and the nuts.
- Pour this mixture in a baking pan and bake for 1.15 minutes at 350 °F.
- For the glaze mix all the glaze ingredients together and boil the mixture for one minute.

- When the cake is baked remove it from the oven and white it is worm pour the glaze on it.
- Apple cake is ready.

BANANA CHOCOLATE CAKE

Relish this culinary bliss of banana chocolate cake with following ingredients banana, sweet chocolate chips and milk.

Ingredients

1 egg
1½ tsp baking powder
1 cup meshed banana
1½ cup all purpose flour
3/4 cup semi sweet chocolate chips
1/2 cup unsalted butter which is melted
1/4 tsp salt
2/3 cup white sugar
1/4 cup milk

How to Make Banana Chocolate Cake?

- In a large mixing bowl stir together all purpose flour, sugar, salt and baking powder.
- Take another bowl and mix together melted butter milk egg and meshed bananas.
- Now add the banana mixture into the flour mixture until thoroughly blended.
- Be careful not to overmix.
- Add the chocolate chips. Preheat the oven to 350 °F to 175 °C.
- Grease and flour a 9 × 13 inch pan.
- Pour the batter into the pan and bake it for 32–35 minutes or until the toothpick inserted into it comes out clean.
- When the cake gets baked take out the pan from the oven and let it cool for 10–15 minutes.
- This cake will have some melted chocolate but no crumbs.

EGGLESS CAKE

You will love this eggless cake. It is simple to make and does not require eggs.

Ingredients

8 oz plain flour
3 oz margarine
pinch of salt
4 tsp baking powder
3 oz sugar
1 tsp vanilla essence
about 1/2 cup milk and water

How to Make Eggless Cake?

- Mix flour, baking powder and salt.
- Mix in the margarine, add the sugar and vanilla and mix to a dropping consistency with the milk and water.
- Turn into a greased 7 inch tin and bake in a moderate oven for 3/4 to 1 hour.

SUGARLESS CAKE

Learn how to make this sugarless cake. It is very easy to make and delicious to make.

Ingredients

1 tsp cinnamon
2 cup water
1/2 cup shortening
1½ tsp vanilla extract
1/2 tsp salt
1 tsp baking soda
1½ tsp artificial sweetener
1 cup rolled oats
1 beaten egg
1 cup raisins
1 cup flour

How to Make Sugarless Cake?

- In a sauce pan add together raisins, water and cinnamon.
- Heat the sauce pan on low heat for fifteen minutes.
- Take off from fire and let it cool.
- To this mixture add the beaten egg, oats, artificial sweeter, shortening and vanilla extract.
- In a separate bowl sift together flour, baking soda, cinnamon powder and salt.
- Add this dry ingredients to the earlier prepare batter and mix well.
- Pour this mixture in a baking pan and bake for 30–35 minutes at 350 °F.
- When the cake is ready let it cool for 10 to 15 minutes and then serve immediately.

36 Sauces

FRENCH WHITE SAUCE

Ingredients

3 tsp butter
2½ tsp flour
3 cups milk
1 small onion (pyaj)
1/2 tsp chopped coriander leaves (dhania patta)
1 piece bay leaf
4 peppercorns
pinch of nutmeg
pinch of red chilies (lal mirchi)
1 clove (lavang)
1/2 lemon (nimbu)
1/2 tsp salt (namak)

How to Make French White Sauce?

- Put the milk to boil with chopped onion, coriander, clove, bay leaf and peppercorns.
- Melt the butter, stir in the flour and cook a little without browning, then add hot milk.
- Whisk over the fire until it boils and let it simmer for 6 minutes.
- Strain or pass through a sieve, return to the pan, season lightly with a pinch of nutmeg, red chili and salt.
- When cold, add lemon juice.
- Serve with fried dishes.

FRESH TOMATO SAUCE

Ingredients

1½ kg tomatoes (tamatar)
1/4 tsp red chili powder (lal mirchi)
1 cup sugar (cheeni)

4 cloves (lavang)
1 small onion (pyaj)
1 small piece cinnamon (dalchini)
30 gram ginger (adarak) (2 tsps chopped)
6 cloves garlic (lahsun)
1/4 cup vinegar (sirka)
2 tsp salt (namak)

How to Make Fresh Tomato Sauce?

- Wash, dry and chop tomatoes.
- Peel and chop the onions, garlic and ginger. Coarsely crush spices.
- Place tomatoes, onion, garlic and ginger in a degchi and cook over a gentle fire till tender.
- Add spices, sugar, chili powder and cook till thick.
- Strain through a sieve and use.
- This sauce cannot be stored.

MUSTARD SAUCE

Ingredients

7 tsp salted butter
3 tsp flour
1 cup hot water
2 tsp brown sugar
6 tsp vinegar (sirka)
9 tsp mustard powder
1/4 tsp red chili pepper (lal mirchi)
1/2 tsp salt (namak)

How to Make Mustard Sauce?

- Melt the butter and stir in the flour.
- Mix well and cook very gently without browning.
- Add water and stir till it thickens.
- Mix mustard in vinegar, add salt, red chili pepper and sugar, and add to the flour stirring well.
- Store the sauce in a jar.

RED CHILI SAUCE

Ingredients

125 gram red chili (lal mirchi), fresh
2 tsp red chili pepper (lal mirchi)

2 cloves (lavang)
1 tsp mustard seeds (rai/sarson) (tied in a muslin bag)
1/4 cup vinegar (sirka)
250 gram tomatoes (tamatar)
1 tsp sugar (cheeni)
2 tsp salt (namak)
1 tsp glacial acetic acid

How to Make Red Chili Sauce

- Deseed the red chilies and grind.
- Cook tomato pieces till tender and pass through a sieve.
- Cook tomato pulp, ground red chilies, chili powder, salt, sugar, cloves, vinegar and mustard seeds till thick.
- Remove from the fire, take out muslin bag and cloves.
- Mix glacial acetic acid. Pour in a bottle and cork tightly.
- Keep it for one week before using.

Note: If the color of the sauce does not look good, mix with it 1/2 teaspoon tomato red color.

TOMATO KETCHUP

Ingredients

1½ kg tomatoes (tamatar)
1 tsps chili powder
1½ cups sugar (cheeni)
2 cloves (lavang)
1 cardamom (elaichi moti)
1/4″ piece cinnamon (dalchini)
2 tsp chopped ginger (adarak)
4 cloves garlic (lahsun)
1 cup vinegar (sirka)
2 tsps salt (namak)
1/2 tsp glacial acetic acid
2 tsp sodium benzoate

How to Make Tomato Ketchup?

- Chop the tomatoes, garlic and ginger and put in a degchi and cook on a low fire till tender and thick.
- Pass through a sieve.
- Add vinegar, sugar and chili powder and cook until thick.
- Add acetic acid and sodium benzoate mixed in 1/4 cup boiling water.
- Pour the ketchup in bottles and cork tightly.
- Use after one week. This tomato ketchup can be kept for one year.

37 Snacks

ALOO CHAAT

Ingredients

3 aloo (potatoes), peeled
1/2 tsp red chili powder
1 tsp roasted cumin powder
1 tsp chaat masala
Tamarind chutney
Mint chutney
Chopped coriander leaves
Optional garnish-chopped onion, tomato julienne, fresh pomegranate seeds
Oil for frying

Preparation

- Dish aloo (potatoes) into a fairly large dish - 3/4 to 1 inch cubes.
- Heat oil in a wok and deep fry potatoes, till golden brown and cooked through. Drain on paper.
- In a bowl, place the fried potatoes and toss with red chili powder, cumin powder, chaat masala.
- Add mint chutney, tamarind chutney according to taste and toss to coat evenly.
- Serve, with toothpicks, in individual bowls, garnished with coriander leaves.
- You can also additionally garnish the special indian aloo chaat with chopped onion, tomato julienne or pomegranate.

ALOO TIKKI

Ingredients

3 large boiled aloo (potatoes)
1 tsp salt or as per taste
1/4th tsp ground black pepper

For Stuffing:

2/3rd cup matar (green peas) cooked or frozen peas defrosted

1/2 tbsp scrapped and minced ginger

1/4th tsp garam masala

1/4th tsp salt or to taste

Red chili powder to taste (optional)

1 tsp coarsely ground dry-roasted cumin seeds

Oil for pan-frying.

How to Make Aloo Tiki?

- Take the cooked or defrosted peas (matar) and mash them using a spoon or a fork. Add all the stuffing ingredients except oil and mash briefly. Divide the mixture into 10 equal portions and keep aside.
- Peel the potatoes and mash them very finely into smooth mashed potatoes. Add salt and pepper and knead until properly mixed.
- Divide it into 10 equal portions.
- Now wash and dry your hands and rub them with little oil.
- Take each portion of potato mixture and make a ball. Now
- Taking one at a time, gently flatten each ball into a round patty of about 1/2-inch thick and place a portion of stuffing in the center and fold the edges together very finely so that mixture does not come out.
- Now very gently flatten it into a 2-inch patty. Repeat the procedure for all pieces.
- Heat 1 tsp oil in a nonstick pan over a low heat. Slip in the patties, not too many at a time, and pan-fry on both sides till crisp golden brown, adding oil if required, on a very low heat.
- Serve aloo tikki hot with chutney and stirred curd.

Note: Boil potatoes until fork-tender. Preferably, potatoes should be boiled well in advance before use. It would be better if they can be refrigerated for a short time.

BREAD PAKORA (BREAD FITTER)

Ingredients

4–5 bread slices

1 cup gram flour (besan)

1/4th tsp turmeric powder

Salt to taste

1/2 tsp ajwain

Red chili powder to taste

1/4th tsp garam masala powder

Water for batter

Oil for frying

How to Make Bread Pakora?

- Cut bread slices into desired shapes (like triangle, rectangle, etc.)
- In a bowl add gram flour salt, chili powder, garam masala, ajwain and mix it.
- Now by pouring little water at a time make a smooth batter (neither too thick nor too lose)
- Heat oil in a kadai.
- Dip bread piece in the batter and fry till crisp on medium flame.
- Serve bread pakora hot with green chutney and tomato sauce.

CHEESY PIZZA

Ingredients

225 gm flour
1/4 tsp salt
15 gm yeast mix with 4–5 tbsp hot water
1 tbsp sugar
150 ml evaporated milk
2 tbsp butter
1/2 cup tomato sauce
1 pkt grated cheese
2 large onions (cut into rings)
1/2 tsp salt
1/2 tsp pepper powder
2 tbsp butter (melted)

Preparation

- Mix yeast in hot water and leave it to be frosty.
- In a bowl put in the flour, salt, sugar and mix with milk and yeast.
- Add butter. Knead until dough become soft and pliable. Leave the dough to rise double in size.
- For the filling mix chicken in the beaten egg along with salt and pepper powder. Leave aside.
- Punch into the dough with your hands and knead again and make into equal balls shape (as big as you want) and flatten the dough with a rolling pin.
- Sprinkle with flour if the dough is sticky.
- Put the mini round dough in a greased flat baking pan.
- Brush the mini pizza with tomato sauce.
- Add in a bit of chicken pieces in the center, top with onion rings and grated cheese.
- Sprinkle a bit of melted margerine to get a crunchy taste.
- Do the same to all the other pizza.
- Pre heat oven for 180°C and bake for 15–20 minutes. You can serve with chili sauce.

PANI PURI

Ingredients

To make puri

1 cup semolina (rava/suji)
3 tblsp fine wheat flour (maida)
1/4 tsp baking soda
1/2 tsp salt
Oil to deep fry

To make pani

1/2 cup tamarind (imli) pulp
2 cups water
2 tblsp roasted cumin seed (jeera) powder
2 tblsp un-roasted cumin seed (jeera)
1/2 cup coriander leaves
3 green chilly (hari mirch)
1 cup mint leaves (pudina leaves)
1 tblsp black salt (kala namak)
1 tblsp boondi
2 tblsp crushed jaggary (gur)

To make stuffing

2 medium boiled potatoes
1/2 cup boiled dried yellow peas/small chickpeas
salt to taste
Green chutney
Red tamarind chutney

How to Make Pani Puri?

To make puri

- Mix sooji, maida, baking soda and salt in a wide mouth vessel. Now add warm water little by little to knead a stiff dough. The stiffness should be same as for the puris. Cover it with a damp muslin cloth and keep it aside for 30 mins.
- Now make small equal lemon sized balls of the dough. Do remember to keep them covered with damp muslin cloth while making more balls.
- Now with the help of some dry maida, roll out thin rotis. Make them round with the help of a round cookie cutter or lid of any container.

Points to remember before frying

1. Always ensure that the oil is hot before frying otherwise the puris will soak in excess oil and will not puff. Put a small testing puri. If it comes up fast then the oil is rightly hot.
2. Also the oil should not be smoking hot or the puris will get burnt and dark.

- Heat oil in a deep bottom pan or kadai and put 3–4 puris in the kadai and fry them with the help of a slotted spoon.
- While frying, press them in the center allow them to puff up. We want a pocket in each and every puri.
- Now flip them over and let them cook. Take them out on a kitchen towel when they are light brown and crisp. Do not let them get dark in color.
- Let them cool. Later store in an airtight container.

To make pani

- Grind in a hand blender coriander, mint leaves and green chillies to make a fine paste.
- Mix all the ingredients of the pani along with the green paste. Dissolve the gur properly. Adjust the spices and tanginess according to taste.
- Strain through a wire strainer to remove any rough bits. Keep in the refrigerator for 2–3 hours before serving.

To make the stuffing

In a bowl mix yellow peas, roughly mashed potatoes and salt. Keep aside.

- **To serve:** Make a small hole on a puri by tapping slowly on the crisp side. Fill some stuffing in the centre along with some green chutney, tamarind chutney and some chilled pani prepared earlier. Stir the pani before using to mix all the masalas.
- Enjoy home-made pani puri or golgappa or puchkas.

CHOLEY BHATURE

Ingredients

Bhature

2 cup all purpose flour (maida)
1 pouch teast
1 cup yoghurt
2 tbsp vegetable oil
Salt to taste

Choley

1 small can garbanzo beans
1/2 tsp ginger paste
1/2 tsp garlic powder
1 tsp cumin seeds
2 tbsp oil
2 tbsp cilantro
6–7 mint leaves
1/2 tsp turmeric powder
1/2 tsp chilly powder
2–3 bay leaves
2–3 cloves

1/2 tsp garam masala
1 medium-sized finely chopped onion
1 big tomato
1½ cup water
Salt to taste

How to Make Chhole Bhature?

Bhature

- Take yeast and soak in lukewarm water for 5–10 minutes
- Take all other ingredients and mix well. To this add the yeast and make a soft dough like for chappatis. If need be add a little water and keep aside for 4–5 hours, the longer kept, the better it is.
- Roll like puri but this needs to be kept thicker than poori. Fry like poori till both sides are golden brown.

Chole

- Take 2 tsp of oil in a pressue cooker and heat it.
- Add garlic powder and make it dark brown. Then add cumin seeds fry till they start spluttering.
- Now add bay leaves and cloves. Add diced onions. Fry then till they are light brown.
- Now add the rest of ingredients including water except the cilantro and mint leaves.
- Close the pressure cooker and wait for 3 whistles to come or cook for 5–7 minutes.
- Garnish choley with thinly sliced long pieces of onion and a piece of lemon split up into 4 pieces.

DAHI VADA

Ingredients

For vada

1/2 cup urad dal
1/2 cup moong dal duli
Salt to taste
1/4 tsp baking powder
1/2 tsp cumin seeds
1 tsp grated ginger
Oil to fry

For dahi

2 cups dahi (yoghurt)
Finely chopped coriander leaves
1–2 green chilies chopped
Salt to taste

2 tsp roasted cumin (jeera) powder
Red chili powder to taste
1 tsp sugar

How to Make Dahi Vadas?

For vada: Clean, wash and soak the dal overnight or 7–8 hours.

- Separate the water and grind them together into smooth paste without water or if necessary then very little water. The paste should be coarse and not fine.
- Take out the paste in a bowl and then beat the mixture for 10–15 minutes till the mixture becomes fluffy. This will make the vadas soft.
- Add salt, cumin seeds, ginger and baking powder.
- Heat oil in a pan for frying and drop small balls of batter in the oil with the help of a spoon. The flame should be medium. Do not put more than 8–9 balls.
- Fry till golden brown. Then take them out on kitchen paper.
- In a bowl fill 2 cups of warm water with 1 tsp salt and put the vadas in it. Let them soak for 1/2 hour.
- Meanwhile prepare the dahi.

For dahi: Beat the curd smooth and put in a bowl.

- Keep in refrigerator for an hour to get chilled.
- Before serving add salt, red chili powder, sugar and roasted cumin powder to the dahi.

Serving: Squeeze out the vadas from the water and in a deep dish arrange the wadas and pour dahi over them.

- Pour imli (tamarind) chutney and green chutney.
- Garnish with coriander and slit green chilies.
- Serve the dahi vadas chilled.

MASALA DOSA

Ingredients

Dosa shell
1½ cups rice
1/2 cup urad dal
Salt to taste
Oil

Masala filling
2 large potatoes
1 medium onion (chopped)
1/2 teaspoon yellow split peas
1/2 teaspoon mustard seed
1/2 teaspoon turmeric

1–2 green chili
1 tablespoon oil
Salt to taste

Preparation

Dosa shell

- Separately soak rice and urad dal at least 6-hour or overnight in water.
- Grind to paste.
- Mix together, add salt with water to make batter.
- Leave in room temperature overnight.
- Mix onion and chilies to the thin batter.
- Heat pan or griddle with little ghee or oil.
- Spread the mix on pan in circular motion to make thin dosa.
- Cook on both the sides, if desired.

Masala filling (Spicy filling)

- Heat oil. Add mustard seed, peas, onions and spice.
- Fry for about 5 minutes on medium heat or/until onions are turned into golden brown.
- Add potatoes and mix and cook some more serve.
- Add filling inside dosa and roll. Serve hot with chutney.

PANEER PAKORA

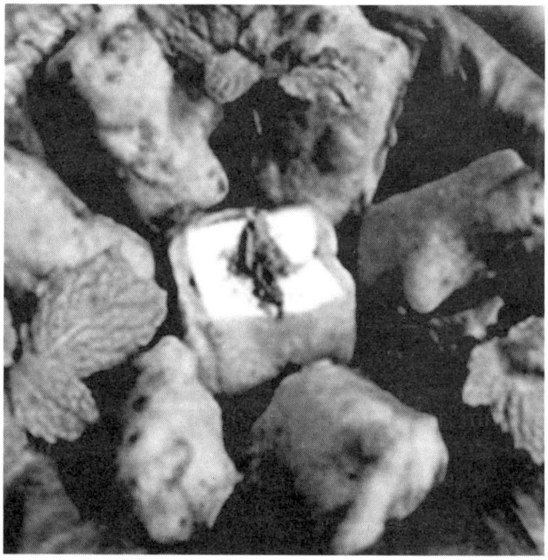

Ingredients

250 gm paneer
1 cup chickpea flour (besan)
2 tsp Oil
1½ tsp salt
1/2 tsp red chili powder
1/2 cup water

How to Make Paneer Pakora

- Beat the chickpea flour with some water to make a thick batter in a blender for 4–5 minutes to incorporate air (this will make the batter fluffier).
- Let the batter rest 1/2 hour in a warm place
- Cut the paneer into thick cubes.
- Sprinkle little salt, chili powder on the cubes
- Dip the cubes of paneer in the batter
- Deep fry in oil that is heated to 375°.
- Drain on paper towels and serve immediately.
- Serve the paneer pakora with coriander or mint chutney.

VEGETABLE SAMOSA RECIPE

Ingredients

For cover

1 cup all purpose flour (Maida)
Water to knead dough
2 tbsp oil
Little salt
1/4th tsp ajwain (optional)

For stuffing

3–4 Potatoes (boiled, peeled & mashed)
1/2 cup green peas (boiled)
1–2 green chilies (finely chopped)
1/2 tsp ginger (crushed)
1 tbsp coriander finely chopped
Few chopped cashews (optional)
Few raisins (optional)
1/2 tsp garam masala
Salt to taste
Red chili powder to taste
1/2 tsp dry mango powder (amchur) (optional)

How to Make Vegetable Samosa?

For cover

- Mix all the ingredients (salt, oil, ajwain) except water.
- Add a little water at a time.
- Pat and knead well for several times into a soft pliable dough.
- Cover it with moist muslin cloth and keep aside for 15 minutes.

For stuffing

- In a bowl add mashed potatoes and all dry masalas (salt, chili powder, mango powder, garam masala) and green chilies, ginger and mix well.
- Add green peas, cashews and raisins and mix well.
- Add coriander and keep aside.

To proceed

- Make small rolls of dough and roll it into a 4"–5" diameter circle.
- Cut it into two parts like semicircle.
- Now take one semicircle and fold it like a cone. Use water while doing so.
- Place a spoon of filling in the cone and seal the third side using a drop of water.
- Heat oil in a kadai and deep fry till golden brown (fry on a medium flame).
- Serve samosa hot with hari chutney, tamarind chutney.

38 Cookies

BUTTER COOKIES

Ingredients

6 cups all purpose flour (maida)
3 tsp baking powder
1 teaspoon salt
2 cup white sugar
2 cup butter or margarine
2 egg
6 tbsp cream
2 tsp vanilla extract

How to Make Butter Cookies?

- Sift flour, baking powder, salt and sugar together. Mix well.
- Add the butter.
- Add egg, cream and vanilla extract thoroughly.
- Wrap this dough into a foil and refrigerate for at least 24 hours.
- Reheat the oven for 400°.
- Now roll the dough into a crust which is 1/4 to 1/8 thick.
- Now with the help of a cookie cutter, cut the cookies.
- Lastly place them on a greased tray and bake them at 400° for 5–8 minutes.

SESAME SEED COOKIES

Ingredients

1/2 cup sesame seeds
4 cup maida
1 cup sugar
1 cup butter
3 eggs
1 tblsp cake seeds (caraway seeds)

1/2 cup milk to mix
Salt a pinch
1/4 tsp baking soda

How to Make Sesame Seed Cookies?

- Sieve flour with salt and baking powder in a bowl.
- Add sugar, butter, 2 eggs, cake seeds, blend well.
- Add milk little by little and knead to a smooth dough.
- Roll out on a floured board 1 cm thick and cut out with fancy cookie cutters.
- Brush with remaining egg (well beaten) and sprinkle heavily with sesame seeds.
- Place on a greased baking tray.
- Bake in a moderate oven for 10 minutes.
- Cool and keep aside. Good to be served with tea.

RAISIN CHOCO OAT COOKIE

Ingredients

3/4 cup fine wheat flour (maida)
1 tsp baking soda
1/4 tsp salt
3/2 cup sugar
3/2 cup brown sugar
3/2 cup butter
1 tsp vanilla essence
1 big sized eggs
1½ cups uncooked oats
1/2 cup currants (kishmish)
1 cup dark chocolate chips

How to Make Raisin Choco Oat Cookie?

- Before you begin preheat the oven to 175 degrees.
- Grease a baking tray.
- Mix flour, baking soda, and salt.
- Cream sugar and butter.
- Add vanilla essence, and eggs one by one while mixing .
- Add the flour and mix the oats.
- Mix well and then add currants and chocolate chips.
- Now drop one spoonful of the batter on inch apart on the greased baking tray.
- Bake for 12–14 minutes or till golden in color.

CHOCOLATE CHIP COOKIES

Ingredients

1¼ cup fine wheat flour (maida)
1/2 tsp baking soda
1/2 tsp salt
1/2 cup butter
1/2 cup brown sugar
1/4 cup sugar
1 small sized egg
1 tsp vanilla essence
1 cup chocolate chips
1/2 cup chopped and roasted walnuts

How to Make Chocolate Chip Cookies?

- Mix the flour, baking soda and salt evenly in a bowl.
- With the mixer running, beat butter, sugar and brown sugar together until creamy.
- Add the egg and vanilla essence.
- Now add flour.
- When flour is fully blended mix the chips and walnuts.
- Preheat the oven to 190°.
- On a tray place a large ungreased cookie sheet.
- Now drop a spoonful of the batter on the sheet 2 inches apart.
- Bake for 10–1 2 minutes.

Bibliography

1. Drugs and Cosmetics Formulations, CBS Publishers and Distributors Pvt Ltd, New Delhi , Ranjan Magazine

2. Drug Index, Passi Publication, 2010.

3. Textbook of Pharmacognosy, CBS Publishers and Distributors Pvt Ltd, New Delhi , Mohammed Ali

4. United States Pharmacopoeia, 23 and NF18, Asian Edition, US Pharmacopocial Convention, Inc.1995.

5. www.google.com

Index